BACKROADS &

Florida

BACKROADS & BYWAYS OF

Florida

Drives, Day Trips & Weekend Excursions

ZAIN DEANE

The Countryman Press
Woodstock, Vermont

We welcome your comments and suggestions.
Please contact
Editor
The Countryman Press
P.O. Box 748
Woodstock
VT 05091
or e-mail
countrymanpress@wwnorton.com

ISBN 978-0-88150-785-0

Book design, map, and composition by Hespenheide Design
Cover and interior photos by the author unless otherwise specified

Published by The Countryman Press, P.O. Box 748, Woodstock, VT 05091

Distributed by W. W. Norton & Company, Inc., 500 Fifth Avenue, New York, NY 10110

Printed in the United States of America

10 9 8 7 6 5 4 3 2 1

Acknowledgments

This book would not have been possible without the small army of people who have helped me, hosted me, and generally gone out of their way to make me feel welcome. My wife had to begin our married life patiently waiting for me to complete this book, and I owe her a huge debt of gratitude. My parents and my sister continue to be my bedrock, my staunchest fans, and a never-ending source of comfort and support.

I must thank Kim Grant, who selected my proposal and recommended it to The Countryman Press; Kermit Hummel, who commissioned the work; and Jennifer Thompson, who had the arduous task of going through the first draft. Without Georgia Turner, Tangela Boyd, Katy Martin, and Bill Voliva, I'd have been lost in Daytona Beach and Polk County. Lorrie Allen was a wonderful host in Amelia Island, and Chris Long helped me discover Kissimmee. Harvey Campbell and Marcheta Keefer guided me through northcentral Florida, and Carol McQueen introduced me to Cedar Key. Gentry Baumline was invaluable in helping me travel through much of the state. John Scherlacher steered me through the Freshwater Frontier, and Leigh Court helped me explore St. Augustine. Mary Deatrick showed me a different side of Orlando, and Ashley Chisolm went out of her way to help me discover Pensacola. Last but not least, a special thank you to Dean Fowler, a true Southern gentleman and a good man to have beside you when you're stuck in the mud.

I wish I could list by name the many people who opened their doors and welcomed me into their homes and their businesses; without them, this book would never have been written. And finally, thank you to all my friends who continue to support, motivate, and inspire me to keep writing.

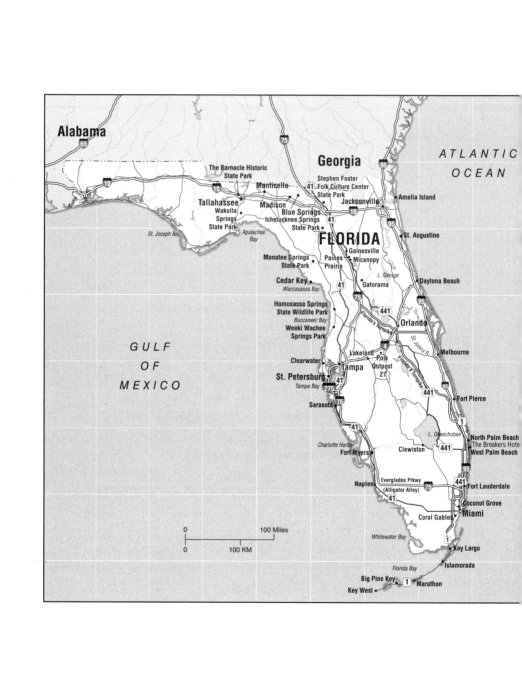

Alabama

Georgia

FLORIDA

ATLANTIC OCEAN

GULF OF MEXICO

The Barnacle Historic State Park
Monticello
Stephen Foster Folk Culture Center State Park
Amelia Island
Tallahassee
Madison
Jacksonville
Wakulla Springs State Park
Blue Springs
Ichetucknee Springs State Park
St. Augustine
St. Joseph Bay
Apalachee Bay
Gainesville
Manatee Springs State Park
Paines Prairie
Micanopy
L. George
Cedar Key
Waccasassa Bay
Gatorama
Daytona Beach
Homosassa Springs State Wildlife Park
Buccaneer Bay
Weeki Wachee Springs Park
Orlando
Florida's Turnpike
St. Johns R.
Lakeland
Melbourne
Clearwater
Polk Outpost 27
Tampa
St. Petersburg
Tampa Bay
Florida's Turnpike
Sarasota
Fort Pierce
Charlotte Harbor
L. Okeechobee
North Palm Beach
The Breakers Hote
West Palm Beach
Fort Myers
Clewiston
Everglades Prkwy
(Alligator Alley)
Fort Lauderdale
Naples
Coconut Grove
Coral Gables
Miami
Whitewater Bay
Key Largo
Florida Bay
Islamorada
Big Pine Key
Marathon
Key West

0   100 Miles

0   100 KM

Contents

Introduction

If you asked me to summarize Florida in one word, I'd have to walk away from you. Even the trite catch-all *unique* doesn't apply, as portions of the state have appropriated so much from other parts of the world. The trademarks that have come to be associated with Florida—hurricanes, retirement homes, amusement parks, sun-drenched beaches, and bikini-clad women—only scratch the surface and ignore much of what makes this a wondrous and surprising place.

For this reason, a Backroads & Byways guide is ideally suited to Florida. This book leaves Disney World and Ocean Drive to other guides and meanders on in pursuit of something more esoteric. In the course of my travels, I've realized that Florida is the perfect state to explore by car. The weather tends to cooperate, and there are so many spectacular, weird, quaint, and interesting places to visit along the way to your destination that you might regret it when you get there. The Florida I'm going to show you is a place of marshes and millionaires; Southern heritage and ancient history; tasteless splendor and pristine paradise. The journeys that make up this book are an exploration of every side of this state, from the slightly bizarre to the surreally breathtaking. And the amazing thing is that I've had to leave so much *out* of this book to keep it manageable.

One of the objectives of this book is to introduce and acknowledge the remarkable diversity of Florida's people. There are major pockets of influence around Florida, encompassing—among others—the Native American, the redneck, the retired, the Jewish, the New Yorker, the Cuban, the Greek, the snowbird, and, of course, the tourist. Each of these communities has stamped its identity on the state, forming a rich social mosaic.

Added to this mix of humanity is a diversity of nature. Because the journey is as important as the destination, many of the most scenic byroads covered in this book are coastal drives, and this is where you find some of Florida's most beautiful towns and cities. But once you leave the water behind, Florida's topography transforms into swamplands, farmlands, and dense forests. Likewise, the native flora, fauna, and marine life include some of the most endangered species in the nation and offer an unparalleled experience for naturalists, bird-watchers, and animal lovers.

Having said all that, there are a few constants for travelers embarking on a road trip in the Sunshine State. The first, as implied by Florida's nickname, is warm weather. Year-round, you'll be hard-pressed to break out a coat in most places (the obvious exception, of course, is hurricane season). In Florida, the earth is flat. Discounting a few hills, this is one massive stretch of even surface. Also, no matter how fast you drive, be prepared to slow down once you step out of the car. Bill Maher once referred to Florida as one of the five stupidest states in the country. I'd like to think of it as people simply taking things a little easier. The hustle and frenzy of New York, the urgency and brisk pace so often found in colder climates, is nonexistent here. So take a deep breath and learn how to go with the Florida flow.

There is great beauty here, and there is some absurdity as well. There are historic highlights and modern marvels. Above all, there is discovery. Let's get started.

Florida's First Coast

A Journey from Amelia Island to St. Augustine

Overview: Walk into a sixth-grade history class and ask the kids to name the oldest settlements in the United States, and you'll probably get half of New England thrown at you. What you're not likely to hear are Amelia Island and St. Augustine. But these two towns, barely 80 miles away from each other, boasted residents long before *The Mayflower* showed up. From Amelia Island, the original FL A1A stretches past Jacksonville Beach and along what is known as Florida's First Coast (so-called because it is the first stretch of coastline as you cross into the state from Georgia) to St. Augustine.

While both make similar claims as to their historical preeminence (both say they're "Florida's Oldest," and both are right), Amelia Island and St. Augustine are quite different. The former is a tranquil anomaly, a tiny strip of land off the northernmost edge of the state that has had a tumultuous and quirky past. Prized for its deep harbor, sweet shrimp, quartz beaches, and Victorian elegance, Amelia Island offers a marked change of pace and scenery from Florida's big cities and theme parks. This is where people come to unwind, commune with nature, and visit another era.

St. Augustine is altogether a different sort of place. Far more developed commercially and as a tourist destination, this is a larger, picturesque city that owes much of its beauty and fame to Henry Flagler, a man who shaped a large part of Florida. (Amelia Island, ironically, owes a very different debt to Mr. Flagler; they thank him for ignoring them.)

This journey tells a tale of two cities that recall five hundred years of history and continue to preserve their legacies.

Total length of trip: A little more than 100 miles over five days. (You can also make two weekend trips and visit these cities separately.)

Getting there: This is an easy road trip, and you even get a rare ferry ride thrown into the mix. From Jacksonville Airport, follow the signs for the airport exit toward Airport Road (FL 102 East). Stay on FL 102 for about a mile and a half until you get to I-95. Head north on I-95 for just under 10 miles to exit 373, and get on Buccaneer Trail (FL 200 East) toward **Amelia Island.** You'll be on this road (which is also A1A) for about 11 miles before crossing into Amelia Island.

From Amelia Island, take A1A south to leave the island and travel about 20 miles until you arrive at the St. Johns River Ferry, the last publicly owned ferry in the state. Drive up and enjoy the all-too-brief ride across the St. Johns River. The ferry deposits you right back on A1A, and it's a straight shot down for about 37 miles before you get to **St. Augustine.**

Highlights: Amelia Island has had so many suitors over its five-century history that it goes by the moniker "Isle of Eight Flags." How exactly does one tiny island get such a distinction? Here's a quick recap: The French Huguenots arrived in 1562 and were greeted by the Timucuan Indians, a rather robust bunch who intimidated the early settlers. The French gave way to the Spanish, who set about diligently Christianizing the natives until they lost Havana to England in 1763. Wanting their Caribbean prize back, Spain offered an even trade: Cuba for Florida. England promptly lost it back to Spain in 1784.

It was the British who christened the island "Amelia" after the daughter of King George II, but in the 1800s things began to fall apart as England increasingly lost all footholds in the New World. Following the colonial powers, a period of debauchery and piracy descended on the island, producing flags of a distinctly poor lineage. In 1812, a group called the Patriots of Amelia Island raised its banner. The flag of the Green Cross of Florida (established by a Scottish adventurer) barely lasted a season before it was usurped by a Mexican rebel. Even Old Glory, which took up residence in 1821, was displaced for one year in 1861 by the Confederate flag, the last of the eight.

It took time to cleanse Amelia Island of its buccaneers and bordellos, but by the late 1800s it had become a summer destination for elite Northerners like Rockefeller and Carnegie. In the 1890s, however, Henry Flagler and his famous railroad bypassed the island and shunted all the tourists south. At the time, it was a crippling blow to the island's tourism, but this neglect had an unforeseen benefit: Over the next several decades, the rapid modernization that engulfed the rest of Florida barely marred Amelia's rustic beauty.

In the early 1900s, the modern shrimping industry was born here, fueled by the leap from traditional cast nets to power-driven seines and trawls. Local shrimpers now harvest almost 80 percent of Florida's sweet Atlantic white shrimp off Amelia Island. But the isolation brought on by Flagler's railroad has remained here, leaving the island small, self-contained, and free of commercial overdevelopment. The rest of Florida—the rest of the world—is simply referred to as "off-island." And all are welcome to visit.

Following A1A, as soon as you cross over the bridge into Amelia Island, you'll see the **welcome center** on your right. Here, you can pick up brochures and literature, and a very helpful staff is on hand to answer questions. If you're hungry, you can head across the street to **Barbara Jean's,** a waterfront eatery that serves up some of the best lump meat crabcakes around in portions to suit any appetite. They also offer rib-sticking Southern home cooking like chicken-fried steak and pot roast.

After the welcome center, A1A immediately forks, with Amelia Island Parkway leading off to the right. Staying on A1A takes you to Eighth Street, which leads you into the heart of the historic downtown. Taking the parkway is the more direct route to the east coast and Amelia's glittering white-sand beaches. Which road you take might well depend on where you're staying on the island, and that decision in turn will be dictated by preference.

Geographically, the island generally offers two categories of lodgings: the beachfront and the historic district. If you want to stay on the beach and have the budget for it, follow Amelia Island Parkway until you arrive at **The Ritz-Carlton, Amelia Island.** You can't beat this resort's location on the water, its championship golf course, and its award-winning spa. The hotel places particular emphasis on family fun (there's a kids' activity center, and a fantastic Our Space recreation area and movie theater just for teens).

Families looking for an apartment to spread out in can reserve a beach-front condo at **Summer Beach Resort,** located behind the Ritz. A large vacation resort complex, Summer Beach has impeccably furnished, full-service apartments that give you more freedom than a hotel room. A more moderate option, located north of these resorts and just across the road from the water, is the **Amelia Hotel and Suites** (look for the tropical pink building on the left as you head up South Fletcher Avenue on the eastern coast of the island). The real draws here are its spacious rooms, better-than-continental free breakfasts, and the pleasant staff.

Rounding out my favorites among the beachfront properties is the unparalleled **Elizabeth Pointe Lodge.** This stately 1890s Nantucket-style inn is right on the ocean and is decorated in an elegant nautical theme. Try to book an oceanfront room for the sound of the rolling surf and the breathtaking views, and enjoy the lodge's main room and wide porches. The staff is also exceptional.

Elizabeth Pointe Lodge

However, you may choose to stay in the island's historic downtown district, in which case you have a selection of fine old bed & breakfast inns and small hotels to choose from. If that is your destination, stick to A1A, which becomes Eighth Street, for just under 4 miles until you reach Centre Street. Take a left and find yourself in the middle of **Historic Fernandina Beach.**

An afternoon stroll is all you need to imagine Rockefeller disembarking at the pier for a weekend getaway in this town, circa 1880. As you walk in the footsteps of titans, sailors, and pirates, it's easy to lose yourself amid Fernandina Beach's proud Victorian mansions and steeped-in-history buildings. Markers around town identify major landmarks, and at night, the amber glow of re-created gas lanterns enhances the town's historic charm. Fernandina Beach is also the island's shopping, dining, and nightlife center. Palm-lined Centre Street, the main thoroughfare, has plenty of mom-and-pop clothing boutiques, antiques stores, and a smattering of more typical, kitschy island shopping.

This is a laid-back place, a cross between a sleepy fishing village, beach town, and Victorian community. The hottest action that Amelia Island sees is during its heralded annual Shrimp Festival, held the first weekend in May. During this celebration of Amelia's favorite crustacean, the island gets overrun by visitors from near and far.

On and around Centre Street are some of the town's best examples of period architecture and some lovely old churches; the visitors center gives out a handy walking or driving tour that covers all the best spots. You can also take a guided horse-drawn carriage tour through the downtown area. **Olde Towne Carriage Company** and **Amelia Island Carriages** both provide knowledgeable guides and comfortable carriages, and are reasonably priced. Another way to stay off your feet is by taking the **Polly the Trolley** downtown tour.

There are several specialty shops and retailers along the main road that might call out to you in a particularly compelling voice. The first is **Fernandina's Fantastic Fudge,** an old-fashioned ice cream parlor where owner Steve Colwell can be found working his handmade-from-scratch fudge with a long paddle. Even the locals line up here for a small slice of decadence. The island has a respectable cluster of antiques shops, and down the block is one of my favorites, **French Market Antiques,** which offers antiques, reproductions, accessories, and gift items with a distinctly Provençal bent.

AMELIA ISLAND'S HISTORIC INNS

Beach lovers might prefer oceanfront lodgings, but if you want to experience Amelia Island's quaint allure, you have to check out one of their B&Bs or downtown hotels. Here are a few of the best:

The Amelia Island Williams House exemplifies the elegance of the island's Victorian inns. Built in 1856, it has kept all the hall-

The Amelia Island Williams House

marks of the era—dark, polished wood; softly lit chandeliers; and Southern-charm dining room and parlor—while updating the ameni-ties. Each room is uniquely, sumptu-ously decorated. Breakfast in the morning is superb.

The Fairbanks House, built in 1885, is a grand old villa that dominates one corner of Seventh Street. Oversized rooms with four-poster beds, claw-foot tubs, and fireplaces can be found here, along with a fairly decent-sized pool—a rare commodity in a B&B—and a two-course breakfast.

The Florida House Inn is Florida's oldest surviving hotel. Presidents, revolutionaries, billionaires, and ghosts have rested here. (The ghosts still do.) The inn has kept its connection with the past. Its 22 rooms are decorated in a romantic vintage style that pays homage to Florida's history. It's the only inn on the island to have a full-service restaurant and a pub (a Southern breakfast is included with your room). And you'll know you're in good hands with innkeepers Diane and Joe Warwick: Before they bought the Florida House, they were married here.

At this point, in case you missed lunch or wanted to wait until you reached Fernandina Beach, you have two dependably good options right off Centre and Third Streets (it's surprising how many establishments are open for dinner only). **La Bodega Courtyard Café** offers light salads and sandwiches in a relaxed, outdoor ambience, and **The Frisky Mermaid Café** inside the Florida House Inn offers basic but tasty lunch fare inside or out (the outdoor courtyard is dominated by a fountain of—you guessed it—a frisky mermaid).

Continue walking south down Third Street for 3 blocks to arrive at the **Amelia Island Museum of History.** Housed in a renovated 1935 jail, this is Florida's only spoken-history museum. Tours are given daily at 11 AM and 2 PM, and as the expert docents guide you through the exhibits, they'll wax eloquent about Timucuan Indian societal behavior, the eight flags, pirate legends, and advances in shrimping. The museum also offers downtown and ghost tours.

Returning on Third Street, you'll pass **Fernandina Beach Winery & Gifts,** where you can sample the store's premium wines and browse the collection of tropical and Florida citrus wine. At Centre Street, turn right and cross the road to get to the **Palace Saloon,** impossible to miss thanks to the rather campy pirate statue just outside the door. Florida's oldest saloon has been sending everyone from sailors to billionaires staggering home since 1878. Order your drink at the original, hand-carved 40-foot mahogany bar. From the saloon, continue to the end of the road to the Fernandina Beach Harbor Marina, where you can catch gorgeous sunsets and watch the shrimp boats return with the day's catch in the evening.

It's always pleasant to walk around the town, especially after the sun goes down and the quiet whisper of the past settles over Centre Street. When you're ready to dine, you'll find two excellent choices within a few blocks of each other on Second Street. **The Crab Trap,** north of Centre, is a lively and casual place. If you get here early, head to the upstairs bar for spectacular sunset views. Then come down to the main dining room, which is decorated in a rustic nautical style (fishnets abound), to sample the local seafood. Don't forget to try those sweet shrimp that Amelia Island is famous for; they get 'em fresh off the boat here.

A fancier destination is **Joe's Second Street Bistro.** A downtown fine-dining stalwart, Joe's manages to be unpretentious while serving up a gourmet, eclectic menu (the crabcakes and the Asian barbecued duckling are superb) along with one of the more extensive wine lists on the island. Try to book a table on the porch overlooking Second Street or in the courtyard.

Amelia Island isn't known for its nightlife (and the locals like it that way), but there are one or two fun late-night haunts. The aforementioned Palace Saloon hosts a variety of live music acts every night at 9:30. My favorite place to go after dark is **Wicked Davey's Fancy Saloon,** billed as Florida's northeasternmost saloon. From Thursday through Saturday, Wicked Davey's features a variety of live acts ranging from blues bands to jazz pianists to rock groups. It has a down-home appeal, a boisterous vibe, a surprisingly good tapas menu, and a ready-to-dance crowd.

On your second day in Amelia, explore the rest of the island. Naturally, fishing and boating are popular activities here. Capt. Chris Holland knows a lot more about this place than where the best fishing spots are, and you can climb aboard the *Misti Lynn* for a half-day or full-day charter, or a scenic tour of the island. **Amelia River Cruises** is another option for sightseeing tours. Among the highlights of each excursion are **Fort Clinch** and Cumberland Island, Georgia's barrier island, where horses run free and where the Carnegies used to have a home (it's now the ultra-prestigious Greyfield Inn).

Sticking to the land, a must-visit highlight is **Fort Clinch,** a short drive across the island on Atlantic Avenue. Perched on the northern edge of a state park, its cannons overlooking pristine beaches, the fort was built in 1847. Never called upon to defend the island, Fort Clinch is an architectural oddity following a coastal defense blueprint known as the Third System, which was duplicated in only a handful of other forts in North America. What really brings the place to life are the two garrulous Union Army soldiers garrisoned here. On the first weekend of each month, a full regiment arrives to re-create military life in 1864. In addition to the fort, nature and bike trails from the main road take you into a dense forest with plenty of opportunity to see the local wildlife and flora.

The Amelia Island Lighthouse is not open often and is not much of an attraction, but once you reach the eastern coast on Atlantic Avenue, you'll hit **Main Beach,** the most popular beach on Amelia Island thanks to its location, ample parking, picnic and playground facilities, and beach cabanas where you can wash off after a dip in the ocean. Keep a discerning eye open as you walk along the sand; shark-tooth hunting is a popular pastime on Amelia's beaches. Savvy explorers head out at low tide along the waterline to seek out the dark, triangular fossilized specimens ranging in size from tiny to fear-inducing.

One of Amelia Island's idyllic beaches

One of the more unique historical beaches on the island is **American Beach,** located farther south off South Fletcher Avenue. In 1935, this became a beach and resort for African Americans at a time when people of color were forbidden access to most beaches in the southern United States. For many years, it was home to one of the most interesting personalities on the island: MaVynne Betsch, also known as the Beach Lady.

Heading south from American Beach on Fletcher, you come to **Amelia Island Plantation,** a ritzy enclave of shops, restaurants, and one of the island's nicer resorts. If you've spent the day on this part of the island, you have a choice of two excellent restaurants for dinner. At the plantation, **PLaE** (People Laughing and Eating) is a swanky lounge and restaurant that serves up creative American cuisine. **Salt,** the restaurant at The Ritz, specializes in inventive and artistic food, and their Chef's Adventure menu is a true culinary journey for the palate. After dinner, you're conveniently close to a moonlight stroll on the beach.

Some of the shops at Amelia Island Plantation

When leaving this tranquil island the following morning, head south on Fletcher, which becomes A1A. You might want to stop a mile or two after crossing the bridge to the mainland at **Kayak Amelia,** where you can rent a kayak and head out on a tour (or on your own) into salt marshes and look out for gators, birds, and jumping mullet. Owners/guides Ray and Jody Hetchka provide the gear, the knowledge, maps, and chocolate chip cookies.

After a rental or a three-hour tour (that's right, a three-hour tour), continue south on A1A for roughly 9 miles before you see a sign on your right for the **Kingsley Plantation.** You'll drive down a 2-mile dirt road to this free historic site, which takes you through the tabby huts that marked the slave quarters up to the barn, garden, and main house of Zephaniah Kingsley, who lived there from 1814 to 1837.

Just a half mile south on A1A, you'll arrive at the **St. Johns River Ferry.** The last public ferry service in Florida (it's in danger of closing down due to expense and lack of traffic), this is a great shortcut that crosses the St. Johns and puts you back on A1A. It's another 40 miles south on A1A to **St. Augustine.**

While Amelia Island makes its own claim for longevity, St. Augustine is celebrated as America's oldest city. (It's a question of semantics, the key difference being that St. Augustine is the oldest *permanently occupied* European settlement.) Founded in 1565 by Don Pedro Menendez de Aviles, St. Augustine—so named because its shore was first sighted by the Spanish sailors on August 28, which is the feast day in honor of the saint—was not an empty tract of land when the colonists arrived. But the Timucuan Indians who lived here were quickly displaced or subjugated by the foreign settlers.

Similar to Amelia Island, St. Augustine changed hands many times. Spain held the city for almost two hundred years before the British took it in 1763. Their reign was much shorter; Spain reclaimed St. Augustine in 1784 and held on to it until 1821, when the United States took over. It was briefly a Confederate city (1861–62) before the Union regained control.

Today, the city remains a historical and cultural national treasure. Not quite timeless—there's too much commercial tourism to imbue the place with a sense of a forgotten era—it is still architecturally stunning and endearingly quaint. Narrow, winding streets intentionally designed to be crooked to prohibit cannon fire from breaching too far into the city) snake their way up from Matanzas Bay amid centuries-old buildings and homes. A 17th-century fort on the northeastern edge of town overlooks the bay, and there is a great variety of museums and cultural sites.

And then there is Henry Morrison Flagler, the entrepreneur and tycoon whose imprint on this city has been vital to its development. Flagler arrived in St. Augustine in 1885, fresh off his retirement from Standard Oil but by no means ready to slow down at age 53. He saw tremendous potential in Florida as a whole and in St. Augustine in particular, but he felt both lacked the proper infrastructure to thrive as a tourist destination. He had the money and the vision to do something about it.

Flagler built two hotels, the magnificent Ponce de León (now Flagler College) and the Alcazar (now the Lightner Museum), which were considered the most lavish of their times. In fact, guests who came to stay at the Ponce de León didn't pay for a night; they paid, in advance, for the season (no refunds). He also purchased a third hotel, renaming it the Cordova (now the Casa Monica Hotel). Then, to help draw crowds from the northeast, he bought a short-line railroad company and so became involved in the railroad business. He also built several churches, a hospital, and critical utilities in St. Augustine. Among other things, Flagler is credited

It's fun to tour any city in a horse-drawn carriage.

with almost single-handedly creating a resort industry in the city, and that legacy continues today.

As you approach the city from the north on A1A, you'll cross the Francis and Marina Usina Bridge. It'll be lunchtime by now, especially if you spent the morning kayaking, and you might as well begin this leg of the trip with a terrific meal. Just over the bridge on your right is the Camachee Cove Marina. Enter the marina, turn right on Yacht Club Drive, and follow the road to the end, where you'll find the **Kingfish Grill.** Located right on the Intracoastal, this restaurant has a casual, contemporary atmosphere to go with excellent fresh seafood and surprisingly good sushi (try the spicy crab roll). It's a bit removed from the heart of the old city, but the food and ambience are so good that it makes for a perfect welcome to St. Augustine.

From here, head back on A1A and go south for 1 mile until you come to San Marco Avenue. Turn left and you'll soon come to the **Old Jail,** where you can buy tickets and pick up the **Old Town Trolley Tours.** You can also continue down San Marco until you get to **Ripley's Believe It or Not!,**

The Inns of St. Augustine

Bed & breakfasts and small inns make up a big part of the experience of visiting St. Augustine. There are close to 30 inns in the city, and the ones below are all fine choices for a quaint and comfortable stay.

Casa de la Paz. If you can, book the Ponce de León room; it's got the nicest period furniture and the best view of the water. Both rooms on the third floor have whirlpool bathtubs.

Casablanca Inn. A departure from the classic Victorian homes you'll find in St. Augustine, this bayfront inn is a stately white building with mini colonnades, a funky martini bar, and 23 unique rooms.

Centennial House. A lovely 19th-century home that's been restored from the ground up to offer the best of both worlds: Think four-poster beds and whirlpool tubs. It's a small inn (only eight rooms) with a pleasant communal area and a fully loaded breakfast every morning.

Inn on Charlotte. With luxuriously appointed rooms, gourmet food (with delicious, freshly made snacks in the afternoon), and a second-floor veranda overlooking scenic Charlotte Street, this 1918 brick home is a serene oasis in the heart of the city.

Old City House Inn & Restaurant. From owners James and Ilsé Philcox to the cuisine and style of the inn, the Old City House celebrates a global theme. The seven rooms are set in a lovely cottage-style building near the heart of the city.

Old Powder House Inn. Large, comfortable rooms; an intimate historic home; and a pleasant second-floor veranda overlooking the street are highlights of this inn, but the star of the show might just be the food. Gourmet breakfasts and afternoon treats will keep you content all day.

St. Francis Inn. "The oldest inn in the oldest city" is the moniker here. Built in 1791 using coquina, the inn has been updated but still retains its old-world charm. It's located in a quiet part of the city near St. Augustine's Oldest House museum.

Old Powder House Inn

where you can get tickets for **Ripley's Sightseeing Trains.** Having ridden both, I can't say there's too much of a difference in the tour, but the Ripley trains are cuter than the trolleys. Whichever one you pick, I recommend a trolley tour as your first activity in town because it will give you a thorough synopsis of all there is to see and let you prioritize where you want to go. Also, you can hop off and back on whenever you like, and your ticket is valid for three days on both tours.

Once you're back in your car, you should have enough time left to enjoy one more attraction before places start to close for the day. From either tour office, continue on San Marco (Ripley's is closer) until you see **Castillo de San Marcos** on your left, overlooking Matanzas Bay. Pull into the parking lot and head up to this ancient guardian of the city. Completed in 1695 using coquina blocks (a mixture of packed shells and limestone that formed the main building materials in St. Augustine's early development), Castillo de San Marcos is the largest and oldest stone fort in the continental United

States. Inside, you can tour the structure, listen to guides in full costume relay the fort's history, and walk up to the ramparts for lovely views of the city, the bay, and, in the distance, the St. Augustine Lighthouse.

After the fort, you'll be ready to check in to your hotel. St. Augustine has a variety of charming bed & breakfast inns, and I would strongly recommend you stay at one. However, if you really prefer hotels and have the budget for it, book a room at the **Casa Monica Hotel,** an architectural gem and a throwback to the era of grand hotels that Flagler was known for (it's now part of the Kessler Collection).

Step out on the town in the evening for a pleasant stroll down St. George Street, the main promenade where shops, galleries, museums, historic sites, and other tourist attractions vie for your attention. Meander around and get a feel for the old city until you've built up a healthy appetite. Depending on your budget, call at one of these two restaurants: **Collage** for sophisticated bistro dining, or **Harry's** for a quintessential (and moderately priced) St. Augustine experience.

Nestled behind blooming pink bougainvilleas, Collage matches an eclectic international menu (with an emphasis on Continental flavors) with a warm, romantic ambience. Located on Hypolita Street right off St. George Street, it's in the heart of the old city. Harry's is on the waterfront, and its classic New Orleans cuisine is best enjoyed at the outdoor patio. The food and atmosphere ensure that it stays packed during peak nights.

End your night with a perfectly St. Augustine adventure and take a ghost tour. Two of the best are **The Original Ghost Tours of St. Augustine** and **A Ghostly Encounter.** Both are terrific, but A Ghostly Encounter is the only one that takes you inside the Old Spanish Military Hospital at night. Your tour guide (Original Ghost Tours offers walking, riding, and sailing tours) leads you around the old city and shares ghost stories and grisly moments from the town's past. Of course, you'll end up taking a million pictures of absolutely nothing in the hope of catching an orb or some other evidence of paranormal activity (and I did catch a perfectly round sphere of light in one photo), but that's all part of the fun. So are all the locals who drive by and honk and hoot at you while you're on the tour.

Your second day in St. Augustine will be a busy one. Chances are you'll want to see and do a lot while you're here. Some places, however, are best avoided. (I have to put the Fountain of Youth atop that particular list; the water tastes foul, and two local historians told me there is no proof that it is the actual location of the fountain.) Starting from the Old City Gate at the north end of St. George Street, you can follow this walking tour (you can also take the trolley, as your ticket is still valid):

1. Walk down St. George Street until you get to the **Colonial Spanish Quarter,** a living-history museum that re-creates 1740s Spanish St. Augustine. Artisans, herbalists, tradesmen, and citizens in period costume will share their skills and stories with you as you walk through the cluster of seven homes and buildings. The excellent and knowledgeable staff makes this my favorite historic attraction in the city.

2. Continue down St. George Street to Hypolita Street and turn right. Walk up the road, passing the lovely **Grace Methodist Church** (it's rarely open to visitors) and turn left at Sevilla Street. You'll now come to **Flagler Memorial Presbyterian Church.** Built by Flagler for his daughter, this is a breathtaking example of Venetian Renaissance architecture and home to the Flagler Mausoleum.

3. Walk south on Sevilla to King Street, where you'll find, facing each other, **Flagler College** and the **Lightner Museum.** The Flagler College tour shows you this magnificent building, which was once the unparalleled Ponce de León Hotel. Check out the largest private collection of Tiffany windows. Visit the unusual Lightner for its architectural grandeur; its three floors of Victorian furniture, musical instruments, toys, and memorabilia; and its Tiffany glass exhibit. (If you have time, squeeze in the **Old St. Augustine Village,** located on Cordova

The magnificent courtyard at Flagler College

A historic home in Old St. Augustine Village

Street behind the Lightner: This is a well-preserved collection of period homes.)

4. Walk down King Street (heading toward the bay) until you get back to St. George Street. You're now at the corner of Plaza de La Constitucion, the center of the old city. Turn left on St. George and walk 1 block to the magnificent **Cathedral-Basilica of St. Augustine.** Completed in 1797, this is the home of the oldest continuously active Catholic faith community in the continental United States. Inside, don't miss the many lovely murals and the blessed sacrament chapel.

Cathedral-Basilica of St. Augustine

5. Time for a quick late lunch (hopefully the hearty breakfast from your B&B should have fueled you until now). Head back along St. George Street to Hypolita Street and turn right. Here you'll come across **Casa Maya,** where you can eat healthy, fresh, and cheap salads, smoothies, and wraps. After, head next door to **Claude's Chocolate** for out-of-this-world, handmade confections by Claude Franques, a pure chocolatier who can do amazing things with chocolate.

6. Follow Hypolita down to the water, where you can walk along the water, with the elegant **Bridge of Lions** on your left, until you return to the Plaza de la Constitucion. Crossing the plaza, you come to Aviles Street, the oldest street in the city. Here you'll find the **Spanish Military Hospital,** a grim but highly entertaining tour of medical practices in vogue in centuries past.

7. From here, walk or take the trolley to **The Oldest House,** which has been occupied by European and American settlers since the 1600s. As such, you'll walk through four hundred years of history as you tour its rooms, adjacent museum, and surrounding grounds.

It's an ambitious tour, but you can do it, and you might even have an hour or so to rest at your hotel before dinner.

If you're here on a Saturday in the summer (May 26–September 1), return to Plaza de la Constitucion by 7 PM to see a reenactment of the changing of the guard, which takes place in front of the Government House. Then, you're just a block or two away from the **Old City House Inn & Restaurant** on Cordova Street, where you can dine on fantastic dishes from around the world, like curried ostrich medallions and pomegranate-glazed rack of lamb. The menu is varied and the food delicious.

Before you leave St. Augustine the next morning, you have one last stop to make. Cross the Bridge of Lions and follow A1A for about 1.5 miles until you reach Red Cox Road. Take a left here and follow the road for less than a half mile to get to the picturesque black-and-white-striped **St. Augustine Lighthouse & Museum.** The 219-step climb up to the top is worth it for the spectacular view and for bragging rights, and the adjacent museum is an interesting look into the origins of the lighthouse and maritime history.

Old City House Inn & Restaurant

Oh, and one last thing: If your way home happens to take you on US 1 South, stop by **Hot Shot Bakery** for fantastic muffins, pastries, cakes, sandwiches, and datil-pepper confections and sauces.

St. Augustine Lighthouse

Contacts:

A Ghostly Encounter, 3 Aviles Street, St. Augustine 32084. Call 904-827-0807 or 1-800-597-7177. Tours at 8 PM nightly (except major holidays) and Sat. at 9:30. Web site: www.ancientcitytours.net.

Amelia Hotel and Suites, 1997 South Fletcher Avenue, Amelia Island 32034. Call 904-261-5735 or 1-877-263-5428. Web site: www.amelia hotelandsuites.com.

Amelia Island Carriages. Call 904-556-2662 to reserve a tour. Web site: www.ameliaislandcarriages.net.

Amelia Island Museum of History, 233 South Third Street, Amelia Island 32034. Call 904-261-7378. Open Mon. through Sat. 10–4, Sun. 1–4. Web site: www.ameliamuseum.org.

Amelia Island Plantation, 6800 First Coast Highway, Amelia Island 32034. Call 904-261-6161 or 1-888-261-6161. Web site: www.aipfl.com.

Amelia Island Tourist Development Council and Welcome Center, 961687 Gateway Boulevard, Suite G, Amelia Island 32034. Call 1-888-228-4975. Open Mon. through Sat. 11–4, Sun. noon–4.

The Amelia Island Williams House, 103 South Ninth Street, Amelia Island 32034. Call 904-277-2328 or 1-800-414-9258. Web site: www.ameliaislandwilliamshouse.com.

Amelia River Cruises, 1 Front Street, Fernandina Beach 32034. Call 904-261-9972. Web site: www.ameliarivercruises.com.

Barbara Jean's, 960030 Gateway Boulevard, Amelia Island 32034. Call 904-277-3700. Open daily 11–9. Web site: www.barbara-jeans.com.

Casa de la Paz, 22 Avenida Menendez, St. Augustine 32084. Call 904-829-2915 or 1-800-929-2915. Web site: www.casadelapaz.com.

Casa Maya, 17 Hypolita Street, St. Augustine 32084. Call 904-823-1739. Open daily 8:30–3:30.

Casa Monica Hotel, 95 Cordova Street, St. Augustine 32084. Call 904-827-1888 or 1-800-648-1888. Web site: www.casamonica.com.

Casablanca Inn, 24 Avenida Menendez, St. Augustine 32084. Call 904-829-0928 or 1-800-826-2626. Web site: www.casablancainn.com.

Castillo de San Marcos, 1 South Castillo Drive, St. Augustine 32084. Call 904-829-6506. Open daily 8:45–4:45 (closed Christmas). Web site: www.nps.gov/casa.

Cathedral-Basilica of St. Augustine, 38 Cathedral Place, St. Augustine 32084. Call 904-824-2806. Web site: www.thefirstparish.org.

Centennial House, 26 Cordova Street, St. Augustine 32084. Call 904-810-2218 or 1-800-611-2880. Web site: www.centennialhouse.com.

Claude's Chocolate, 15 Hypolita Street, St. Augustine 32084. Call 904-808-8395. Open daily 11–6, Fri. and Sat. until 8. Web site: www.claudes chocolate.com.

Collage, 60 Hypolita Street, St. Augustine 32084. Call 904-829-0055. Open daily from 5:30 for dinner, 11:30–2:30 for lunch Sat. and Sun. Web site: www.collagestaug.com.

Colonial Spanish Quarter, St. George Street, St. Augustine 32084. Call 904-825-6830. Open daily 9–5 (closed Christmas).

The Crab Trap, 31 North Second Street, Amelia Island 32034. Call 904-261-4749. Open nightly 5–closing.

Elizabeth Pointe Lodge, 98 South Fletcher Avenue, Amelia Island 32034. Call 904-277-4851. Web site: www.elizabethpointelodge.com.

The Fairbanks House, 227 South Seventh Street, Amelia Island 32034. Call 904-277-0500 or 1-800-261-4838. Web site: www.fairbankshouse.com.

Fernandina Beach Winery & Gifts, 25 South Third Street, Fernandina Beach 32034. Call 904-583-3394. Open Sun. through Thurs. noon–6, Fri. and Sat. noon–8. Web site: www.fernandinabeachwinery.com.

Fernandina's Fantastic Fudge, 218 Centre Street, Amelia Island 32034. Call 904-277-4801. Open Sun. through Thurs. 10–8:30, Fri. and Sat. 10–10. Web site: www.fantasticfudge.com.

Flagler College Tours, 74 King Street, St. Augustine 32084. Call 904-823-3378. Tours run at 10 and 2 daily. Web site: www.flagler.edu/news_events/tours.html.

Flagler Memorial Presbyterian Church, 32 Sevilla Street, St. Augustine 32084. Call 904-829-6451. Web site: www.memorialpcusa.org.

The Florida House Inn, 20 and 22 South Third Street, Amelia Island 32034. Call 904-261-3300 or 1-800-258-3301 (reservations only). Web site: www.floridahouseinn.com.

Fort Clinch State Park, 2601 Atlantic Avenue, Amelia Island 32034. Call 904-277-7274. Park open daily 8–sunset; visitors center open 9–4:30. Web site: www.floridastateparks.org/fortclinch.

French Market Antiques, 203 Centre Street, Amelia Island 32034. Call 904-491-0707. Open Mon. through Sat. 10–5:30. Web site: www.french marketantiques.com.

The Frisky Mermaid Café, at the Florida House Inn, 22 South Third Street, Fernandina Beach 32034. Call 904-261-3300. Open daily for lunch 8–2, for dinner 5–9 (weekends until 10). Web site: www.frisky mermaid.com.

Harry's, 46 Avenida Menendez, St. Augustine 32084. Call 904-824-7765. Open Sun. through Thurs. 11–10, Fri. and Sat. 11–11. Web site: www.hookedonharrys.com.

Hot Shot Bakery, 1962 US 1 South, St. Augustine 32084. Call 904-824-7898. Open Tues. through Fri.

Inn on Charlotte, 52 Charlotte Street, St. Augustine 32084. Call 904-829-3819 or 1-800-355-5508. Web site: www.innoncharlotte.com.

Joe's Second Street Bistro, 14 South Second Street, Amelia Island 32034. Call 904-321-2558. Open nightly 6–9. Web site: www.joesbistro .com.

Kayak Amelia, 13030 Heckscher Drive, Jacksonville 32226. Call 904-251-0016. Open daily 9–5 for rentals; call ahead for tours. Web site: www.kayakamelia.com.

Kingfish Grill, 252 Yacht Club Drive, St. Augustine 32084. Call 904-824-2111. Open Sun. through Thurs. 11:30–9, Fri. and Sat. 11:30–10. Web site: www.kingfishgrill.com.

Kingsley Plantation, Fort George Island 32226. Call 904-251-3537. Open daily 9–5 (closed Thanksgiving, Christmas, and New Year's Day). Web site: www.nps.gov/archive/timu/indepth/kingsley/ kingsley_home.htm.

La Bodega Courtyard Café, 19 South Third Street, Fernandina Beach 32034. Call 904-321-1922. Open for lunch Mon. through Sat. 11:30–2:30. Web site: www.labodegacafe.com.

Lightner Museum, 75 King Street, St. Augustine 32084. Call 904-824-2874. Open daily 9–5 (closed Christmas). Web site: www.lightner museum.org.

Misti Lynn Charters, at the Fernandina Beach Marina, Fernandina Beach 32034. Call 904-321-5650 to schedule a charter or tour.

Old City House Inn & Restaurant, 115 Cordova Street, St. Augustine 32084. Call 904-826-0113 for the inn, 904-826-0184 for the restaurant. Web site: www.oldcityhouse.com.

Old Powder House Inn, 38 Cordova Street, St. Augustine 32084. Call 1-800-447-4149. Web site: www.oldpowderhouse.com.

Old St. Augustine Village, 246 St. George Street, St. Augustine 32084. Call 904-823-9722. Open Mon. through Sat. 10–4:30, Sun. 11–4:30. Web site: www.old-staug-village.com.

Old Town Trolley Tours, 167 San Marco Avenue, St. Augustine 32084. Call 904-829-3800. Tours run 8:30–5. Web site: www.trolleytours.com.

Olde Towne Carriage Company. Call 904-277-1555 to reserve a tour. Web site: www.ameliacarriagetours.com.

The Oldest House (González-Alvarez House), 14 St. Francis Street, St. Augustine 32084. Call 904-824-2872. Open daily 9–5. Web site: www.oldesthouse.org.

The Original Ghost Tours of St. Augustine, City Gate Plaza on the north end of St. George Street, St. Augustine 32084. Call 904-461-1009 or 1-888-461-1009. Tours nightly at 8 and at 9:30 PM on Fri. and Sat. (from Memorial Day through Labor Day, 8 and 9:30 nightly). Web site: www.ghosttoursofstaugustine.com.

Palace Saloon, 117 Centre Street, Fernandina Beach 32034. Call 904-491-3332. Open daily noon–2 AM. Web site: www.thepalacesaloon.com.

PLaE, 80 Amelia Village Circle, Amelia Island 32034. Call 904-277-2132. Open daily at 5:30 PM. Web site: www.plaefl.net.

Polly the Trolley, end of Centre Street, Fernandina Beach. Call 904-753-4486. Tours at 10 and 4 daily. Web site: www.pollythetrolley.com.

Ripley's Sightseeing Trains, 170 San Marco Avenue, St. Augustine 32084. Call 904-829-6545 or 1-800-226-6545. Tours run 8:30–5. Web site: www.redtrains.com.

The Ritz-Carlton, Amelia Island, 4750 Amelia Island Parkway, Amelia Island 32034. Call 904-277-1100. Web site: www.ritzcarlton.com.

Salt, at the Ritz-Carlton, 4750 Amelia Island Parkway, Amelia Island 32034. Call 904-491-6746. Open Tues. through Sat. 6–9:30 for dinner, Sun. brunch 11–2. Reservations recommended.

St. Augustine Lighthouse & Museum, 81 Lighthouse Avenue, St. Augustine 32080. Call 904-829-0745. Open daily 9–6. Web site: www.staugustinelighthouse.com.

St. Francis Inn, 279 St. George Street, St. Augustine 32084. Call 904-824-6068 or 1-800-824-6062. Web site: www.stfrancisinn.com.

St. Johns River Ferry, 4610 Ocean Street, Mayport 32233. Call 904-241-9969. Operates Mon. through Fri. at 6, 6:20, and 7 AM, continuing on the hour and half hour, with the final departure at 7 PM; Sat. and Sun. at 7, 7:20, and 8 AM, continuing on the hour and half hour, with the final departure at 8:30 PM. Web site: www.stjohnsriverferry.com.

Spanish Military Hospital Museum, 3 Aviles Street, St. Augustine 32084. Call 904-827-0807. Open daily 10–5.

Summer Beach Resort, 5456 First Coast Highway, Amelia Island 32034. Call 904-277-0905 or 1-800-862-9297. Web site: www.summerbeach.com.

Wicked Davey's Fancy Saloon, 232 North Second Street, Fernandina Beach 32034. Call 904-321-4224. Open daily 5:30–midnight or later.

CHAPTER

The Keys to the Kingdom

A Journey to and through the Florida Keys

Overview: Let's face it. The vast majority of people who head out to the keys are only there for one reason: Key West. Countless motorists have raced down US 1, ignoring everything around them in their haste to get to Florida's most famous island retreat. And I do admit, there is a lot to see and do in Key West, even if all you want to do is find the nearest bar and claim a small portion of it for a week or two.

But there's a reason someone came up with the "stop and smell the roses" adage, and it applies here. Key Largo, Islamorada, Marathon, Big Pine Key . . . each offers reasons to slow down, get out of the car, and discover something special.

Total length of trip: About 160 miles over a three- or four-day period.

Getting there: From Miami International Airport, take LeJeune Road south to FL 836 West. Follow the road for about 6 miles until you get to the Florida Turnpike. Head south toward **Key West** for about 36 miles. The turnpike ends at US 1 in Florida City. From here, it's a straight shot all the way down to Key West. Follow US 1 south about 22 miles to **Key Largo,** which is the start of the Florida Keys. At this point, US 1 becomes Overseas Highway, the main—check that, the *only*—thoroughfare through the keys. From here, you'll notice mile markers along the side of the road. These are

the best way to track where you are and where you're going (many businesses and attractions in the keys use mile markers, or MM, as their
address). The mile markers begin in Florida City with number 127, and end
at 0 in Key West. The distance from Key Largo to **Islamorada** is approximately 18 miles; it's another 35 miles to **Marathon,** and from here, 17
miles to **Big Pine Key.** The last leg of the journey is 31 miles to
Key West.

Highlights: Key West occupies the spotlight and is a hot tourist hub, world
famous for its Hemingway look-alikes and six-toed cats. By and large, the
other keys offer a more rustic experience, with Old Florida attractions and
institutions that have been here for decades. Some are no fancier than buying a few dollars' worth of food and hand-feeding hyperactive tarpon. The
interesting thing is, each key has its own identity, its own claim to fame.
We begin, naturally, in Key Largo, the first and the largest of the keys.

Key Largo

It won't take you long to get to Key Largo from Miami, but you'll feel the
change in the air once you arrive. It's not so much a difference in climate
as it is a change in culture. The keys are famous for their easygoing lifestyle,
and the buzz of Miami will have long vanished by the time you enter their
domain. Key Largo is your door to the archipelago, and it is unique in that
it straddles two very distinct environments: the sun-kissed isles to the
south, and the Everglades National Park to the north.

Indeed, it is Key Largo's natural wonders that make it worth a stop, both
above and beneath the water. The keys are known as the "Dive Capital of
the World," and Key Largo deserves part of the credit: It's home to the
John Pennekamp Coral Reef State Park, the first undersea park ever
built in the United States. You might think that would make the park the
exclusive province of divers, but it is equally accessible for those who like
to snorkel, canoe, or ride in glass-bottom boats and admire the spectacular, shallow coral reef below.

Another way to get out on the water is with **Caribbean Watersports,**
located at the **Key Largo Grande Resort & Beach Club.** Caribbean
Watersports has the usual array of water sports—parasailing, personal
watercraft, snorkeling and sailing tours, and hobie cats and sailboards for
rent—that you can find in the keys. But what they also offer, which sets

Mrs. Mac's Kitchen

them apart, are terrific Everglades ecotours. This isn't an alligator show, incidentally; rather, it's a much more serene excursion out into mangrove islands and shallow, crystal clear waters. On my tour with the able and knowledgeable Captain Matt, we spotted bonnethead sharks (these are very small and quite harmless), lobster, horseshoe crabs, a variety of jellyfish, and even a seahorse or two, along with a variety of sponges and other colorful sea life.

A few hours on the water will build up an appetite, and not far from the Key Largo Grande, at Mile Marker (MM) 99.4, is a truly "keys" joint: **Mrs. Mac's Kitchen.** You'll pass a couple of local landmarks before you get there. There is a beautifully painted building in the middle of the highway showing an underwater scene dominated by a manta ray; this is one of many murals in the Keys by marine artist Guy Harvey. Also, at MM 100, just before the restaurant, is a famous steamboat, a relic from the classic movie *The African Queen,* starring Humphrey Bogart and Katharine Hepburn.

On to Mrs. Mac's. (When you get here, you can park nearby in front of a second, ludicrous yet strangely appealing mural with a giant shark literally leaping out of it.) Upon entering, you'll notice that the walls are plastered with license plates from around the country, and even the ceiling lamps are made of them. At this down-home eatery you can get local specialties like conch (they call it "konk" in the keys) chowder and the excellent Superfishwich (a sandwich of crispy, golden fried grouper or mahi with Swiss cheese and Thousand Island dressing).

If you're taking your time through the keys, you might want to spend a night in Key Largo. You could do a lot worse than The Key Largo Grande, a modern, newly renovated hotel right on the ocean. But dive enthusiasts will probably want to check out **Jules' Undersea Lodge,** the only aquanaut hotel in the world. Located in the Emerald lagoon and accessible only to divers, it's a pricey alternative, but a unique one. If you are spending a night at Key Largo, then I'd save Mrs. Mac's for dinner and check out **Harriette's Restaurant,** a roadside diner that oozes old-time American nostalgia.

After lunch you'll continue south, passing by Tavernier; the town is believed to be named after the many taverns that once awaited sailors and "wreckers" during the 19th century, although it may also simply be a mispronunciation of the original Spanish name *Cayo Tabona*. Wreckers play an interesting role in keys history: They were the people who made a rather profitable industry of sailing out to ships that had foundered on the sharp rocks of the reef and scavenging, or rescuing, what they could before the ships were lost. This was a very different, and harshe, time on the islands, and as you pass through Tavernier you'll come across a small historic district with homes and buildings from the 1900s.

Islamorada

Islamorada stretches from MM 90 to MM 72 and includes a chain of interconnected islets. Hailed as the "Sport Fishing Capital of the World" (see what I mean about each key preserving its own identity?), it has a plethora of marinas, docks, and fishing/boating–related businesses. In fact, this is home to one of the largest charter boat fleets in Florida, and whether deepsea angling or "backcountry" (uninhabited bayside islands) flats fishing is your thing, you'll find it here. But there are interesting sights for nonanglers, havens for artists and art collectors, and plenty of up-close interaction with sea life.

The Theater of the Sea

One stop that you'll come to early on in Islamorada is **The Rain Barrel,** an artists' village where you can often find the artists-in-residence at work. Some longtime residents, like Dwayne and Cindy King of the **Rain Barrel Sculpture Gallery,** have been showcasing their marvelous work here for more than 20 years. Others, like John David Hawyer, whose paintings capture keys' landscapes in a timeless and beautiful way, are Florida natives but relative newcomers to the village.

Just across from the Rain Barrel is a giant lobster. This massive crustacean is an effective mascot and a sure-fire way to draw attention to **Treasure Village,** a second cluster of artisan and gift shops. Continuing south from here, you'll come to one of my favorite destinations in the keys: **The Theater of the Sea.** Another "Original Florida" attraction, this family-owned park was established in 1946 and is the second-oldest marine mammal facility in the world. Part Sea World Jr., part education center, and part environmental mission, it remains a must-see on the way to Key West.

Give yourself a few hours at the park to make the most of it. Included in the admission are continuous daily shows featuring dolphins, sea lions, and parrots. At the end of the show, a lucky few will be able to walk down and pet the dolphins and get a kiss (or hug) from Seth the sea lion. There's also a bottomless boat ride (accompanied by leaping dolphins) and nature tour. For a special treat (naturally at an additional price), book an interactive program that takes you in the water with your choice of dolphins, sea lions, or stingrays. The dedication of the staff and the humane focus on animal rescue and health (quite a few of the animals here are injured or crippled) make this an experience as heartwarming as it is entertaining.

For lunch, head south to the **Spanish Gardens Café,** located on MM 80.9. Don't let the plain exterior of the mall deter you. This café, owned and run by a charismatic Spaniard with a local reputation as the "Salad Nazi" (he doesn't like it when customers mess with his food or ask for substitutions), offers terrific salads and sandwiches on fresh-baked baguettes made from fine, fresh ingredients. There is a very nice market adjacent to the small café, and a pleasant outdoor seating area surrounding a small fountain. (The café also has excellent tapas and seafood paella at night.)

While Key West is generally pricy when it comes to its accommodations, Islamorada is a good option for budget travelers. The **Pines and Palms Resort** is one such place, offering individual and shared cottages by the ocean. The interior is pretty bare-bones, but it's clean and well maintained, and the complex has an oceanfront heated pool. On the other side of the spectrum is the **Cheeca Lodge,** which is about as swanky as it gets on Islamorada. A favorite haunt for movie stars and celebrities in its heyday, the lodge offers a range of accommodations from a typical resort double to a beach bungalow, and boasts one of the best pools and spas on the island.

Fishing and all things nautical dominate life in Islamorada, as a quick tour of these islands will confirm. On MM 81.5, there's a beautiful, if relatively small, **Worldwide Sportsman** store whose proud centerpiece is *Pilar*, sister to Hemingway's famous boat, behind which is a marina where you can book a boat trip through **Easy Adventures.** Farther south, on

MM 77.5, it's almost a right of passage to stop by at **Robbie's.** This one-stop-shopping institution has a marina where you can charter fishing trips, catamaran snorkeling cruises, boat rentals, Jet Skis, and other aquatic activities. But most everyone comes to feed the tarpon. For a few dollars, you get a bucket of baitfish with which you walk out to the edge of the docks. Dangle the bait in front of you, and in a blink you'll have a massive tarpon leap up out of the water to grab it. If you're not quick enough (and there are ample photos in the bait shop to prove this), the tarpon will swallow your entire hand in its bid to get its snack. This doesn't hurt, but it is quite a sight.

Speaking of sights, there are a few here that will make you chuckle. A mammoth fake shark hangs from a motel/fishing charter; a mermaid billboard beckons you to the **Lorelei;** and, of course, there is the aforementioned giant lobster. Of the three, the Lorelei is the place you'll want to go for dinner. The lilting name is derived from a German mermaid legend (hence the billboard).

Located on the water (much of the original restaurant was destroyed by Hurricane Wilma, but the cabana still stands, and the place is being rebuilt), this restaurant is a local hangout with outdoor seating, a lively bar area, and live music every night. The menu ranges from burgers to fresh seafood and prime rib (their conch fritters are outstanding). It's also a lovely place to watch the sun set over the water. If you want to try something a little different than keys' flavor, check out **Kaiyo,** a Japanese restaurant that's a welcome anomaly. From the rock garden outside to the cool, artfully decorated interior, Kaiyo combines inventive Japanese cuisine (try one of their signature maki rolls) with an ambience that you won't find elsewhere on the island.

Islamorada doesn't exactly come alive at night. Most people who come here want to be up early to get on the water, and you'll want to do the same to continue your journey. Before you leave, however, stop by the **Midway Café** for breakfast. Located squarely at the midpoint between Miami and Key West, this warm, inviting little restaurant has excellent breakfast fare (and tasty wraps for lunch).

Marathon

Continuing the theme of "to each his own identity," Marathon falls under the moniker, "The Heart of the Keys." This is the midpoint of the archipelago, and its name and claim to fame arise from its role in the construction of the famous Seven Mile Bridge. The bridge lies on the southern end of the island. Before you get to it, there are two places that are worth your time.

As you're making your way down, keep an eye out on the right for the large leaping mother and baby dolphin statues that mark the entrance to the **Dolphin Research Center.** This not-for-profit educational facility is devoted to the study and better understanding of dolphins (there's a secondary focus on sea lions), but it also serves as an attraction where visitors can learn about one of humanity's best friends. Through daily narrated sessions, you'll get to learn about the dolphins' different personalities and watch how humans and dolphins interact. You'll also meet Tursi, a minor celebrity who is the daughter of one of the original five dolphins who starred in *Flipper* (the show was filmed here). It's not a fancy water park, but rather a research center where there is obvious and open love between the staff and the dolphins. There are also several programs that let you get in the water with the animals, and even be a dolphin trainer for a day.

Less than 10 miles south of the Dolphin Research Center is a very different highlight of Marathon. The **Crane Point Museum & Nature Center** is spread across 63 acres and is really a collection of different experiences; the main building houses a museum of natural and nautical history, and adjacent to this is a children's area (highlighted by two Wyland murals) that includes marine touch tanks and a mini pirate's ship deck where kids can dress up in costume and play. You can then hike along one of the many nature trails on the property and walk through one of the last remaining thatch palm hammocks in the country. The loop around the entire site takes you to a wild-bird center; two historic properties—the Crane House (a classic example of 1950s architecture) and the Adderley House (an early-1900s home built from "tabby," or crushed seashells, by a Bahamian immigrant); and a rotating "Creature Feature" exhibit.

From here, it's on to the Seven Mile Bridge. You'll be driving on the new, modern Seven Mile Bridge, of course. But the original one leads to an interesting collection of historic homes and museums called **Pigeon Key,** which chronicles the lives of the workers who built the bridge between 1908 and 1923 for Henry Flagler's railroad (also known as "Flagler's Folly"). At the time, it was a backbreaking—one could say *marathon*—endeavor.

Big Pine Key and the Lower Keys

The first thing you'll come across in Big Pine Key happens to be one of the natural treasures of the archipelago. **Bahia Honda State Park** has the only natural sand beaches in the keys, and they are breathtaking. Loggerhead, Calusa, and Sandpiper Beaches have been counted among the best in the country, and they're more than worth the entrance fee into the park.

You also get spectacular views of the water, the remnants of the old bridge, and tiny islets in the distance where you can go snorkeling. The park has excellent concessions and offers snorkeling tours out to Looe Key National Marine Sanctuary. Bahia Honda is one of the most popular camping destinations in South Florida, but the park also has a secret: You can rent one of six cabins here (they are located across the highway), complete with kitchen, living, and sleeping areas, for a bargain. This is one of the best and most secluded lodging bets in the keys, but those who know about it make sure they have one reserved: As a result, the cabins are often booked months in advance.

Bahia Honda State Park

Big Pine Key and the Lower Keys are the animal kingdom of the keys. As soon as you come off the bridge, you'll see signs telling you to slow down and watch for deer. And these aren't any ordinary deer: Big Pine Key is where you'll find the **National Key Deer Refuge,** home to a tiny, almost toylike subspecies of the Virginia white-tailed deer. There are only about seven hundred of these beautiful creatures, which stand no taller than 32 inches high, and they inhabit the 25 islands that make up the refuge. You can spot one or two (I did) if you're willing to drive off the main road onto Key Deer Boulevard, which takes you through the refuge. For the best chance of seeing the deer, go at dawn or dusk.

While you're here, turn right onto Watson Boulevard and head toward No Name Key. Eventually, you'll come to the **No Name Pub,** a legendary landmark with the character and history of a place that has seen and been through a lot. In 1931, the business opened as a general store, but it was also, for a while, a bait-and-tackle shop and a brothel. Since the late 1930s, it's been serving food, and it is now known for its pizzas. Dollar bills cover the walls and ceiling, and the atmosphere is downhome, backcountry authentic Florida Keys. Grab a table and settle down for a rewarding lunch.

There is one last place worthy of mention before you arrive at Key West: **Boondocks Grille & Draft House,** on Ramrod Key (MM 27.5), is a fun, family-oriented place. In addition to the only miniature golf park in the keys, Boondocks has live music and tasty comfort food, and it always seems to be celebrating one event or other under its massive tiki-hut roof. If you like karaoke, don't miss the Tuesday and Wednesday karaoke competition, where the grand prize winner gets a vacation to the Bahamas.

Key West

Depending on how easy you take it and how often you decide to bunker down for the night, you'll arrive in Key West on either day two or day three of your trip. And while it's a little bit of a reach to discuss "The Conch Republic" in a Backroads & Byways book, it also can't be ignored. After all, this is your final destination, and I would be a poor guide if I didn't have anything to say about it.

However, for the purposes of this book, I'll stay away from Duval Street and focus on what there is to do and see beyond Key West's world-famous main strip. The first item to settle is lodging. You won't be driving much—

A Fury Water Adventures catamaran

this is a town made for walking or trolley rides—so where you stay is important. As nice as some of the hotels are here, I'd also recommend one of the island's many fine inns or bed & breakfasts, which really seasons your experience with island flavor and laid-back hospitality.

For something a little different, check out **The Eden House,** a tucked-away inn with airy rooms (the light-colored wood makes a huge difference), pleasant pool, a small niche in one corner where you can go pick up a hammock if you want one, and a friendly, ultracasual staff. For a more typical

B&B experience, you'll have numerous options, and one of the better ones is the **Artist House** (try to book the Turret Suite). This gorgeous, renovated Victorian mansion has quite a history, and it has kept much of the ambience and look of the past while installing the modern amenities you need.

If this is your first time in Key West, an **Old Town Trolley Tour** is the way to go to see and learn the most in a short amount of time. In 90 minutes, you'll know which museums and attractions you'll want to visit. Of course, many people who travel to this island want to get off the island and head to the reef for some wonderful snorkeling or diving. As this is the only living coral barrier reef in North America, it's kind of a special treat, to put it mildly, and there are several companies that will help you see it up close. If you want the party-boat experience, book a catamaran tour with **Fury Water Adventures** (which also offers a range of other on-the-water excursions and a glass-bottom boat for those who don't want something too rigorous); for a more private and relaxed experience, sail with **Danger Charters.** Both are located at the Westin Marina on the northwest corner of the town.

You can take a half- or full-day tour, but on a short trip, I'd stick with the half day so you can head back to your hotel, freshen up, and hit the town for some sight-seeing and lunch. Do the latter first and head to Eaton Street (2 blocks away from Fleming Street). At Eaton and White Streets, you'll find the new location of **The Art of Baking by Henrietta,** a sweet, sweet institution. Burgers and sandwiches, along with some Spanish-Cuban specialties, are the lunch fare at this eatery, but the stars of the show are the baked goods. Henrietta's Coconut Strips and Conch Rolls, in particular, are decadent delights that have been featured nationally on the Food Network. In my mother's opinion, she also makes the best key lime pie in Key West.

From Henrietta's, you have a bit of a trek (you might want to grab a cab) to get to the **Hemingway Home and Museum.** Walk west on Eaton toward Duvall Street for about a half mile, and turn left on Whitehead Street. In another half mile, you'll reach the landmark. The author's onetime home chronicles "Papa's" time on the island, and it is the best place to see those famous six-toed cats you've heard so much about.

Meander down Duval Street (heading north) in the afternoon, enjoying the sights and sounds of Key West. You'll want to get to Mallory Square in time for sunset, but before that, try to make time for another of Key West's quirky museums. My vote—kitschy as it sounds—goes to **Pat**

Croce's Pirate Soul Museum, on Front Street a block east off Duval. Interactive displays, elaborate rooms, and, above all, real-life histories of the world's most famous buccaneers make this an enjoyable cross between Disney-like artifice and Caribbean folklore.

Mallory Square in the hour or two leading up to sunset is home to a daily street festival with performers, food, and arts and crafts stalls. The performances range from magicians to high-wire acts to sword-swallowers; but the action stops by the time the sun sets, because this is what people come to see. It's a picturesque sight.

I highly recommend **The Original Ghost Tours of Key West** as a nighttime activity, but before that (the tours start at 8 and 9 nightly), you'll

Hemingway Home and Museum

Guy Harvey's Island Grill

probably want to eat dinner. To make the 9 PM show, you'll want something near the square, and I'd head to the new **Guy Harvey's Island Grill,** just off Duval on Greene Street. Guy Harvey has spent his life on the water. A researcher, artist, conservationist, and explorer, he is a crusader for ocean life. At his restaurant, you not only get live music and fresh seafood in a pleasant atmosphere; you also help his conservationist efforts. A portion of all the money spent here goes to his research institute.

After dinner, head south on Duval (away from the water) to La Concha Hotel to meet your ghost tour guide and enjoy a nighttime walk through Key West. The stories you'll hear alternate between spooky and just plain twisted, and you'll hear about a certain doll named Robert. I won't say more here, but on your next day, before you leave Key West, head to the **East Martello Museum & Gallery,** where Robert lives . . . if you dare.

Contacts:

The Art of Baking by Henrietta, 1111 Eaton Street, Key West 33040. Call 305-295-0505. Open Mon. through Sat. 9–6. Web site: www .henriettakeywest.com.

Artist House, 534 Eaton Street, Key West 33040. Call 305-296-3977 or 1-800-582-7882. Web site: www.artisthousekeywest.com.

Bahia Honda State Park, 36850 Overseas Highway, Big Pine Key 33043. Call 305-872-3210 or 1-800-326-3521. Open daily 8 AM–sunset. Web site: www.floridastateparks.org/bahiahonda.

Boondocks Grille & Draft House, 27205 US 1, Ramrod Key 33042. Call 305-872-4094. Restaurant open daily 11–11, mini golf open 10–10:30. Web site: www.boondocks.us.com.

Caribbean Watersports and Enviro-Tours, at the Key Largo Grande Resort & Beach Club, 97000 Overseas Highway, Key Largo 33037. Call 305-852-4707. Web site: www.caribbeanwatersports.com.

Cheeca Lodge & Spa, 81801 Overseas Highway, Islamorada 33036. Call 305-664-4651 or 1-800-327-2888. Web site: www.cheeca.com.

Crane Point Museum & Nature Center, 5550 Overseas Highway, Marathon 33050. Call 305-743-3900. Open Mon. through Sat. 9–5, Sun. noon–5. Web site: www.cranepoint.net.

Danger Charters, Westin Marina, Slip #7, Key West. Call 305-296-3272 or 305-304-7999. Half-day tours depart daily at 9 and 2 (3:30 in the summer), full-day tours leave at 9 (10 in the summer). Web site: www.dangercharters.com.

Dolphin Research Center, 58901 Overseas Highway, Grassy Key 33050. Call 305-289-1121, or 305-289-0002 for program reservations. Open daily 9–4:30 except major holidays. Web site: www.dolphins.org.

East Martello Museum & Gallery, 3501 South Roosevelt Boulevard, Key West 33040. Call 305-296-3913. Open daily 9:30–4:30 except Christmas. Web site: www.kwahs.com.

The Eden House, 1015 Fleming Street, Key West 33040. Call 305-296-6868 or 1-800-533-5397. Web site: www.edenhouse.com.

Fury Water Adventures, at the Westin Marina, Key West. Call 1-877-994-8898. Half-day three-hour tours depart at 9:30 and 1, full-day tours leave at 9:30. Web site: www.furykeywest.com.

Guy Harvey's Island Grill, 511 Greene Street, Key West 33040. Call 305-295-0019. Open Sun. to Wed. 11–midnight, Thurs. to Sat. 11–2 AM. Web site: www.guyharveysislandgrill.net.

Harriette's Restaurant, MM 95.7, Key Largo 33037. Call 305-852-8689. Open daily 6 AM–2 PM.

Hemingway Home and Museum, 907 Whitehead Street, Key West 33040. Call 305-294-1136. Open daily 9–5. Web site: www.hemingway home.com.

Hilton Key Largo Beach Resort, 97000 South Overseas Highway, Key Largo 33037. Call 1-888-871-3437. Web site: www.keylargoresort.com.

John Pennekamp Coral Reef State Park, MM 102.5, Overseas Highway, Key Largo 33037. Call 305-451-6300. Web site: www .pennekamppark.com.

Jules' Undersea Lodge, 51 Shoreland Drive, Key Largo 33037. Call 305-451-2353. Web site: www.jul.com.

Kaiyo, 81701 Old Highway, Islamorada 33036. Call 305-664-5556. Open Mon. to Sat. for dinner 5–10. Web site: www.kaiyokeys.com.

Lorelei, 81924 Overseas Highway, Islamorada 33036. Call 305-664-4656. Open for breakfast daily 7–11 in season, on weekends only 7–11 in off-season; open for lunch 11–9 weekdays, 11–10 weekends.

Midway Café, 80499 Overseas Highway, Islamorada 33036. Call 305-664-2622. Open weekdays 7–3 (closed Wed.), 6–3 on weekends. Closed October.

Mrs. Mac's Kitchen, MM 99.5, Key Largo 33037. Call 305-451-3722. Open Mon. through Sat. 10:30–9:30.

National Key Deer Refuge Visitor Center, 28950 Watson Boulevard, Big Pine Key 33043. Call 305-872-0774. Web site: www.nationalkeydeer .fws.gov.

No Name Pub, North Watson Boulevard, Big Pine Key 33043. Call 305-872-9115. Open daily 11–11. Web site: www.nonamepub.com.

Old Town Trolley Tours, Mallory Square Depot, Key West 33040. Call 305-296-6688. Tours run daily 9–5. Web site: www.trolleytours.com/key-west.

The Original Ghost Tours of Key West, 423 Fleming Street at La Concha Hotel, Key West 33040. Call 305-294-9255. Tours run at 7 and 9 nightly. Web site: www.hauntedtours.com.

Pat Croce's Pirate Soul Museum, 524 Front Street, Key West 33040. Call 305-292-1113. Open daily 9–7. Web site: www.piratesoul.com.

Pines and Palms Resort, MM 80.4, Islamorada 33036. Call 305-664-4343 or 1-800-624-0964. Web site: www.pinesandpalms.com.

The Rain Barrel artists' village, 86700 Overseas Highway, Islamorada 33036. Call 305-852-3084. Open daily 9–5.

Robbie's, MM 77.5, Islamorada 33036. Call 305-664-9814 for boat rentals and tarpon feeding, 305-664-8070 for charter fishing, or 1-877-664-8498. Open 8–4 daily for tarpon feeding (sometimes later); call for charters and trips. Web site: www.robbies.com.

Spanish Gardens Café, MM 80.9, Islamorada 33036. Call 305-664-3999. Open Mon. through Sat. 11–9, Sun. 11–3.

The Theater of the Sea, 84721 Overseas Highway, Islamorada 33036. Call 305-664-2431. Ticket office opens at 9:30 AM daily. Web site: www.theaterofthesea.com.

Worldwide Sportsman, 81576 Overseas Highway, Islamorada 33036. Call 305-664-4615. Open daily 9–8:30 (Fri. and Sat. until 9). Web site: www.worldwidesportsman.com. For **Easy Adventures** boat tours, call 305-451-8393. Web site: www.easyadventures.net.

CHAPTER

3

Passport to the Everglades

The Alleys of Alligator Alley and the Trails of Tamiami Trail

Overview: No book on Florida byways would be complete without mentioning Alligator Alley and the Tamiami Trail. This is not because these are hidden, seldom-traveled roads that you need four-wheel drive to reach. Alligator Alley is the name of the portion of I-75 that cuts through the Everglades from Fort Lauderdale to Naples. It's one of the principal highways that cross Florida from east to west, and it's pretty much the quickest way to travel between these two large, well-known cities; a straight shot along level, flat ground; a well-paved, four-lane highway and also a toll road.

The Tamiami Trail Scenic Highway is a more meandering road beginning just south of Naples and crossing the heart of the Everglades. The "scenic highway" section is part of a 275-mile-long road that runs from Tampa to Miami. The Tamiami Trail is quite famous. Considered one of the great engineering accomplishments of its time, the highway was completed in 1928, an $8-million urbanization of some of the wildest and most inhospitable wilderness in the country.

You might think all of these credentials would disqualify Alligator Alley and the Tamiami Trail from contention as true back roads. And I would've been inclined to agree with you until I started discovering where the roads lead from these highways. There's a reason that this part of Florida—encompassing Everglades City, Marco Island, and Naples—is known as the Paradise Coast.

Alligator Alley

Total length of trip: About 100 miles over a weekend.

Getting there: From I-95, take exit 24, I-595 West. Drive along I-595 about 10 miles, and you'll get to an interchange that marks the beginning of Alligator Alley (I-75). From the tollbooth, it's 84 miles to **Naples,** but the hour and 15 minutes it takes to get there are pretty much wasted if you don't indulge your adventurous spirit and explore what the exits have to offer. Drive along Alligator Alley for 25 miles until you get to exit 49. Take a right off the exit ramp, heading north, to enter the Big Cypress Seminole Indian Reservation. You'll be on County Route 833 (CR 833), also called Snake Road (and later Government Road). From here, it's 17 miles to the **Ah-Tah-Thi-Ki Museum,** 17.5 miles to **Big Cypress Hunting Adventures,** and 19 miles to **Billie Swamp Safari.** Once you return to Alligator Alley, it's another 37 miles to exit 80. Take a left off this exit, heading south, and travel along FL 29 for about 12 miles to **Fakahatchee Strand Preserve State Park.** Once you're back on Alligator Alley, it's approximately 20 miles to Naples.

Highlights: I'm going to throw out a disclaimer, right off the bat. Alligator Alley is somewhat of a misnomer, because you might not see any alligators here. It's not that they don't frequent the canal that runs adjacent to the road; they do. But you're going too fast to see them, or if you do see them, it's a neck-snapping glimpse as you zoom by. You'll have more luck if you crawl through the 70 mph road and stop at all the rest areas, which are right on the edge of the canal, to scan the water for a protruding snout. I tried that. The first time I took the road, I was completely seduced by the name and kept my neck firmly craned to the right in hopes of catching a veritable swarm of gators sunbathing by the road. But alligators have no particular desire to be seen, and so it is up to us to go and search them out.

Alligator Alley wasn't always this way. When it was completed in 1969, it was a two-lane freeway that divided traffic by a double yellow line. Back then, it was dangerous not just because of gators, but because of oncoming cars flying by with very little room to maneuver. In fact, the drama surrounding the building of Alligator Alley is a quirky anecdote in the annals of Florida's history. While many clamored for the vital link between the east and west coasts, and the project was supported by the Seminole tribe who

Alligator Alley

owned the land through which the road must pass, there was stiff local and national opposition. The swirling, bickering parties who fought all the way to the Supreme Court over the road prompted the Associated Press to label it, "the most controversial road ever built in Florida." A catchier moniker was "Alligator Alley."

When it was first built, Alligator Alley didn't have the wire fencing that now runs along both sides, so the wildlife had as much access to it as the motorists. It also didn't have the development of bridges that engineers and conservationists have put into place to let alligators and other residents of the Everglades flourish and travel unmolested through the area. Don't worry, though. We'll get to the gators in just a bit.

Alligator Alley is unlike your typical U.S. interstate highway. There are no fast-food chains interrupting your drive. There is only one gas station along the entire road, and it's not visible until you take the exit. With the exception of small stretches at either end, there are no lights. There are few public restrooms.

What the Alley does give you is swamp grass, near unbroken miles of it. You see the flat, marshy immensity of the Everglades stretching out on both sides of the highway. For most of the way, the vista is punctuated in places by random clusters of trees that look like they arrived here by accident and don't know how to get out. It's very appropriately known as the "River of Grass," and while some will think the unchanging landscape makes for a boring, even grueling, ride, I found it to be a swampy oasis. This is the time to roll down your windows (if it's not too hot), put on your favorite driving music, and just cruise. This is timeless Florida, the land of the Calusa Indians who first settled here and survived against some of Mother Nature's (and the U.S. army's) most aggressive ambassadors.

It's rough land, so isolated that there are emergency call boxes placed at 1-mile intervals throughout the road. Proposals are in place to build a firehouse near the Naples end of the road, but until that happy day, you do not want to get stuck at night on Alligator Alley. Even the rest areas have been stripped down to the bare basics. Most are little more than parking lots, picnic tables, and boat ramps. I still recommend pulling off the road at one of these, not just because you might see one of those infamous alligators, but because you'll *hear* what the Everglades is all about. The constant chattering of bird, bug, and beast echoes in the air at all times, drowning out even the roar of traffic zooming by.

While it may seem untamed and unspoiled, the land here has been meticulously irrigated and managed by the Florida Fish and Wildlife Conservation Commission. Water management is huge in the swamp, and the massive network of more than 200 miles of canals and waterways that crisscross this area is a mark of the ingenuity and dedication that has gone into preserving the natural habitat. In addition to helping to protect the native flora and fauna, these hydrological improvements contribute to Florida's water supply. It's a subtle reminder that, while the Everglades looks wild, it does come with one 20th-century luxury: modern plumbing.

Many people come to Alligator Alley to fish, either angling by the side of the road or taking a boat along the 285 miles of canals or the more natural "flats." The Everglades gives them quite a bounty, and the dry season, beginning in the fall, is the best time to cast your line and try your luck. People also come here to hunt. Hogs, deer, turkey, coot, duck, and quail headline the list of potential prey, along with less edible game. There's an archery-only season from mid-August to mid-September. In addition to holding valid hunting and fishing licenses while you're on state soil (as opposed to native tribal land), you need to be aware of all rules and restrictions regarding guns, vehicles, and what you can, and can't, bag for the ride home. For up-to-date information, call the Fish & Wildlife Conservation Commission South Region Office at 561-625-5122.

When you enter Alligator Alley from Broward County in the east, heading toward Naples, the second rest area you encounter is a good place to stop. (The rest stop is on the other side of the road, but there is a meandering underpass that will get you there.) In addition to restrooms and a cornucopia (for Alligator Alley) of snack machines, there is an informative exhibit depicting the Glades, the conservation efforts in place to keep it the way it is, and displays of the native wildlife.

Once you're back on the road, you can cruise along until you get to exit 49. It's not like you have many options: This is the first exit off the main road that goes anywhere, and it's located roughly at the halfway point of Alligator Alley. Here you'll find, on the corner of the exit ramp and CR 833, the only gas station along the road. This is a good place to stock up on the basics, and inside the store are coupons to area attractions. From here, head north into the Big Cypress Seminole Indian Reservation. You're in Seminole land now.

At this point, you have a few options. You can go into full safari mode, taking what the road gives you and striking out on your own along trails and byways. If you do this, you'll quickly leave what civilization there is behind, and the alligators will not disappoint. In 12 minutes of driving, I found four of them, three small specimens and one larger one, none of them caring that I had jumped out of my car to point excitedly at them.

But it's not just the alligators that will excite you. There are several worthy denizens of the marshes, some more elusive than others: The Florida panther, wild hogs, river otters, brown water snakes, and white-tailed deer can be found here. Herds of water buffalo are visible. Snow-white egrets seemed frozen in place along the side of the road. Larger species, also easy to find, included a variety of herons and storks. Hawks circled overhead as I drove.

If you prefer guided tours to do-it-yourself adventures, head straight along CR 833, which is also called Snake Road. You won't find much beyond grazing water buffalo and cows for miles until you reach **Big Cypress Hunting Adventures,** a hunter's wonderland. Here a hunting guide will take you on a custom-built buggy deep into the heart of the Everglades, where you have the potential to see just about every animal this wilderness has to offer. Your vantage point on the elevated buggy gives you an excellent field of vision across the fields of swamp grass; you can also jump off and travel on foot or sit perched high above the ground in a tree stand. Rifles, handguns, and muzzle loaders can be supplied, although many people bring their own.

As for game, it all depends on the season. It's best to call Big Cypress Hunting Adventures, or visit their Web site, to find what's available when you're going. You can't hunt the panther, which is an endangered species, but wild hogs (for meat), boars (for trophies), deer, and Osceola turkeys are in abundance. An additional advantage to newcomers and out-of-towners is that no hunting license is required. Again, this is Seminole land, and their license is included in the hunting package.

Once you've made a kill and taken the "Look ma, I did it!" photos, your guide will have it skinned, cleaned, and quartered for you. For an additional fee, you can have your prize sent to an on-site processing plant, where the meat can be dressed, prepared, packed into sausages, and/or wrapped for the ride home. If one day of hunting just isn't enough, overnight accommodations are available. *Note:* You need to call in advance to set up an outing, and be prepared to put down a deposit to hold your reservation.

If you bypass the hunting extravaganza and continue straight along Snake Road, you'll soon enter the main part of the Seminole community. The roads are well paved but are narrow in places, and large trucks going the opposite way can give you a close shave as they pass. Once you reach the community, you'll see schools, administrative buildings, and residential areas, all belonging to the tribe, which numbers about three hundred people. The Big Cypress Reservation is home to a proud people, a tribe that celebrates its status as Florida's "Unconquered" Seminoles. And your first major destination on the road will tell you all about them.

At the corner of CR 833 and West Boundary Road (17 miles north of Alligator Alley), you'll find the **Ah-Tah-Thi-Ki Museum.** *Ah-Tah-Thi-Ki* means "a place to learn," and the museum houses the largest exhibition relating to Seminole life and culture in the country. Visiting Ah-Tah-Thi-Ki is a multifaceted introduction to the Seminole tribe and the Everglades. It's Native American history as told by Native Americans.

Start your tour with a brief but excellent introduction to the Seminole people and their history. You can take a guided tour of the facility or wander through the various exhibits depicting life-sized models of Seminole Indians engaged in day-to-day activities such as fishing, cooking, and sewing. The displays show how the tribe settled and survived in this rough land for the past two hundred years. Marriage, folklore, and spiritual ceremonies are also portrayed, as are collections of colorful clothing, tools, weapons, and instruments used by past settlers. At the Legends Theater, visitors can gather in a camplike environment to hear about Seminole legends and traditional beliefs.

After touring the main building, you can take a walk along a 1.5-mile boardwalk that stretches from the museum out into the Big Cypress Swamp. There are markers along the way that identify the local flora and describe how many of the plants were used by the tribe. Along the way is a re-created Seminole village, complete with chickee huts, ceremonial grounds, and artisans in action. From here, Ah-Tah-Thi-Ki takes you to the present day. Part of the museum includes a "living village" experience; visitors visit an actual Native American village and learn about traditional cooking, arts, and crafts from local tribal members.

Once you leave Ah-Tah-Thi-Ki, continue on West Boundary Road for 3 miles and you'll see the sign for **Billie Swamp Safari** on your right. For those of you on the hunt for gators, I have two words: *buckle up.* Billie Swamp might not look like much at first glance. Once you park and walk up to the main area, you'll see a few thatched roofs, a pathway disappearing into a thick growth of Everglades foliage, and a gift shop. On your left is a shy-looking wild boar in an enclosure. An even more timid deer is in a nearby pen.

But then you step onto the path and enter a wild, wild world. You'll see, in low-walled enclosures, native creatures including large turtles and small alligators. There's a row of glass cages with snakes, spiders, and other little bugs and beasts. Next to that is another, larger enclosure where scores of alligators laze in the sun, and the **Swamp Water Café,** an excellent place for Indian tacos and burgers, frog's legs, and gator-tail nuggets. Make sure to try the traditional flat, round Seminole fry bread.

If I learned one thing at Billie Swamp, it was that walking alone along a wooden boardwalk over an alligator pit is a mildly unnerving experience. But this is the path to Billie's most popular attraction: the swamp buggy ride. So, with a wary eye, I crossed the pit, peering down at a bevy of full-grown gators, one of which had its mouth wide open, waiting for its teeth to be cleaned, and another that was so large that it looked like it had cleaned out the menu at the Swamp Water Café.

Once you're over this threshold (if you're feeling squeamish, there's a safer path), you can board one of the custom-made, 9-foot-high swamp buggies, which look a bit like prehistoric Hummers. Because of their massive tires, these transports provide you with an elevated viewpoint of all there is to see out here. The canopy above you is equally important, as it blocks out the Florida sun. The hour-long guided tour is a bumpy, bouncy joyride through the wetlands, and the exuberant guides are pleasant hosts.

Not every animal at Billie's is native, so if you see an ostrich on your tour, don't suddenly start questioning your grasp of Florida fauna. But the locals are the stars of the show: water buffalo, razorback hogs, wild turkey, indigenous and exotic deer, antelope, bison, raccoons, panthers (good luck finding one of them), and the ubiquitous gators.

If you want to get closer to the alligators, Billie's will take you on an airboat ride. The drone of the giant fan propelling you across the marsh can make you feel like you're directly under the engine of a small airplane, but if you can handle the noise (the earplugs help), these are fun romps through the swamp. Your driver, perched atop a high chair, will be happy to point out the turtles, birds, fish, and other creatures that thrive in the water. And when the boats stop, you're likely to see your fair share of alligators in their natural environment.

Back on dry land, you can catch one of the two shows Billie's offers daily. The snake and alligator show is, naturally, an exhibition of snake handling and alligator wrestling. The swamp critter show is a little kitschier, involving nonnative animals. There's also a nature trail and a re-created traditional Seminole village deep in the heart of the swamp.

Hardy tourists can enhance their commune-with-nature zeal exponentially by opting to stay the night at Billie's. Overnight packages include a night safari in the swamp buggy, which will give you new respect for the untamed power of this land. After your ride, you'll check in at your thatched-roof *chickee*, the Seminole word for "house" or "home." The Seminoles used to build these palmetto-thatched huts at various points along the Everglades, and they were used as free lodgings for any Seminole traveler. Today, you'll pay for the privilege, but this is as close as you'll get to nature short of packing a tent and marching out into the wetlands. There is no electricity or running water. At night, when even the museum staff is absent, you'll feel like the only person within a thousand-mile radius. The only sounds you'll hear are the scurrying, splashing, and skittering of the land's residents.

The morning after (or the day before, if the chickee-hut experience is your idea of torture), you'll find yourself back on Alligator Alley. By now, you'll likely have seen your fill of gators and won't be scanning the canals and horizons feverishly for these creatures. You can continue toward

Naples, and if you don't veer from your path, you'll be there in about 40 minutes. Before you get there, however, there is one other exit that will tempt you off the beaten path.

The road, which is FL 29, isn't all that special; that is to say, it's more of the same: The Everglades doesn't change its colors or vistas all that much. You do pass through a panther habitat, and there are several signposts telling you to be wary of crossing panthers. It's not going to happen. If you park your car and hold your breath for a few hours . . . nah, still won't happen. There's a reason they're on the endangered list: There are fewer than a hundred of these native big cats left, and they live and roam across a huge section of land.

This doesn't mean the trip is wasted, however, because there is one destination on FL 29 that is worth exploring: the wildlife-packed sanctuary of the **Fakahatchee Strand Preserve State Park.** Travel along FL 29 for roughly 12 miles, and you'll see a road leading off to your right. This is James Memorial Scenic Drive, and it takes you to the Fakahatchee Park office. The park is an unusual place, even in the Glades. The largest drainage slough in the Big Cypress Swamp, the Strand has been called the "Amazon of North America," and if you take one of the tours, you'll understand why.

You'll hear words like *only here*, *largest*, and *rare* a lot in reference to the plant and animal life of the Strand. For example, this is the only ecosystem in the world where bald cypress trees grow along with royal palms. It holds the largest variety and concentration of orchids in North America. And it is home to some of the rarest species on the continent—Florida panther, Florida black bear, Everglades mink, bald eagle (although these are making a healthy comeback), and West Indian manatee—in addition to a tremendous diversity of birds, animals, reptiles, and marine life.

You have a few options for enjoying the park. A 2,000-foot-long boardwalk cuts its way through the preserve, giving you ample opportunity to experience the dense forest, wetlands, and native flora and fauna. If you want to get up close and personal with the Strand, you can take a swamp walk with a trail guide. You need to be relatively fit for this one, and you need to make sure you leave the designer jeans at home. By swamp walk, I mean literally wading waist deep through the sloughs. For the less fit, the less inclined, and the less eager to be dipped into a swamp for four hours, there's a guided canoe trip. There are no paths, let alone restaurants, so bring food and water. And insect repellent and sunblock, especially in summer, are as mandatory as water in a desert.

Once you leave the Strand and return to Alligator Alley, you're just a few miles away from Naples. It's difficult to imagine a more dramatic transition than leaving the desolate swamp and coasting into this small, opulent resort town. The landscape of Old Naples was painted with the finest brush. Alligator Alley practically drops you into tree-lined Fifth Avenue South, the manicured thoroughfare through the heart of the city. This section of town is replete with posh boutiques, swanky restaurants, and fancy cars.

After your trek through the swamp, you might feel you deserve some pampering. If so, head straight to the charming **Inn on Fifth** and check yourself in for a night. This romantic boutique hotel overlooking the most fashionable street in town is worth every penny. From its stately Mediterranean architecture to its spacious rooms (try to get either a poolside view or a balcony suite) to its top-class amenities, the hotel epitomizes the understated grandeur of Old Naples. And its award-winning Asian-themed Spa on Fifth is a virtual guarantee to wash away any lingering grime from the Everglades. (Incidentally, because the summer season is the off-season in Naples, this is a good time to check the inn's rates, as there are typically some terrific deals.)

After checking in, take a stroll or a drive down Fifth Avenue, enjoying the immaculate sidewalks, tucked-away fountains and sculptures, and exclusive boutiques lining the road. But don't tarry too long here, because you want to make it to **Naples Pier** (at the end of 12th Avenue, it's a short drive or quite a long walk) for its magnificent sunset views and pristine white-sand beach. A long wooden boardwalk built in 1888 and extending out into the Gulf of Mexico, the pier brings the city together to fish, relax on the beach, and watch the sun dip beneath the blue horizon. On any given day, you might see dolphin, manatee, jellyfish, and other marine life breaking the clear surface of the water. It's a top highlight in Naples, and it's free.

By now, you've built up quite an appetite; fortunately, you're in luck. This town has an array of restaurants that do not disappoint. Those who want to splurge should check out **Truluck's,** which is located at the back of the Inn on Fifth but isn't part of the hotel. An amalgamation of "truly lucky," Truluck's will make you feel just that as you dine on one of their succulent steaks, seafood entrées, or the pièce de résistance (when available), fresh king crab legs (the chef has been seen on Discovery Channel's *The Deadliest Catch*). For a more eclectic meal, check out **Café Lurcat,** where the quality of the food is matched by the architecture of the build-

Naples Pier

ing, highlighted by the gorgeous Chagall-inspired domed ceiling on the second floor. Budget-minded travelers can enjoy tasty and hearty pub grub in a warm, authentic setting at **McCabe's Irish Pub** on Fifth Avenue.

Start your next morning with breakfast at the **5th Avenue Coffee Co.,** which should fortify you for the morning's stroll through Fifth Avenue South's colorful architecture, hidden fountains, eclectic art galleries, ritzy jewelers, and interesting boutiques like **Trendy With a Twist** (on the more cost-effective end), **Brodeur Carvell** (high-end menswear), and **Chic Rustique** (a must-see for any home- and garden-decor enthusiast). Fifth intersects with Third Street South, which continues the upscale shopping district. There are many galleries and cafés in this part of town, as well as two polished shopping complexes that stand out from the crowd. The pink and white building houses **Marissa Collections,** a very swanky retailer where you can get your D&G fix or pick up that Prada bag. Across the street is the Plaza on Third, recognizable by its herons fountain. Naples is known for its clothiers, and one worth a call is Victoria at **The Artful Diva,** who will custom-fit her designs for you. She offers private, one-on-one consultations.

If shopping isn't your thing, try a more interactive, in-depth tour of the city with **Naples Bicycle Tours.** The two-and-a-half- to three-hour guided ride through the town is an informative and pleasant way to learn about the city, explore its residential architecture, and get some exercise in the bargain. Don't feel like biking? There's always the reliable **Naples Trolley Tours,** which cover a large territory and hit all the major spots. If you stuck to your shopping guns, you can always take a quick drive along Gulf Shore Boulevard and the Port Royal community to gape at the multimillion-dollar mansions that make up the wealthiest part of the city.

After seeing how the rich live, check out the more rustic side of Naples at **Tin City.** This is an old clam-shelling facility converted to a collection of shops, galleries, and restaurants. It's worth it to meander around Tin City and find the hidden places of interest among the more kitschy souvenir shops. One of my favorite stops is **Docks By Jen,** where owner/artist Jennifer Norqual makes quaint miniatures of local buildings, landscapes, and landmarks. There are also some fine waterfront restaurants here, and my recommendation is **Riverwalk,** where you can sample a deliciously crispy grouper sandwich or fried grouper tacos at the edge of the dock.

There's more to Naples than its downtown glamour. In fact, if the hotels in the ritzier part of town are too much buck for your bang, try the **Inn at Pelican Bay,** situated in the northern section of the city, near the white sands of Vanderbilt Beach. This is a large but inviting hotel with well-appointed, comfortable rooms and reasonable rates. There are several reasons to venture beyond Old Naples. The **Naples Museum of Art** is a cultural treasure (with a magnificent Chihuly sculpture gracing the lobby) with a varied collection of permanent and temporary exhibits. Adjacent to the museum is the **Philharmonic Center for the Arts,** where the Naples Philharmonic Orchestra, which debuted in 1983, continues to attract some of the biggest names in the industry.

Secondly, there is golf. The National Golf Foundation rated Naples as the city with the most avid golfers per capita in the nation, and these majestic greens have earned the city the tagline of "Golf Capital of the World" (how's that for a measuring stick of the per capita income in this city?). With more than one hundred golf courses across the Paradise Coast, it's a title well earned, but check with each course to see if they are open to the public (some are in summer season only) or are affiliated in any way with your hotel (both the inns mentioned above have partnerships with several courses). And by the way, did you know that if your ball ends up anywhere near an alligator, you're entitled to a free drop?

GOLF COURSES IN NAPLES

Naples has long been a premier golfing destination, even by Florida's lofty standards. Here are just a few of the highly rated courses, many of which have been designed by the game's all-time greats.

Flamingo Island Course. A picturesque and highly decorated course designed by Robert Trent Jones Sr., it was declared one of America's best by *Golfweek* and awarded a four-star rating by *Golf Digest*.

Grandézza. A challenging championship course with holes named Devil's Backbone, Mission Impossible, and the Hour Glass.

Naples Beach Hotel & Golf Club. The city's first championship course opened in 1929 and has been voted the "Best Public Course in Southwest Florida" by *Gulfshore Life* magazine.

Palmira Golf Club. Designed by Gordon Lewis, this is where the Palmira Open is played.

Raptor Bay Golf Club. Designed by Raymond Floyd, a World Golf Hall of Fame inductee, it's the first resort golf course in the country to receive Audubon International's Gold Certification.

Tiburón. Named after and designed by "the Shark" himself (Greg Norman, that is), this course is also home to the Rick Smith Golf Academy.

Valencia Golf & Country Club. One of the few public courses around, this one was awarded three and a half stars by *Golf Digest*.

All of Naples's vaunted shopping isn't centered on the old part of town. A pleasant open-air center north of Fifth Avenue is **Waterside Shops,** complete with trickling waters and sculptures guiding you to all the major brand names. There are some good restaurants here as well, and **BrickTop's** makes for a tasty end to your shopping excursion. The American bistro menu is simple but well prepared, and the flatbreads are an excellent way to start the meal. For something far more casual, head to **Grouper & Chips** for a Floridian take on a British favorite.

Naples and the Everglades are diametric opposites, and the contrast makes for an interesting excursion into—and out of—Florida's wilderness.

Contacts:

Ah-Tah-Thi-Ki Museum, HC-61, Box 21-A, Clewiston 33440. On the Big Cypress Reservation at the corner of CR 833 and West Boundary Road. Call 863-902-1113. Open Tues. through Sun. 9–5. Call for holiday hours. Web site: www.seminoletribe.com/museum.

The Artful Diva, Naples. By appointment only. Call 239-530-4494. E-mail: victoria@theartfuldiva.com.

Big Cypress Hunting Adventures, HC-61, Box 46, Clewiston 33440. On the Big Cypress Reservation, about 17 miles away from Alligator Alley. Call 863-983-1190 or 1-800-689-2378 to make a reservation. Web site: www.seminoletribe.com/enterprises/bigcypress/hunting.shtml.

Billie Swamp Safari, HC-61, Box 46, Clewiston 33440. On the Big Cypress Reservation, 19 miles from Alligator Alley. Call 863-983-6101 or 1-800-949-6101. Open daily 9–5 (closed Christmas). (Park gates close at 9 pm, but rides and tours end at 5.) The Swamp Water Café, located on the premises, is open 7:30–6. Web site: www.seminoletribe.com/safari.

BrickTop's, 5555 Tamiami Trail North (at Waterside Shops), Naples 34108. Call 239-596-9112. Open Sun. through Thurs. 11–10 and weekends 11–11.

Brodeur Carvell, 850 Fifth Avenue South, Naples 34102. Call 239-261-7767. Open Mon. through Wed. and Sat. 10–6, Thurs. and Fri. 10–9. Web site: www.suitup.net.

Café Lurcat, 494 Fifth Avenue South, Naples 34102. Call 239-213-3357.

Open for dinner Sun. through Thurs. 5–10 (until 9:30 in summer) and Fri. and Sat. 5–10:30 (until 10 in summer).

Chic Rustique, 340 Fifth Avenue South, Naples 34102. Call 239-403-1733. Open Mon. through Sat. 10–5. Web site: www.chicrustiqueof naples.com.

Docks By Jen, 1200 Fifth Avenue South, Suite 402, Naples 34102. Call 651-226-7397. Web site: www.docksbyjen.com.

Fakahatchee Strand Preserve State Park, P.O. Box 548, Copeland 34137. Call 239-695-4593. Open daily 8–sundown. Web site: www.florida stateparks.org/fakahatcheestrand/default.cfm.

5th Avenue Coffee Co., 599 Fifth Avenue South, Naples 34102. Call 239-261-5757. Open daily 7 am–9 pm, but summer hours vary.

Flamingo Island Course, 8004 Lely Resort Boulevard, Naples 34113. Call 239-793-2223. Web site: www.lely-resort.net.

Grandézza, 11471 Grande Oak Boulevard, Estero 33928. Call 239-948-1913 or 1-866-472-6336. Web site: www.grandezzacc.com.

Grouper & Chips, 338 Tamiami Trail North, Naples 34102. Call 239-643-4577. Open Mon. through Sat. 11:30–9. Web site: www.grouperand chips.com.

Inn at Pelican Bay, 800 Vanderbilt Beach Road, Naples 34108. Call 239-597-8777 or 1-800-597-8770. Web site: www.innatpelicanbay.com.

Inn on Fifth, 699 Fifth Avenue South, Naples 34102. Call 239-403-8777 or 1-888-403-8778. Web site: www.innonfifth.com.

Marissa Collections, 1167 Third Street South, Naples 34102. Call 1-800-581-6641. Open Mon. through Sat. 9:30–6, Sun. noon–5. Web site: www.marissacollections.com.

McCabe's Irish Pub & Grill, 699 Fifth Avenue South, Naples 34102. Call 239-403-7170. Open daily 8 AM–9:30 PM; bar open until midnight or later. Web site: www.mccabesirishpub.com.

Naples Beach Hotel & Golf Club, 851 Gulf Shore Boulevard North, Naples 34102. Call 239-261-2222 or 1-800-455-1546. Web site: www.naplesbeachhotel.com.

Naples Bicycle Tours. Book by phone at 239-455-4611.

Naples Museum of Art and Philharmonic Center for the Arts, 5833 Pelican Bay Boulevard, Naples 34108. Call 239-597-1900 or 1-800-597-1900 to order tickets. Web site: www.thephil.org.

Naples Trolley Tours, 1010 Sixth Avenue, South Naples 34102. Call 239-262-7300. Tours run daily 8:30–5. Web site: www.naplestrolley tours.com.

Palmira Golf Club, 28501 Matteotti View, Bonita Springs 34135. Call 239-949-4466. Web site: www.palmiragolfclub.com.

Raptor Bay Golf Club, 23001 Coconut Point Resort Drive, Bonita Springs 34134. Call 239-390-4600. Web site: www.raptorbaygolf club.com.

Riverwalk Restaurant, 1200 Fifth Avenue South at Tin City. Call 239-263-2734. Open daily 11–10. Web site: www.riverwalktincity.com.

Tiburón Golf Club, 2600 Tiburón Drive at the Ritz-Carlton Golf Resort, Naples 34109. Call 239-593-2000. Web site: www.ritzcarlton .com/en/Properties/NaplesGolf/Default.htm.

Tin City, US 41 East at Goodlette Road, Naples. Call 239-262-4200. Open Mon. through Sat. 10–9, Sun. noon–5. Web site: www.tin-city.com.

Trendy With a Twist, Colonnade Building, 600 Fifth Avenue South, Naples 34102. Call 239-261-2060. Open Sun. through Thurs. 10–9, Fri. and Sat. 10–10.

Truluck's, 698 Fourth Avenue South, Naples 34102. Call 239-530-3131. Open daily for dinner Sun. through Thurs. 5–10, Fri. and Sat. 5–11. Web site: www.trulucks.com.

Valencia Golf & Country Club, 1725 Double Eagle Trail, Naples 34120. Call 239-352-0777. Web site: www.valenciagolfand countryclub.com.

Waterside Shops, Seagate Drive and Tamiami Trail North, Naples 34108. Call 239-598-1605. Open Mon. through Sat. 10–7, Sun. noon–5. Web site: www.watersideshops.com.

The Tamiami Trail

Total length of trip: About 275 miles over four or five days.

Getting there: From the Florida Turnpike, take exit 25, Southwest Eighth Street, which is also US 41, or the Tamiami Trail. It's a straight shot on this road for almost 60 miles before you turn right on CR 29 to get to **Everglades City.** Once you get back on the Tamiami Trail, it's another 16 miles until you take a left on CR 92 and travel about 10 miles to **Marco Island.** You'll leave Marco Island following North Collier Boulevard (FL 951 North), which connects back to the Tamiami Trail in less than 9 miles. From here, you'll stay on US 41 all the way to **Tampa.** Along the way, you'll pass through **Naples** (8 miles from Marco Island) and **Fort Myers** (about 30 miles from Naples).

From here, you can choose the first of two detours from US 41. Bearing left on CR 865 (which becomes CR 869 and then CR 867), you can travel east for 17 miles to **Sanibel Island.** When you get back on the trail, it's roughly another 100 miles to **Sarasota.** From Sarasota, it's about 60 miles to Tampa.

Highlights: The history of the Tamiami Trail—along with much of the Everglades—is tied to one Barron G. Collier. Construction of the trail began in 1915, but it proved a difficult and expensive endeavor from the start. Hacking through the unforgiving swamplands of the Everglades in that era was no small task; workers toiled in near total isolation from civilization, under extreme heat and surrounded by Florida's least-friendly residents. By 1919, construction ground to a halt as Lee County ran out of money to complete its portion of the road. By 1922, the state had also run out of funds to complete the east-west section of the road. In stepped Barron G. Collier, a New York advertising mogul who, for reasons best known to himself, decided that southwest Florida was the place to be.

From 1911 to the mid-1920s, Collier acquired more than a million acres of land here, making him the largest private landowner in the state. He also invested heavily in Everglades City and, when the money ran out on the Tamiami Trail, financed its completion. In exchange, he had a county named after him. Thirteen years and $8 million after its construction had begun, the trail officially opened in April 1928. More than 2.5 million sticks of dynamite had been used to clear its path through the swamp.

At that time, the road was a vital artery, and many roadside tourist attractions popped up during its heyday. However, the opening of Alligator Alley, a quicker, more direct link between Florida's east and west coasts, decreased the significance of the Tamiami Trail. Today, the trail is a mix of scenic roadway and congested urban thoroughfare. It's also a unique, if lengthy, way to explore a diverse stretch of Florida that takes you past bucolic villages, opulent towns, beachfront paradises, pristine parks, and a plethora of interesting attractions.

The Everglades

You start your journey on Miami's famous **Calle Ocho,** which is part of US 41. This road takes you through Little Havana, and since you want an early start, I'd recommend stopping by **Versailles Restaurant** for a *cortadito* (a Cuban espresso) and a guava and cheese *pastel* (pastry). Now you're ready to hit the road—or trail.

It won't be long before you start seeing signs for airboat rides, Everglades safaris, and similar roadside attractions. Some of these guys have been doing this for decades, and you can stop by one if you feel the urge, but you don't have to; we're going to go adventuring later on. One place that is worth a stop is the **Miccosukee Indian Village** at Mile Mark (MM) 70. This is a combination of tribal museum, cultural exhibits (you can see woodworking, beadwork, patchwork, basket weaving, and doll making on the premises), airboat ride (with a bonus of a scenic re-created Indian camp along the way), and alligator show.

Thirty miles west of Miami, you'll come to **Shark Valley Tram Tours,** a good way to see the Everglades without exerting yourself too much. These tours conducted by National Park Service rangers are two-hour excursions through a 17-mile loop that takes you deep into the Everglades (there's an observation tower midway through the tour that gives panoramic views of the swamp). You can also bike the trail (bring plenty of water with you). It's not far from here to Ochopee. Keep a lookout on the left-hand side of the road for the nation's smallest post office (it was formerly an irrigation pipe shed).

A quarter mile later, you'll come to **Joanie's Blue Crab Café,** a local favorite for salads, sandwiches, and homemade soups. Joanie's fried green tomatoes, gator, grouper sandwiches, and homemade blue crab soup are excellent. The restaurant has a rustic, homey vibe and great live music on the weekends. Down the road from Joanie's is the Skunk-ape Research Center, a bizarre place that you can't beat for sheer kitsch factor (check out the enormous panther statue).

It's just a few miles farther to the intersection of the Tamiami Trail with CR 29, which takes you into **Everglades City.** This sleepy seaside fishing village located on a mangrove island is home to fewer than five hundred souls and is a place that evokes memories of what small-town America used to be. The first settlers here were the Calusa Indians, who lived in these parts for about two thousand years. In 1868, George Storter Jr. came along and decided to settle here. He built a house (I guess you could call it the Storter starter home) and in 1889 managed to buy the land for $800. But the town remained little more than a fishing village and trading post until Barron G. Collier began scooping up territory and transforming the landscape.

Downtown Everglades City

Everglades City's moment in the Florida sun came with the construction of the Tamiami Trail, which would literally and figuratively place the city on the map. Everglades City was the original county seat of Collier County and enjoyed a relatively prosperous existence. Then, Hurricane Donna struck in 1960, causing widespread devastation. One year later, the county seat moved to Naples.

Today, Everglades City relies on the land for its economy, and the land provides: This is the gateway to the 10,000 Islands region and the headquarters of the Everglades National Park. The city is known for its seafood and for its crabs in particular; its moniker is the "Stone Crab Capital of the World." If you're planning your trip in February, make sure to inquire about the **Everglades Seafood Festival,** the city's biggest annual fair. Fishing and boating are two principal reasons why people flock here in the winter months. (In the summer, as I found, the mosquitoes can make your life truly miserable.)

Beyond its natural appeal, it is the town's quirky history and quiet charm that make it worth the trip, and it's worth spending a night here to enjoy its yesteryear appeal. You have a few lodging options, but two places come to mind above all others. The original Storter residence was converted into the historic Rod & Gun Club—now called the **Rod & Gun Lodge—** in 1925. Also purchased by the redoubtable Mr. Collier, this private club was the one-time haunt of notable hunters, fishermen, and celebrities, including Ernest Hemingway, Mick Jagger, John Wayne, Burt Reynolds, and Presidents Eisenhower, Truman, and Nixon. Today, it remains a bastion of the glory days. (In case you're not staying here, you can have lunch or dinner if you want to enjoy the ambience; the lodge frowns upon the casual visitor.)

Less famous but a worthy and popular choice is **The Ivey House Bed & Breakfast,** which offers three types of accommodations: a room by the small but pleasant pool at the inn; the lodge, which was built in the 1920s as a boardinghouse; or a separate cottage. Also, the Ivey House's "Adventure Desk" is a good resource for kayaking, fishing, and other outdoors activities.

Spend your first day here exploring Everglades City. Along Collier Avenue, the main road through the town, you sweep past cabins and houses raised on wood pilings. Water and swamplands extend around you in all directions, and you get a feel for how isolated this town must have been before the Tamiami Trail improved its access to the rest of the state.

Old-fashioned general stores, fishing-related businesses, and restaurants greet you as Collier Avenue winds down and you get closer to the town center. There are no chains, brand-name stores, or other examples of bustling Americana. The nearest McDonald's is more than 30 miles away. Collier feeds into Broadway, which takes you to the town center. Drive around the roundabout to get to the town's old laundry building, now the **Museum of the Everglades.** It seems almost unfair that a land as vast and unique as the Everglades should have such a small museum, but this little pink building does a nice job chronicling two thousand years of human experience in the swamp, from the Calusa and Seminole Indians to the later settlers. A large portion of the museum is devoted to Collier's exploits.

After the museum, continue following the roundabout and take your next right onto Copeland Avenue. You can stop by **Everglades Scoop** for ice cream and some very good sandwiches before continuing on Copeland toward Chokoloskee Island. On your right, a few miles down the road, you'll come to a parking lot and boathouse belonging to the Florida Everglades National Park, which is a part of the largest wetlands ecosystem in the United States.

Crossing over to Chokoloskee, you enter an almost entirely residential portion of town, but on the edge of town on Mamie Street (it's a bit hard to find, but follow the signs) is the **Smallwood Store** historic "ole Indian trading post" and museum. This red-painted wooden building raised on pilings is a must-see when you're in town. Smallwood is not so much a museum as it is a perfectly preserved general store. From 1908 to 1982, it served as a store and trading post (and also was a post office during Ted Smallwood's time). Inside, more than 95 percent of the goods are original artifacts that were sold in the store, and these include such bygone items as elixirs, pelts, old photographs, and household items from brands long forgotten.

Wake up early on your second day in Everglades City, because it's time to enjoy the swamp. Capt. Charles Wright is a good man to know if you want to hit the water or experience the outdoors. His **Everglades Area Tours** operates year-round and has a variety of fishing charters in addition to biking tours, aerial tours in a private Cessna (in winter), photography trips, ATV tours through the Big Cypress Swamp, boat rides through the 10,000 Islands region, and kayak/canoe tours.

Everglades Rentals & Eco Adventures, which is partnered with the Ivey House, also runs kayak tours (day and overnight trips) from November to April. These can be challenging, as you will have to fight your way through mangrove tunnels and narrow channels, but gliding along the water and spotting birds and alligators in this setting is unparalleled. **Everglades Guided Cycling Tours** takes you into hard-to-reach areas and provides an excellent opportunity to view the native flora and fauna. From my bike, I spotted boar and otters in addition to a bevy of gators (however, my tour guide, Marcy, quickly informed me that I was one of the lucky ones). Finally, airboat rides abound in Everglades City. The Everglades National Park is a good place to take one, or to hire out a fishing boat.

Beyond the Swamp

After your morning adventures, it's time to leave the Everglades behind. And what better way to do that than to turn left on CR 92, about 15 miles west along the Tamiami Trail from the junction that takes you into Everglades City? From here it's a 10-mile journey to **Marco Island.** The largest of the 10,000 Islands, Marco is also the *least* like the rest of its brothers. Cultivated, modernized, and built for beach lovers and condo developers, Marco is more reminiscent of Fort Lauderdale and Sarasota than it is the swamp.

You'll be hungry after your morning excursion, and fortunately there is a worthy outpost just as you enter into Marco Island from the east: **Stan's Idle Hour** is the oldest family-operated restaurant on the island. The menu is seafood-driven (especially of the fried variety) and the ambience laid-back—that is, until Sunday, when the place goes nuts and people come from all over to see and do the Buzzard Lope Dance, an ungainly sight that must be experienced to be appreciated.

Marco Island has the unique geographic luxury of boasting spectacular beaches facing the Gulf of Mexico on its eastern coast and the swampland of the Everglades on its western coast. Coming from the latter, you might naturally be interested in enjoying the former. If so, spend a few hours on one of the island's two public beaches: **South Marco Beach,** on the southern end of the island, or **Tigertail Beach,** closer to the northern edge. Both offer soft white sands, a vista of soaring condos, and the calm, warm waters of the Gulf. If you elect to spend your second night here, you'll have quite a few hotels and resorts to choose from, and a plethora of condo rentals for extended-stay visitors. A pleasant alternative from the norm is the **Marco Island Lakeside Inn,** a midrange option that offers 17 suites

South Marco Beach

in a cozy white cottage setting. Even though it's a lakefront property, you're still only about a mile from the beach.

Leaving Marco Island, you quickly return to the Tamiami Trail and head to Naples, which is covered in detail in the "Alligator Alley" section of this chapter. Continuing north, you'll travel through **Fort Myers.** It's worth taking a left at Bonita Beach Road to go through **Lovers Key Carl E. Johnson State Park,** which has a romantic history (it is said in the early 1900s, when the islands that make up the park were only accessible by boat, only lovers made the effort to come here), unspoiled beaches, mangrove swamps, and excellent facilities. You can park and take a free tram down to the beach, rent kayaks and canoes, or go shelling on your own or with a ranger as your guide.

If you decide to stick to the Tamiami Trail instead of checking out Lovers Key, don't miss the **Koreshan State Historic Site** at the intersection of US 41 and Corkscrew Road (you can't do both the park and Koreshan without backtracking, so you'll have to pick one). This is the

Kayaking at Lovers Key Carl E. Johnson State Park

original home of the Koreshan Unity Settlement, a movement started in 1880 in New York. The Koreshans, in search of a religious utopia, moved here under the guidance of Dr. Cyrus (which translates into Hebrew as "Koresh") Tweed. Their views may have been unorthodox, but as you stroll

Koreshan Unity Settlement

around the buildings and workplaces that once thrived here, you can't help but realize that this was not a dysfunctional cult, but rather an education-driven, self-sustaining, and prosperous community. It's a unique destination that chronicles both a part of pioneer Florida and one of the many communal societies that flourished in the United States at the turn of the 20th century.

An Island Detour

After Lovers Key, you'll continue along Estero Boulevard until you come to Summerlin Road. Here, you have a choice of making a rather substantial detour off your journey or heading back to the Tamiami Trail. Turn right, and you'll hit Gladiolus Drive, which will feed into US 41 in less than 2 miles. However, if you turn left, in roughly 15 miles you'll be on **Sanibel Island,** an idyllic barrier island that continues Florida's spectacular Gulf Coast beaches. Sanibel started life as a meager sandbar, but it has grown to a much-loved retreat full of natural splendor.

Once you cross the Sanibel Causeway onto the island (the toll is a hefty $6), you'll be ready to explore the island, but you'll also likely be ready to eat. If it's the latter, **Gramma Dot's** will do nicely. This self-styled "seaside saloon" is an island institution that serves up delicious grouper sandwiches and salads.

Sanibel's beaches are glittering white and its Gulf waters deliciously tranquil. **Tarpon Bay Road Beach** and **Bowman's Beach** are perhaps the most popular, but I prefer the beach at the lighthouse because, well, it's near the lighthouse. This stark, skeletal brown iron tower was first lit in 1884. It's not open to the public, but it makes for a nice landmark that you can see from the water.

One of the biggest surfside attractions at Sanibel are the seashells; because the island lies east and west, as opposed to north and south, it is geographically suited to snag an abundance of seashells, and it's quite common to see droves of people, bucket in hand, stooping to pick up their favorites. If you do come for the shells, don't forget to visit the **Bailey-Matthews Shell Museum.** In addition to learning about and seeing virtually every kind of shell, you can explore several interesting exhibits; my favorite is the shell valentines that sailors' wives would make while their men were at sea (at the gift shop, you can pick up a do-it-yourself valentine kit for a truly memorable souvenir).

Sanibel's lighthouse

Nature lovers also have access to a hidden jewel in the **J. N. "Ding" Darling National Wildlife Refuge.** This sprawling sanctuary spans more than 6,400 acres and is a habitat to more than 220 species of local and migratory birds, sea turtles, manatees, alligators, and other wildlife. Most people elect to experience the refuge by taking the wildlife observation drive through the refuge (4 miles long, or an 8-mile loop). Visitors can also hike and canoe here. Nearby, **Tarpon Bay Explorers** offers nature cruises, tram tours, and touch-tank exhibits. They also rent kayaks, canoes, boats, bikes, and fishing gear.

Captiva continues the natural beauty of Sanibel Island and has a more homey feel to it (there are plenty of cottages and small shops, and a very quaint chapel on the sea). One reason to come here is the 'Tween Waters Inn, a warm and friendly resort that offers a range of accommodations from beautifully appointed seaside cottages to efficiency rooms. Dinner here is pretty good, too, at the inn's **Old Captiva House,** for fine dining, or the adjacent **Crow's Nest,** for more casual fare. The inn offers a range of aquatic activities, tennis courts, bikes, golf, and a very cool retro-styled spa.

After breakfast at 'Tween Waters, it's time to hit the road. One last stop on your way out, however, should be the **Sanibel Historical Village & Museum,** a charming re-creation of pioneer life in the early 20th century. A boardwalk takes you down Periwinkle Way with stops at an old school-house, post office, and residences. This is located close to the bridge that will return you, in less than 20 miles, to our beloved Tamiami Trail.

Sarasota

There are scores of interesting diversions along the Tamiami Trail that this book doesn't cover, simply because few people have the luxury of being on the road for that long, but I'll try to name a few. The first of these, for base-ball fans, is a few miles north of where you rejoin US 41. Roughly half a mile away from the bridge that takes you into North Fort Myers, you pass Edison Boulevard. To the right is **City of Palms Stadium,** where the Boston Red Sox have their spring training games. (Yankee fans like me can get down and per-form whatever voodoo rain dance they feel will help for next season.)

You can also take a left turn at Edison, continue on Larchmont, and turn left on McGregor Boulevard (total travel time is roughly three min-utes) to reach the **Edison & Ford Winter Estates.** This tour of the win-ter residences of two of the most influential men of their era is a trip back through time. Among the highlights are Edison's lab, his home (which has some remarkably advanced features), botanical gardens, antique car garage, and the second-largest banyan tree in the world.

McGregor Boulevard takes you back to the Tamiami Trail and on toward Tampa. You'll be driving for close to 70 miles before your next stop, and much of this trip is visually not the most appealing: Think strip malls and gas stations. However, just as you enter Sarasota County, you'll come to **Historic Spanish Point.** Three different communities, representing five thousand years of history, have lived at this site, and evidence of their time here exists today. A burial mound and two shell mounds point to a prehistoric Indian tribe. More obvious to the eye are the buildings that were left by the early pioneers in the late 19th century: a citrus packing-house, several dwellings, a lovely chapel, and a pioneer cemetery. Finally, you can visit Bertha Matilde Honoré Palmer's winter estate and land-scaped gardens, built in the early 1900s. Spanish Point has several nature trails, a butterfly garden, and a wooden path and footbridge through a mangrove swamp. You can visit the site on your own or take a guided tour.

The chapel and pioneer cemetery at Historic Spanish Point

It's only 11 miles on US 41 from Historic Spanish Point to downtown **Sarasota,** and you get a lovely view of the city and the dozens of boats dotting the harbor as you approach. Sarasota deserves a two-night stay so you can enjoy both the city and its three keys, which offer an altogether different experience. With its beautiful, Mediterranean-inspired architecture; elegant shopping districts; diverse restaurants; and plethora of cultural and natural attractions, Sarasota will keep you active and well fed.

Where to stay while you're here? Your choice will be dictated by budget, location, and type of accommodation. At the high end of the

The pool at the Hyatt Sarasota

scale, the **Ritz-Carlton** is unparalleled, even by Ritz standards. This is a full-service hotel with shuttle service to a private beach club, a family-friendly focus on keeping the kids entertained, a members-only golf club for guests, and all kinds of add-ons and extra touches that make the price worth it. Beyond the elegance of the hotel, it's the service and go-the-extra-mile amenities that make this hotel stand out. (To be *really* pampered, book a room at the club level.)

The Ritz shares a private marina with the **Hyatt Sarasota,** another excellent option that has just completed a multimillion-dollar renovation.

The hotel features spacious, newly updated, iPod-ready rooms; a revamped lobby; and an excellent open-air heated pool complete with rock formations, waterfalls, and palm trees. For those who prefer B&Bs, **The Cypress** is a small, lovingly kept inn with an intimate and personal charm.

Conversely, you might want to forego the city and stay on one of Sarasota's three island gems: Siesta, Longboat, and Lido Keys. Again, your options here vary from opulent to budget. On the latter side, the **Siesta Key Bungalows** is a collection of cozy cottages on the Heron lagoon (with free kayaks for guests). For more expensive budgets, I'd recommend the **Bungalow Beach Resort** on Anna Maria Island at the northern end of Longboat Key, which is a beachfront, retro-styled property that artfully combines the glamour of a 1930s resort with modern amenities.

Your itinerary will depend on where you stay, but generally, you can spend one day exploring the mainland and another on the keys. A great way to start your day in Sarasota is by taking a scenic and historic Segway tour of the city. **Florida Ever-Glides, Inc.** is the first tour company in the United States to offer guided tours on Segway Personal Transporters, and given how much the idea has spread, you can tell owner Tom Jacobson was on to a good thing. Segways are fun and remarkably easy to use, and the tour takes you through artist villages, small homes that once belonged to little people who performed for P. T. Barnum's circus, and the oldest parts of the city.

After the tour, you can explore the nearby **Towles Court Arts District,** a colorful community where a variety of artists have set up galleries and workshops. From here, you can do one of two things while still in the downtown district: If you've brought the kids, check out **G.Wiz, The Hands-On Science Museum,** a children's educational wonderland divided into a first floor dedicated to traveling exhibits and a second floor devoted to more than 80 hands-on stations where children and adults can learn about electricity, sound, light, and basic scientific principles. If the kids aren't in the picture, check out the **Marie Selby Botanical Gardens,** a lush oasis famous for its collection of more than six thousand orchids. You can also explore downtown Sarasota and visit interesting niches and boutiques on Herald Square, Main Street, and Lemon and Orange Avenues. On Saturday mornings, vendors set up a farmer's market along Lemon Avenue and Main Street.

There are plenty of options for lunch; Sarasota prides itself on the quality of its food and the caliber of its chefs. A popular spot for a casual lunch

G.Wiz, The Hands-On Science Museum

is **The Boathouse,** which is part of the Hyatt but located off the main building, right on the water. Their signature dish is fish-and-chips, but their burgers and sandwiches are also pretty good. For a completely no-frills, nontourist experience, check out **Pho Cali** on Main Street for authentic Vietnamese specialties like noodle soups and grilled beef short ribs over rice.

After lunch, travel north along the Tamiami Trail for about 2 miles before turning left on Myrtle Street and making another left on Bay Shore Road to reach **Sarasota Jungle Gardens.** There are numerous shows and creature exhibits here, but the absolute highlight is buying bird food from one of the dispensers and hand-feeding the large and completely tame flock of flamingoes that wanders freely through the park. From here, drive north on Bay Shore Road for another mile to get to one of the more unusual cultural attractions in the area: the **John and Mable Ringling Museum of Art.** This sprawling complex includes a fantastic circus

The statuary and gardens at the John and Mable Ringling Museum of Art

museum, the highlight of which is the world's largest miniature circus, a replica of the Ringling Bros. and Barnum & Bailey Circus from 1919 to 1938; a museum of art with a fantastic baroque collection; the magnificent Venetian-inspired Cà D'Zan, home of John and Mable Ringling; the Historic Alonso Theater, an 18th-century playhouse; and sculpted grounds and gardens.

By the time you return to the downtown district, you'll likely be in the mood to eat, and you might as well enjoy one of Sarasota's better restaurants. **Derek's Culinary Casual,** a relative newcomer to the scene, is a hidden treasure well worth the trip to sample the food of one of the most creative chefs in the city. Derek Barnes calls his food "progressive American cuisine"; with superb inventions like foie gras torchon, duck two ways, and poached pear with homemade goat cheese ice cream, he can call it whatever he likes: It's all delicious.

Day two in Sarasota belongs in the keys, and there is no better way to start it than by having breakfast at **The Broken Egg,** a fun, lively local eatery in Siesta Key. As you can imagine, the egg is king here, and the concoctions and combinations they come up with are quite scrumptious. Thus fortified, you can move on to a full day of activities ranging from the beach, nature excursions, golfing, and shopping.

As far as beaches go, there are a few options. On Siesta Key, **Siesta Beach** on Beach Road is the crown jewel, boasting some of the finest, whitest sand in the world and lifeguards year-round. **Turtle Beach** doesn't have such pure sand but is less populated and lies hidden near the southern end of the island off Midnight Pass Road. **Lido Beach** on Ben Franklin Drive in Lido Key is a full-service beach with all the amenities and a large parking area. **North Lido Beach,** off John Ringling Boulevard, is more secluded.

Siesta Key has a string of casual beachside hangouts catering to a younger and more laid-back crowd. Places like the **Daiquiri Deck,** with its wall of cocktails and finger-food "snacketizers," are fun throughout the day and well into the night. More family-friendly is **Big Oläf,** where you can get excellent homemade ice cream in freshly made waffle cones. Traveling north, you leave Siesta Key and return to the mainland via Siesta Drive. Take a left on Tamiami Trail to John Ringling Boulevard, which will take you to Lido Key. In addition to its beaches, Lido Key has the picturesque **St. Armand's Circle,** an elegant shopping and dining district that's worth a stroll. Meander around, and make sure you stop at **ScoopDaddy's,** a blast-from-the-past 1950s ice cream parlor that also sells memorabilia from the '50s and '60s.

Save enough time (at least an hour or two) for the **Mote Marine Aquarium.** Mote has been conducting research and promoting a better understanding of the sea since 1955. Today, the learning continues in the aquarium, which allows you to learn about sea life as you wander through its exhibits. There is a jellyfish tank, a large touch tank, and manatee and shark habitats. One of the more inventive experiences here is the Immersion Cinema, a 40-foot-wide screen depicting interactive games that let you play along on your own console. There is also Shark Attack theater, which puts you in the shark's place as it goes hunting for prey. In a separate building but still part of the facility is a dolphin, whale, and sea turtle hospital that's accessible to the public. Mote is an incredible place of learning that also displays a love of the sea. At the aquarium, you can also book a boat ecotour or kayak tour with **Sarasota Bay Explorers,** a private company that also promotes conservation and understanding of the marine ecosystem.

Your last night in Sarasota should end with a good dinner. From Mote, you can continue north on John Ringling Parkway, which becomes Gulf of Mexico Drive, for just over 8 miles before arriving at the serene and homey **Euphemia Haye,** one of Sarasota's best restaurants. In this warm and intimate setting, Chef Raymond Arpke serves up a varied menu; his roast duckling and prime peppered steak are among his most mouth-watering dishes. After dinner, walk up to the Haye Loft for drinks, coffee, and terrific homemade cakes and pies in a more relaxed, lounge-style atmosphere. If you want to return to St. Armand's Circle for the evening (which usually stays active as the sun sets), book a table at **The Crab & Fin,** a cozy place right off the circle that prides itself on the variety and quality of its seafood. If you've had your fill of grouper and want a more exotic fish like arctic char or French turbot, this is the place to come (the local fish dishes are quite good as well). Try to get a table outdoors and enjoy the action in St. Armand's.

The Last Leg

Sarasota is your last stop before Tampa, and it's roughly a 60-mile trip. If you avoid the interstate and remain faithful to the Tamiami Trail, you'll bypass St. Petersburg, but you will drive through **Gibsonton,** a nondescript town with a curious history. Approximately 12 miles south of Tampa, Gibsonton is where carnival workers, or "carnies," have lived in and retired to for decades. When they're not on the road, you're likely to find an interesting mix of people here. Sadly, Giant's Camp Restaurant, one of the local institutions that was truly representative of the community, closed its doors in 2007. The restaurant had been started in the 1950s by Al Tomaini, who was over 8 feet tall, and his wife, Jeanie, who was 2 feet, 6 inches. The other local hangout, **Showtown USA,** is still going strong, drawing a steady, and mixed, crowd.

The Tamiami Trail ends somewhat incongruously in Tampa's industrial and entirely nonscenic east side. It's an abrupt conclusion to a remarkable odyssey through swamp, sand, and seaside paradise that captures Florida both at its wildest and its finest.

Contacts:

Bailey-Matthews Shell Museum, 3075 Sanibel-Captiva Road, Sanibel Island 33957. Call 239-295-2233. Open daily 10–5. Web site: www.shell museum.org.

Big Oläf, 5208 Ocean Boulevard, Sarasota 34242 (Siesta Key). Call 941-349-9392. Open Sun. through Thurs. noon–10, Fri. and Sat noon–11.

The Boathouse, 1000 Boulevard of the Arts, Sarasota 34236. Call 941-953-1234. Open Mon. through Sat. 11–10, Sun. for breakfast from 6:30–11:00 AM.

The Broken Egg, 140 Avenida Messina, Sarasota 34242 (Siesta Key). Call 941-346-2750. Open daily 7:30–2:30. Web site: www.thebroken egg.com.

Bungalow Beach Resort, 2000 Gulf North Drive North, Bradenton Beach 34217. Call 941-778-3600. Web site: www.bungalowbeach.com.

City of Palms Stadium, 2201 Edison Avenue, Fort Myers 33916. Call 239-344-5208 or 617-482-4SOX for tickets and schedule.

The Crab & Fin, 420 St. Armand's Circle, Sarasota 34236. Call 941-388-3964. Open Mon. through Thurs. 11:30–10, Fri. and Sat. 11:30–10:30, Sun. noon–10. Web site: www.crabfinrestaurant.com.

The Cypress—A Bed & Breakfast Inn, 621 Gulfstream Avenue South, Sarasota 34236. Call 941-955-4683. Web site: www.cypressbb.com.

Daiquiri Deck, 5250 Ocean Boulevard, Sarasota 34242 (Siesta Key). Call 941-349-8697. Open daily 11 AM–2 AM. Web site: www.daiquiri deck.com.

Derek's Culinary Casual, 514 Central Avenue, Sarasota 34236. Call 941-366-6565. Open Tues. to Fri. 11:30–2:30 for lunch, Tues. to Sat. 5–10 for dinner. Web site: www.dereks-sarasota.com.

Edison & Ford Winter Estates, 2350 McGregor Boulevard, Fort Myers 33901. Call 239-334-7419. Open daily 9–5 (closed Christmas and Thanksgiving). Web site: www.efwefla.org.

Euphemia Haye Restaurant & Haye Loft, 5540 Gulf of Mexico Drive, Longboat Key 34228. Call 941-383-3633. Open daily for dinner from 6–10; loft opens at 5 and closes late. Web site: www.euphemia haye.com.

Everglades Area Tours, P.O. Box 670, Everglades City 34139. Call 239-695-9107. Web site: www.evergladesareatours.com.

Everglades Guided Cycling Tours. Call 239-455-4611 to arrange a tour.

Everglades Rentals & Eco Adventures, at the Ivey House, Everglades City 34139. Call 239-695-4666. Web site: www.iveyhouse.com.

Everglades Scoop, 203 South Copeland Avenue, Everglades City 34139. Call 239-695-0375. Open daily 11–6, until 5 in the summer.

Everglades Seafood Festival, P.O. Box 5029, Everglades City 34139-5029. Call 239-695-4100. Held annually during the first week of February. Web site: www.evergladesseafoodfestival.com.

Florida Ever-Glides, Inc., 200 South Washington Boulevard, Suite #11, Sarasota 34236. Call 941-363-9556. Tours offered daily at 9 AM (two hours), 9:30 AM (one hour), and 6 PM (two-hour sunset tour). Web site: www.floridaever-glides.com.

Gramma Dot's Seaside Sanibel Saloon, 634 North Yachtsman Drive, Sanibel Island 33957. Call 239-472-8138. Open daily 11:30–7:30.

G.Wiz, The Hands-On Science Museum, 1001 Boulevard of the Arts, Sarasota 34236. Call 941-309-4949. Open Mon. through Fri. 10–5, Sat. 10–6, Sun. noon–6. Web site: www.gwiz.org.

Historic Spanish Point, 337 North Tamiami Trail, Osprey 34229. Call 941-966-5214. Open Mon. through Sat. 9–5, Sun. noon–5. Web site: www.historicspanishpoint.org.

Hyatt Sarasota, 1000 Boulevard of the Arts, Sarasota 34236. Call 941-953-1234. Web site: www.hyatt.com.

The Ivey House Bed & Breakfast, 107 Camellia Street, Everglades City 34139. Call 239-695-3299. Web site: www.iveyhouse.com.

J. N. "Ding" Darling National Wildlife Refuge, 1 Wildlife Drive, Sanibel Island 33957. Call 239-472-1100. Wildlife Drive open daily 7:30 AM to half hour before sunset (closed Fri.). Web site: www.fws.gov/ding darling.

Joanie's Blue Crab Café, 39395 US 41, Ochopee 34141. Call 239-695-2682. Open Tues. through Sun. 9–5, until 6 on Fri. and Sat. Closed Tues. in summer.

John and Mable Ringling Museum of Art, 5401 Bay Shore Road, Sarasota 34243. Call 941-359-5700. Open daily 10–5:30. Web site: www.ringling.org.

Koreshan State Historic Site, US 41 and Corkscrew Road, Estero 33928. Call 239-992-0311. Open daily 8–5; attached park grounds open 8–sundown. Web site: www.floridastateparks.org.

Lovers Key Carl E. Johnson State Park, 8700 Estero Boulevard, Fort Myers Beach 33931. Call 239-463-4588. Open daily 8–sundown.

Marco Island Lakeside Inn, 155 First Avenue, Marco Island 34145. Call 239-394-1161 or 1-800-729-0216. Web site: www.marcoisland lakeside.com.

Marie Selby Botanical Gardens, 811 South Palm Avenue, Sarasota 34236. Call 941-366-5731. Open daily 10–5 (closed Christmas). Web site: www.selby.org.

Miccosukee Indian Village, MM 70, US 41, Miami 33144. Call 305-552-8365. Open daily 9–5. Web site: www.miccosukee.com/indian _village.htm.

Mote Marine Aquarium, 1600 Ken Thompson Parkway, Sarasota 34236. Call 941-388-4441 or 1-800-691-MOTE. Open daily 10–5. Web site: www.mote.org.

Museum of the Everglades, 105 Broadway Avenue West, Everglades City 34139. Call 239-695-0008. Open Tues. through Sat. 10–4. Web site: www.colliermuseum.com.

Pho Cali, 1578 Main Street, Sarasota 34243. Call 941-955-2683. Open Mon. through Thurs. 11–9, Fri. and Sat. 11–9:30.

Ritz-Carlton Sarasota, 1111 Ritz-Carlton Drive, Sarasota 34236. Call 941-309-2000. Web site: www.ritzcarlton.com.

Rod & Gun Lodge, P.O. Box 190, Everglades City 34139. Call 239-695-2101. Web site: www.florida-secrets.com/Bed&Breakfast/SWBeds/Rod.htm.

Sanibel Historical Village & Museum, 950 Dunlop Road, Sanibel Island 33957. Call 239-472-4648. Open Wed. through Sat. 10–4 from November 7 to April 30 and Wed. through Sat. 10–1 from May 1 to August 11.

Sarasota Bay Explorers, 1600 Ken Thompson Parkway at Mote Aquarium, City Island, Sarasota 34236. Call 941-388-4200. Web site: www.sarasotabayexplorers.com.

Sarasota Jungle Gardens, 3701 Bay Shore Road, Sarasota 34234. Call 941-355-5305. Open daily 9–5 (closed Christmas). Web site: www.sarasotajunglegardens.com.

ScoopDaddy's, 373 St. Armand's Circle, Sarasota 34236. Call 941-388-1650. Open Mon. through Thurs. 10–10, Fri. and Sat. 10–11, Sun. 11–10. Web site: www.scoopdaddys.com.

Shark Valley Tram Tours, Shark Valley Loop Road, Miami 33194. Call 305-221-8455. Open daily, May through December 9:30–3, December through April 9–4. Web site: www.sharkvalleytramtours.com/index.html.

Showtown USA, 10902 US 41 South, Gibsonton 33534. Call 813-677-5443. Open daily 6 AM–10 PM; lounge stays open until 3 AM. Web site: www.showtownusa.com.

Siesta Key Bungalows, 8212 Midnight Pass Road, Siesta Key 34242. Call 941-349-9025. Web site: www.siestakeybungalows.com.

Smallwood Store, 360 Mamie Street, Chokoloskee 34138. Call 239-695-2989. Open daily 10–5 (opens at 11 from May to November).

Stan's Idle Hour Seafood Restaurant, 221 West Goodland Drive, Goodland 34140. Call 239-394-3041. Open Tues. through Sun. 11–10. Web site: www.stansidlehour.net.

Tarpon Bay Explorers, 900 Tarpon Bay Road, Sanibel Island 33957. Call 239-472-8900 for rates and reservations. Web site: www.tarponbay explorers.com.

Towles Court Arts District, located between Adams Lane, Links Avenue, West Morrill Street, and US 301 in downtown Sarasota. Web site: www.towlescourt.com.

'Tween Waters Inn, 15951 Captiva Road, Captiva 33924. Call 239-472-5161 or 1-800-223-5865. Web site: www.tween-waters.com.

Versailles Restaurant, 3555 Southwest Eighth Street, Miami 33135. Call 305-444-0240. Open Mon. through Thurs. 8 AM–2 AM, Fri. 8 AM–3 AM, Sun. 9 AM–1 AM.

CHAPTER

4

Emerald Cities

Postcards from the Panhandle

Overview: The "Redneck Riviera"; that's what they used to call the beaches along the Panhandle. Then, a socially conscious and politically correct majority demanded a name change, and the beaches and seaside towns became known as "The Forgotten Coast" and "The Emerald Coast." In truth, Florida's Panhandle has multiple personalities. Parts of this region identify more with the South than with Florida; you'll even find cotton fields near the Georgia border. The topography is different, with tall, dense forests replacing the swamps and marshes that make up so much of the state; there are miles upon miles of beaches of the whitest sand in the world, and yes, the water is a lovely shade of emerald.

Driving from one end of the Panhandle to the other—in effect, from Florida's capital of Tallahassee to Pensacola, at the western edge of the state—takes you through quiet fishing villages; towns so idyllic they were featured in movies; some of the best historical landmarks in the state, if not the region; and nature at its most dramatic. Come and discover which part of the Panhandle suits you best.

Total length of trip: This is a long one. From Tallahassee to Pensacola, hugging the coast and then returning via I-10, is a 436-mile round-trip, stretched over a weeklong adventure.

Getting there: Fortunately, it's an easy road, and a pleasant one. From Tallahassee, follow South Monroe Street to FL 61 South, and continue on Crawfordville Road (US 319). You'll be on 319 for almost 10 miles before turning left on Bloxham Cutoff Road (FL 267). After 3.5 miles, turn right on Wakulla Springs Road to reach **Wakulla Springs.**

From here, continue along Wakulla Springs Road for about 2 miles before turning right and driving along Shadeville Road (FL 61) for another 2 miles. Turn left on Spring Creek Highway (County Route 365 [CR 365]) and travel 4 miles before making a right on Coastal Highway (US 98). You'll be on this road for 6.5 miles, and then bear right on Sopchoppy Highway (US 319). Travel roughly 27 miles to reach **Carabelle.** You'll follow US 319, which becomes US 98/30, as it hugs the coast, passing **Apalachicola, Port St. Joe, Panama City, Seaside, Destin, Fort Walton,** and finally culminating in **Pensacola.** Carabelle to Pensacola is 190 miles.

From Pensacola, you'll take the quicker route back, following I-110 North for about 5 miles, and then getting on I-10 heading east. You'll be on the highway for 9 miles to exit 22. Turn left on Avalon Boulevard (FL 281 North) for 5 miles, and then turn right on US 90 East. In less than 2 miles, turn left on Dogwood Drive (FL 89 North) for about 3.5 miles, and then left again on FL 87 North. Drive 9 miles and turn right on Neal Kennington Road. In half a mile, the road jogs right at Lewis Road; continue on Springhill Road for just over 3 miles. Turn right on Tomahawk Landing Road to arrive at **Adventures Unlimited** in Milton.

Continue on Springhill Road, heading east for 3 miles, and then turn left on Munson Highway (County Route 191). Travel 8 miles and turn right on FL 4; you'll be on this road for about 18 miles before bearing right on US 90. In just over 4 miles, turn right onto FL 85, which in less than 3 miles will put you back on I-10, heading east. You'll be on I-10 for 80 miles to exit 136. Turn left on Kynesville Road (FL 276 East) and drive less than 2 miles. Continue on South Street for less than 2 miles, and then turn left on Jefferson Street (County Route 167). Follow this road for roughly 3 miles to arrive at the **Florida Caverns State Park.**

Return to I-10 East and continue for 32 miles to exit 174. Turn left on Greensboro Highway (FL 12 East), which becomes Veteran's Memorial Highway (US 90) before reverting back to FL 12. It's about 18 miles from the freeway to Ninth Avenue, which leads you to **Havana.** Continue on Ninth Avenue to US 27 South, which will take you back to **Tallahassee** in about 16 miles.

Highlights: People come to this part of Florida to enjoy the water and the beach in a more relaxed and laid-back environment. You won't find Miami's hot nightlife here, or even the festive surf-centric ambience of Cocoa Beach. This chapter honors the take-it-easy spirit of the Panhandle. You could pick and choose what you want to do, spend a weekend here, and still enjoy what the Panhandle has to offer; I chose to stretch it out over five days to give you ample time to see and do it all.

Appropriately, the first stop on this journey is a place of pristine natural beauty. Leaving Tallahassee, follow the directions listed on the previous page and in about a half hour you'll come to **Wakulla Springs State Park,** home to one of the world's largest, deepest freshwater springs. The water is so clean and clear that you can easily see fish swimming below the surface, and the observation tower/diving platform stands ready to launch you into the natural lagoon. Wakulla also has glass-bottom boat and riverboat tours, as well as several nature trails and an elegant 1930s lodge with a hotel and a restaurant. There is a deep tranquility and sense of timeless beauty here that you won't want to leave.

However, I recommend leaving Wakulla and traveling a few miles to the **Cherokee Sink,** which is a hidden treasure within the grounds (you can get a map and directions at the main lodge). When you leave the main

Wakulla Springs State Park

park, turn left on FL 267, and then left again onto CR 61. In just over a mile, turn right onto an unpaved road. In roughly a mile you'll come to the sink, a perfect circle of deep water with natural rock banks and unspoiled nature all around you. It's possible that you will be the only visitor at this lovely, secluded spot that most people overlook when they visit Wakulla.

From the Cherokee Sink, get back on CR 61 and continue west for about 8 miles to Crawfordville Highway (US 319). If you like barbecue, stop for lunch here at **Hamaknockers Bar-B-Q.** (Remember, you're closer to the Deep South than you are to Calle Ocho, so good barbecue is plentiful in this part of Florida.) A rustic joint with a basic menu tacked on the wall, Hamaknockers has excellent chicken and ribs at bargain prices. However, if it's seafood you crave, then keep going.

Stay on US 319 heading south, which turns into the very cool-sounding Sopchoppy Highway, for roughly 30 miles to reach **Carabelle.** There are some unusual and funky landmarks along the way down to this tiny fishing village: In Crawfordville, there is the onion-shaped River of Life temple, and after that, in the middle of nowhere (but just off the highway, so keep your eyes peeled for it), there is an artist's display of rusted, vintage cars lined up in an arc. It's oddly beautiful and practically compels your

Rusty vehicles in Carabelle

camera to start clicking (in fact, several noteworthy photographers have come here to shoot this weird but cool monument to . . . rusty vehicles). You're also driving along the coast, so the sight, smell, and sound of Gulf and forest is invigorating. You can't escape the feeling that you're in a remote part of the state—the country, for that matter—and this is appropriate, because you're now in The Forgotten Coast.

Carabelle is a good introduction to this slice of Florida. A tiny village snug on the coast, you can drive through it in a few minutes, but then you'd miss the **World's Smallest Police Station** (which was formerly a phone booth), right off US 98, and **The Fisherman's Wife** across the street. It might not be much to look at, but this colorful roadside eatery serves up deliciously plump fried shrimp and other seafood platters. Round off your meal with a fried peanut butter sandwich; the first bite will have you wondering what you're eating, but about two seconds later you'll realize it's all gone.

As you leave Carabelle, continue on US 98 and make your way toward Apalachicola, which is 20 miles away. Just before you reach this historic town, namesake of those world-famous oysters, you'll pass by **Eastpoint,** a humble, old-fashioned fishing town where you can still see the oyster harvesters (or tongers) bring in their haul every day. (Franklin County harvests more than 90 percent of Florida's oysters.) If it's an unspoiled, secluded beach you're hunting for, then turn left at Island Drive (FL 300) and cross the nearly 5-mile-long bridge to **St. George Island,** a barrier island well known for its pristine beaches and back-to-nature tranquility. From May to October, this is a good place to see (but not interfere with) nesting loggerhead turtles.

Apalachicola boasts a cluster of Victorian-era homes nestled in a picturesque historic district, and a walking tour of the area is a nice way to spend an afternoon, if you're not hitting the beach. Check out the **Orman House Museum,** a grand antebellum home built in the 1830s by cotton merchant Thomas Orman. Linger in the quaint heart of the Forgotten Coast, and then return to US 98 to continue your journey west. In roughly 7 miles, you'll hit a fork in the road. Take the scenic route (CR 30A), which takes you along the coast in a winding but rewarding tour of truly forgotten parts of the Forgotten Coast. Another good reason to take this road less traveled is to come to the **Indian Pass Raw Bar,** about 10 miles from the fork. This is a favorite local hideout where you can sample raw, baked, or steamed local oysters. They have other items on the menu (shrimp,

burgers, and other basic fare), which you can briefly consider before order-
ing your dozen oysters.

Much as I would recommend exploring this area, especially Cape San
Blas, you'll want to get back on US 98 (another 10 miles on CR 30A will
connect you to the main road) and keep going toward Pensacola. You'll pass
by **Port St. Joe** and, in another 30 miles or so, **Panama City,** a classic
Floridian beach town complete with surfside motels and a sun-loving
crowd. At this point, you have bidden a fond farewell to the Forgotten
Coast and welcomed its wealthier, more dashing, and more popular bigger brother: The Emerald Coast.

To continue the analogy, you'll find this part of the Gulf Coast dressed
in much ritzier trappings. Small towns, polished and shining with the lus-
ter of prosperity, line the road to Pensacola. Some are famous, like **Destin,
Sandestin,** and **Seaside.** Others, like **Watercolor** and **Seagrove,** are
almost completely unknown. But they share a common sense of elegance
and luxury that lives up to the "Riviera" part of "Redneck Riviera."

Of course, the big draw here is the combination of emerald waters and
bright, white sand, which form a near-irresistible duo. Unlike the Forgotten
Coast, the hotel chains have not left this part of the coast unblemished;
high-rise vacation homes and resorts line the beach at Destin and
Sandestin. I prefer the quieter towns that lie along the beaches of South
Walton, closer to Panama City. Your first stop for the night is 30 miles west
of Panama City. You'll continue on US 98 for about 21 miles before you
get to another fork in the road; again, choose the scenic road (CR 30A).
Now you're entering some of the loveliest vacation communities that
Florida has to offer. One of the first you'll pass is **The Village of South
Walton Beach,** whose central plaza boasts a cute semicircle of stalls around
a large fountain where kids can be seen at play during the day.

Just beyond lies **Alys Beach,** with its palm-lined main road, beautiful
bleached white buildings, and two small towers that mark its boundaries.
This place is manicured perfection (but it was also the only place in the
entire state during my travels where a policeman stopped me for appar-
ently looking suspicious—a fact that naturally left a blemish on the experience). Continue on the road until you get to Lakewood Drive (less than
6 miles from where US 98 forks) and turn left. In a half mile, bear left on
Beachwood Trail, and then continue on Lakewood Drive to arrive at the
Dunes of Seagrove. One of the larger properties in the area, the Dunes
doesn't dominate the landscape. A ResortQuest property, it consists of

Fonville Press

comfortably appointed two- and three-bedroom apartments. You'll be here for two nights (a minimum at most ResortQuest properties), and you'll cherish the spacious rooms, the resort's location (right on the beach), its large split pool, and the opportunity to explore the area.

If you've taken your time to enjoy the Forgotten Coast, you'll likely get to the hotel with an hour or two to spare before dinner. **Café Thirty-A** is close by, just across CR 30A, and it serves gourmet seafood and pizzas in a casually refined setting (don't forget to try their renowned martinis while you're here).

You'd be doing yourself a great disservice if you didn't spend a healthy chunk of time at the beach outside your apartment. When you're ready for breakfast, you have two choices. For something light, head back along 30A toward Alys Beach. Take a left onto La Garza Lane and you'll come to a nondescript white building called **Fonville Press.** Originally a bookstore, this is now a very sophisticated café and newsstand. The building has tremendous character and still retains elements of its former life, with a row of magazines and an eclectic collection of books; but now, Fonville offers coffee, pastries, their signature ice cream, and, on weekends, wine and cheese in a pleasant outdoor setting. This is a chic place unlike any other in this area.

For something heartier, get on CR 30A and turn left. In roughly 5 miles, you'll come to **Another Broken Egg,** a mini chain of restaurants—with branches in nearby Destin and Sandestin—that have consistently been hailed as the best place in town for anything to do with breakfast. The menu is a combination of old favorites and new twists (like blackberry grits and a Cajun-seasoned crawfish omelet).

After breakfast, you have a choice of continuing east and exploring Destin and Sandestin, which are the more developed stretches of the Emerald Coast. I prefer to head east up to Dune Allen Beach, to enjoy the homey elegance of this stretch of CR 30A, and then retrace my path west toward **Seaside.** Even those who have never heard of this tiny, cozy little community might recognize it. This was the setting for the movie *The Truman Show,* and the filmmakers could not have picked a better location to imitate their pretend utopia. Seaside is clean, safe, pretty, and full of friendly people. The small town has a special vibe that easily seduces. Let your feet take you around the town's central plaza, with its eclectic shops and eateries, and then enjoy the beachfront area of town.

When it's time to eat, you'll want to go to **Bud & Alley's Restaurant and Bar.** One of the best spots on this coast, Bud & Alley's is a local fixture; situated on the water with an outdoor lounge area complementing a fine, pleasant indoor dining room and a lively upstairs bar, it draws a happy and relaxed crowd. The food is ingredient-driven and focuses on fresh seafood. After your meal, you can wander around the beachfront boardwalk or enjoy one the restaurant's other environments. The upper deck is a fine place for sunsets and ocean views.

On your next morning, leave the Dunes and head west toward Pensacola. CR 30A will meet up with US 98 again, and, past Destin and Sandestin, will lead to downtown Fort Walton. Follow the road (it will become the Miracle Strip Parkway) all the way until you arrive at the **Indian Temple Mound Museum,** which chronicles ten thousand years of Native American history in northwest Florida. Despite the numerous well-preserved artifacts in its exhibit halls, the museum's greatest asset is the temple mound itself. A ceremonial and political center from A.D. 800 to 1400, it is among the largest prehistoric earthworks on the Gulf Coast, measuring 17 feet tall and 223 feet wide at the base. After the museum, continue heading west on US 98 for 40 miles, which will take you straight into **Pensacola.**

Of all the cities in Florida, I have to admit that Pensacola surprised me the most, simply because I had no idea there was such a deep reservoir of history, culture, and tradition here. The westernmost city in Florida, Pensacola has a few other nicknames and monikers. Not to be outdone by St. Augustine and Amelia Island, it claims to be the first European *settlement* in America (for a lesson in semantics, see what Florida's other two elder statesmen call themselves); "The Cradle of Aviation," it is called, for its prestigious naval air station; and, finally, it is known as "The City of Five Flags" since it has belonged at one time or another to the Spanish, English, French, the Confederacy, and the United States.

The squeaky beaches will tempt you with their siren song (yes, they really do squeak in this part of the state), but you won't do this city justice unless you explore its fascinating historical and cultural highlights. As such, begin your stay here in the downtown area—and you might as well begin with lunch. Follow US 98 to Palafox Street, which is the main road through the city's beautiful historic district. In about a mile you'll turn left on Zaragoza Street, and in a few blocks, onto South Barracks Street. The **Fish House** will be on your left.

True to its name, seafood is king at this large waterfront restaurant, but within these boundaries, the Fish House spreads out quite a bit; you can try unique sushi rolls, a few Asian-accented dishes, or stick to the happy marriage of seafood and Southern cooking. Their Grits à Ya Ya, smoked Gouda cheese grits topped with Gulf shrimp, sautéed spinach, mushrooms, and bacon, is practically a rite of passage. The restaurant is popular both during the day and in the evening, with live music on weekend nights.

Duly fed, immerse yourself in Pensacola's history with a tour of **Historic Pensacola Village.** Head back on Zaragoza and look for the Tivoli House, where you can purchase tickets for this cluster of 20 historic 19th-century homes and buildings, including the lovely Old Christ Church and the Julee Cottage, built in 1805 and owned by a "free woman of color." Parts of the tour are self-guided, but I'd wait for the guide, who does a great job explaining the history of these structures and the stories of the people who lived and worked in them.

Following the tour, meander around this part of town and check out the arts and culture scene. A short walk west along Zaragoza Street to Jefferson Street brings you to Plaza Ferdinand VII, one of two large, green plazas that bookend the historic district (the other is Seville Square, across from the old church). On your right is the **T. T. Wentworth, Jr. Florida State Museum,** housed in a large and beautiful Spanish Revival–style building that was once the town's city hall. This museum chronicles local history through the stunningly diverse and immense private collection of historical artifacts of its namesake.

Across from the plaza on Jefferson Street, the **Pensacola Museum of Art** is housed in the old city jail. A small museum, it nevertheless garners some impressive local and national exhibits (Picasso, Tiffany, Dale Chihuly, and Ansel Adams are among the big names to be exhibited here). Just across from the museum is the **Pensacola Cultural Center,** home to the **Pensacola Little Theater,** the oldest continuously operating community theater in the Southeast. Call and see what's playing while you're in town.

As with the Dunes at Seagrove, I'd recommend two nights in Pensacola to make the most of your trip. Where you stay will depend on what you're looking for. If you have the family with you and want to be removed from the bustle of city life, then see what ResortQuest has to offer on Perdido Key. The properties here, like the **Palacio,** are the more typical high-rise vacation rentals, with the same excellent standard of furnishings and spacious accommodations. And Perdido Key, a sliver of a barrier island, is about as remote as you can get in Florida; it's little more than a pristine, squeaky beach (the squeakiness, incidentally, is evidence of finely ground, almost pure quartz).

To get here, take Zaragoza to Tarragona Street and turn right. This will lead you to East Garden Street (US 98). Turn left and go 1 mile before bearing left on Barrancas Avenue. In 3.5 miles, Barrancas will lead into Gulf Beach Highway (FL 292). Continue on this road for 12 miles. After you cross the bridge onto Perdido Key, watch for the Palacio building on your left.

However, if you want to remain in the downtown area, turn left on Tarragona Street and follow it for roughly a half mile to Gregory Street. Turn left here and in another half mile or so, you'll see the graceful **Pensacola Victorian Bed & Breakfast.** A throwback to another era, this restored inn has retained the charm of Pensacola's past. Your hosts, Barbee and Chuck Major, are attentive and pleasant, and maintain a casual, friendly ambience. And the rooms are quite spacious, with rich wood floors and paneling, and some with antique four-poster beds.

Before you head out to dinner, call the **Belmont Arts & Cultural Center** and see if they have any evening workshops on their schedule. At

Plaza Ferdinand VII

this way-off-the-beaten-path facility (a large space that was once a window factory), you can take evening workshops on a variety of arts, including glassblowing, bead making, pottery, and jewelry making. From the Pensacola Victorian, it's an easy drive. Take Gregory Street 2 blocks to North Reus Street and turn right. The center will be on your left.

Whether you're in Perdido Key or the Pensacola Victorian, you'll want to head to **Jerry's Drive In** for dinner. A Pensacola institution since 1939, this low-key diner is known for a local classic: fried mullet. Because mullet is a bottom feeder, it's generally a baitfish and not something people go out of their way to eat. But here, because the water is so clean, the fish is tender and delicious. Jerry's also has burgers, seafood dinners, and an extensive breakfast menu. To get here from the downtown area, take Palafox to Cervantes Street and turn right. The restaurant is roughly 2 miles down the road, past the bridge.

If diners aren't your thing and you crave a little more elegance, forget Jerry's and try **Jamie's.** Located downtown on Zaragoza Street (a few blocks east of the Historic Village), Jamie's offers superb French cuisine in a home built during the 1800s. The setting is romantic and intimate (there are only 16 tables), and the food is outstanding. Jamie's takes great pride in its sauces and reductions, which are essential to classic French cooking. A good way to sample the local seafood is to try the *Deux Poisson* ("Two Fish"), which combines two fresh catches of the day with the chef's choice of sauces.

After dinner, if you're not too tired, you can walk or drive to the **Seville Quarter** on Government Street, which runs parallel to Zaragoza. The quarter houses a cluster of bars and restaurants that makes for lively nightlife, and in the summer, there are free live concerts every Thursday evening.

Day two in Pensacola will be an air and sea show—sort of. Begin your morning with a visit to the city's most visited attraction: the **National Museum of Naval Aviation.** To get here, take FL 292 (Gulf Beach Highway from downtown or Perdido Key Drive from Perdido Key) to Blue Angel Parkway. Turn right and follow the road for roughly 4 miles to the checkpoint at NAS Pensacola.

The navy has been in Pensacola since 1824, and this museum is a tribute to their legacy. More than 160 vintage aircraft are on display here, including some one-of-a-kind restorations like the resident *Brewster*

National Museum of Naval Aviation

Buffalo. The museum is located on the grounds of NAS Pensacola, which is also the home of the vaunted Blue Angels. From March through November, on Tuesday and Thursday, you might catch this elite flight team soaring through the sky during their practices. (The "Blues" are in full form on Pensacola Beach the weekend after July 4th and in November, their last show of the season.)

In addition to a myriad of aircraft (and a very cool mock-up of the flight deck and island of an aircraft carrier) and the suspended-in-midflight Blue Angels exhibit, the museum has an excellent IMAX movie called *The Magic of Flight*, F-14 flight simulators, a neat gift shop, and a café modeled after NAS Cubi Point in the Philippines. Amazingly, the museum is free. Nearby within the NAS compound are **Fort Barrancas,** a 19th-century fortification that was partner to nearby Fort Pickens in the defense of the bay, and the black-and-white **Pensacola Lighthouse,** the fourth tallest in the nation. (It's only open to the public on Sunday from May to October.)

After the museum, it's time for the "sea" portion of the day. Take a left on Taylor Road and drive less than 2 miles to Duncan Road (CR 295). Turn left and follow the road for about 2.5 miles before turning right on

Fort Barrancas

Barrancas Avenue. In another 3.5 miles, bear right on West Garden Street (US 98). The road curves at this point and then gets a bit muddled, but turn right on Chase Street and in less than a mile you'll reconnect with US 98 and cross over the Pensacola Bay Bridge. In less than 2 miles, take the ramp to Gulf Breeze Parkway (CR 399) toward Pensacola Beach. Here you'll see one of Pensacola's most recognizable landmarks: a big, neon billfish sign pointing toward the beach. Believe it or not, when lit up, the fish can be seen from space. It'll cost you a dollar toll to get on the beach. Once over the bridge, look out on your right for the large yellow building that marks the **Cabana Club.**

Architecturally modeled after a ship's prow, the club is a one-stop shop for the Pensacola tourist. Want to get on the water? Hop aboard the *Vitamin*

Cabana Club

Sea for deep-sea fishing (walk-on or private charters) and sunset and dolphin cruises. Need supplies? The market here is surprisingly well stocked. Hungry? The Cabana serves breakfast, lunch, and dinner, highlighted by a mean plate of shrimp grits.

There are at least three reasons to take a boat ride: The first is that you get great views of **Fort Pickens,** the largest of Pensacola's forts and principal defender of its naval yard in the 1800s. (As of this writing, the road to the fort is still closed due to recent hurricane damage, but it is scheduled to open in 2008.) You also have a great chance of seeing dolphins and birds. Finally, if you're lucky, like I was, you can be out on the water when the Navy or Coast Guard is conducting training exercises.

After your boat tour, you can rent bicycles at the market and ride down to the beach or to Fort Pickens, or continue down to **Casino Beach,** instantly recognizable for a second landmark: the giant beach-ball-shaped water tower. Pensacola Beach is part of Santa Rosa Island, one of the longest barrier islands in the world. In addition to glittering white sands and emerald waters, Casino Beach has a lively boardwalk with shops, bars and restaurants, and free concerts at its Gulfside Pavilion on Thursday. Also here is the longest fishing pier in the Gulf of Mexico. It's worth the dollar access fee to walk to the end; watch for fish, jellyfish, and dolphin; and enjoy postcard-perfect views of the beach and the iconic water tower.

A short distance east and west of this popular main beach is a less crowded and more natural beachfront that is little more than dunes, sea grass, and sand. You can get away from the crowd and find a spot of isolated paradise. If you head west along Fort Pickens Road, watch for **The Island Cross,** a 10-foot cast-iron cross that commemorates the first Christian mass in the United States. The cross was originally planted in 1559 and was later moved to this spot.

It's also fun to drive east along Via de Luna (CR 399) and duck into the residential roads on the island; amid some lovely seaside homes are some truly bizarre structures, like the alien home and the space-age-looking dome house. If you continue along CR 399, the residential community soon slips away, and you'll find yourself on a beautiful drive along the **Gulf Islands National Seashore,** with nothing but Santa Rosa Island's natural beauty around you.

For dinner, treat yourself to something special by returning to the historic downtown area and heading to **Jackson's.** Located on the corner of Palafox and Zaragoza, Jackson's is widely considered the premier fine-dining establishment in the city, and one look inside will confirm this: Beautiful wrought-iron chandeliers resembling branches; murals behind the long, polished-wood bar and in the private function room; an exceptional staff; and world-class cuisine combine to make this place memorable. The menu is a creative upgrade of the steaks-and-seafood standards you'd expect to find at upscale restaurants. For example, you can top your Kobe New York strip, Kurobuta pork chop, or other meat selection with anything from white truffle oil to jumbo lump crab. This is where people come for special occasions, like engagements, anniversaries, and their last night in Pensacola.

However, leaving Pensacola doesn't mean your vacation is over. You'll be taking a different route back to Tallahassee, enjoying a completely different scenic route that leaves the beaches behind and plunges through the forests (and caves) of the Panhandle. From downtown, you can follow US 98 to I-110, heading north for about 6 miles before taking the ramp onto I-10 East, heading toward Tallahassee. In 9 miles, get off at exit 22 and turn left on Avalon Boulevard (FL 281). In 5 miles, you'll meet US 90. Turn left, and in a half mile turn right on Anna Simpson Road. In another half mile, turn left on Mill Pond Lane to arrive at **Arcadia Mill.**

At press time, there was still a lot of work and research being done at Arcadia, but the boardwalk through the site, complete with swinging footbridges, gave visitors a sense of the scope of this site (don't expect to see ancient buildings here; you'll need to bring your imagination). Arcadia was the first and largest water-powered industrial complex in Florida. It was an incredible undertaking in a land that was almost entirely bereft of the infrastructure needed to survive and prosper, but the mill operated for almost 40 years, from 1817 to 1855, as a sawmill and shingle mill, and later on as a cotton textile factory. An interesting historical anecdote about this latter operation is that the labor force was entirely composed of young female slaves, a rare gender disparity. By 1853, Arcadia had become the largest textile factory in Florida.

The mill is a monument to the intrepid nature of Florida's early pioneers. To get an idea of what the land must have looked like when they came here—or simply to enjoy a canoe ride along a winding river—make your way to **Adventures Unlimited Outdoor Center,** but before you do that, stop by **Red Barn Bar-B-Q** for an early lunch. It's right on US 90 (in fact, you passed it on your way to Arcadia). The name and the sign kind of say it all: It's a large red barn, with a fat and happy pig in overalls serving as its mascot, which offers tender, smoky, slow-roasted barbecued meats.

After lunch, continue east on US 90 for roughly 2 miles. You'll drive through the small and scenic town of Milton, turning left on Stewart Street. In just over 3 miles, this road will meet up with FL 87 North. Follow it for 9 miles before turning right on Neal Kennington Road. You'll start to see signs for Adventures Unlimited, which is roughly 4 miles away.

Truly hidden in the woods, Adventures Unlimited is an interesting place. Specializing in group and corporate retreats, it offers obstacle courses, team-building excursions, and a way-off-site location where coworkers can bond. But it also offers a rustic back-to-the-land experience for the casual visitor. You can book a canoe or tubing river trip here along the beautiful Coldwater Creek, which combines forests and an occasional white-sand beach. These excursions can range from less than two hours to overnight trips.

Adventures Unlimited also has a surprisingly cozy assortment of lodging options, from its large schoolhouse with its high-ceilinged, spacious rooms, to individual cottages, to cabins ideal for campers (think bunk beds and attached bathhouses). If you can spare an added night on this trip, I highly recommend booking a night here. (Check if Granny Peasden's cottage is available; built in 1901, it's true Florida Cracker living.) However, note that there is no food served here, so dinner will likely be in Milton.

After Adventures Unlimited, you're in for a long drive before your next stop. Follow the directions at the start of the chapter to return to I-10 East, and in roughly 80 miles take exit 136 toward Marianna and the **Florida Caverns State Park.** Thirty-eight million years in the making, this cave system is an awesome sight and well worth the 45-minute guided tour of spectacular stalactites, stalagmites, and rock formations. After the caves, you can enjoy the many nature trails in the park or go for a swim in the park's Blue Hole spring.

After the caverns, head back to I-10 East and travel close to 40 miles to exit 181. Turn left on FL 267 North and head toward **Quincy,** a town with an interesting story to tell. Established in 1828, the town's fortune changed for the better (the *much* better) when the president of the Quincy State Bank believed in a certain company's future growth potential and encouraged his friends, neighbors, and patrons to invest in its stock. That company was Coca-Cola, and Mr. Munroe was quite right to reason that a cold, refreshing drink would be popular. His foresight produced a town chock-full of "Coca-Cola Millionaires," which made Quincy the wealthiest town per capita in the state.

Today, Quincy's prosperity is more modest, but its history and cultural highlights make it an interesting, albeit little-known, destination. Your last night of this tour will be spent here, at **The Allison House Inn.** A touch of England in the heart of Quincy, this B&B, built in 1843 by the sixth governor of Florida, offers cozy, beautifully appointed rooms with European accents. On weekends a full breakfast is served (weekday guests get a deluxe continental breakfast), featuring, in grand English style, homemade marmalade. To get here, follow FL 267 North for about 4 miles before turning right on Jefferson Street (US 90 East). Travel 1 mile, passing the beautiful yellow-brick **Gadsden County Courthouse** on your left, to Madison Street. Turn left and drive to the corner of Madison and King Streets to reach the inn.

If you have time (you can do this on your way out of town tomorrow as well), head back toward the courthouse to check out the **Gadsden Arts Center,** which is right across it on Madison Street. A beautiful space that was once the Bell & Bates Hardware Store (the intentional remnants of its predecessor, like the rolling ladder and raised office, are a nice touch), the arts center is divided into three galleries that host diverse exhibitions throughout the year.

Round out your day with a stroll around the historic district and admire the homes that Coca-Cola built. On the corner of Madison and Jefferson Streets is a Coca-Cola mural, a perfect tribute to this town. (Don't miss the stained-glass windows, including a signed Tiffany, at the **Centenary United Methodist Church** a block away from The Allison House on Madison Street.)

On your last leg of your tour of the Panhandle, you'll travel to Havana and to a Spanish mission. And both are within a short drive from Quincy. Begin by traveling east on King Street (FL 12) for about 11 miles to get to **Havana.** Turn left on Second Street Northwest and park at this small town built by the railroad, named for its tobacco and now known for its antiques shops. Havana had a special trade relationship with Cuba; it grew the outer leaves used to make those famous cigars. Naturally, when the trade embargo hit the United States, both Havanas suffered, but the Floridian town has reinvented itself into an antiques-shopping destination.

A walk along picturesque First Street will give you an idea of its new bread and butter: stores like **Wanderings** (which specializes in home decoration with a global accent), **Mirror Images Antiques and Little River General Store** (which houses a diverse collection of curios and artifacts, along with gourmet foods and toys from the 1950s and '60s), and **H&H Antiques** (specializing in fine furniture). On Second Street, the **Planter's Exchange** brings together more than 50 antiques and furniture merchants, and it has a little bit of everything. And there are five art galleries here—not bad for a town of roughly two thousand people. It's also become known for a more modern, and slightly wacky, tradition: The annual lawnmower contest, held in December, is part costume party and part lawnmower-turned-parade-float.

Browse around the town and enjoy the hospitality of the local residents, and when you're ready for lunch, walk along First Street to **The Mockingbird Café** for salads, sandwiches, or, naturally, a Havana Cuban Sandwich, followed by the homemade dessert of the day. After lunch, follow Second Street to Seventh Avenue, and then turn right on the Florida-Georgia Highway (US 27) to leave Havana. Follow US 27 for 8 miles before turning right on Capital Circle Northwest (FL 263). In roughly 5 miles, turn right again onto West Tennessee Street (US 90 East) and travel about 2.5 miles to Ocala Road. Turn left and an immediate left again onto West Mission Road to reach your final destination.

Little River General Store

From a historical perspective, you could say I've saved the best for last. Your last stop on this journey is a unique and inspiring place, where history, archaeology, and a dedicated team of people come together to present you with something altogether different. Welcome to **Mission San Luis.**

What makes this place so special? For one, the story behind the mission is fascinating. Spanish missions were a common phenomenon, with more than one hundred in operation in Spanish Florida during the 16th and 17th centuries. But the powerful Appalachee tribal rulers actually requested the presence of Spanish friars in the early 1600s. More astonishing still, the two groups learned to coexist, each keeping their customs and practices intact. In a time of subjugation and assimilation, this mutual tolerance was rare. (San Luis remains the only mission in the United States with living Native American descendants.)

The original mission was burned and abandoned in 1704, but it has been meticulously re-created. Now, it's a living-history museum. A tour of the mission takes you to the massive Council House, thought to be the largest period Indian building in the Southeast; a Franciscan Church; Spanish residences built and decorated according to the era; and a re-created fort. But what makes this place incredible is the staff, who help connect you with another time. As you tour the place, talk to a Spanish soldier and hear him describe how Indian and Spanish warriors fought together to defend the mission. Then visit a few of the Spanish "residents" at the mission and learn about their food, lifestyle, and culture. Talk to a Franciscan friar who, if you're lucky, will expertly play the flute for you.

This is an educational, transporting, and memorable experience; there's nothing quite like it in Florida, and it's a clear highlight of any trip to the Panhandle.

Contacts:

Adventures Unlimited Outdoor Center, 8974 Tomahawk Landing Road, Milton 32570. Call 850-623-6197 or 1-800-239-6864. River trips run every hour on the hour, starting at 8 AM. Web site: www.adventure sunlimited.com.

The Allison House Inn, 215 North Madison Street, Quincy 32351. Call 1-888-904-2511. Web site: www.allisonhouseinn.com.

Another Broken Egg, 51 Grayton Uptown Circle, Grayton Beach 32459. Call 850-231-7835. Open daily 7:30–2. Web site: www.another brokenegg.com.

Arcadia Mill Site, 5709 Mill Pond Lane, Milton 32583. Call 850-626-4433.

Belmont Arts & Cultural Center, 401 North Reus Street, Pensacola 32501. Call 850-429-1222 for workshop schedules. Web site: www .belmontartscenter.com.

Bud & Alley's Restaurant and Bar, 2236 Easy County Highway 30A, Seaside 32459. Call 850-231-5900. Open daily 11:30–3 for lunch; dinner Mon. through Thurs. 5:30–9 and Fri. and Sat. 5:30–9:30. Web site: www.budandalleys.com.

Cabana Club, 657 Pensacola Boulevard, Pensacola Beach 32561. Call 850-336-1924. Open daily 8–8 (closed Tues.). Web site: www.cabana clubpbeach.com.

Café Thirty-A, 3899 East Scenic Highway 30A, Santa Rosa Beach 32459. Call 850-231-2166. Restaurant opens daily at 6 PM for dinner. Web site: www.cafethirtya.com.

Dunes of Seagrove, 396 Lakewood Drive, Santa Rosa Beach 32459. Call 850-534-0296 (office) or 1-888-475-9055. Web site: www.resortquest nwfl.com.

The Fisherman's Wife, 111 St. James Avenue, Carrabelle 32322. Call 850-697-4533. Open Tues. through Thurs. 11–8, Fri. and Sat. 11–9.

Fish House, 600 South Barracks Street, Pensacola 32502. Call 850-470-0003. Open Mon. through Thurs. 11–midnight, Fri. and Sat. 11–2:30 AM, Sun. 11 AM–2 PM. Web site: www.goodgrits.com.

Florida Caverns State Park, 3345 Caverns Road, Marianna 32466. Call 850-482-9598. Open daily 8–sunset. Web site: www.floridastate parks.org/floridacaverns.

Fonville Press, 147 La Garza Boulevard, Alys Beach 32461. Call 850-213-5906. Open Wed. through Sun. 7:30–4:30 and Fri. nights. Web site: www.fonvillepress.com.

Fort Barrancas, Taylor Road, NAS Pensacola 32508. Call 850-455-5167. Visitors center open daily 9:30–4:45 March through October, 8:30–3:45

November through February. Guided tours conducted at 11 and 2.

Gadsden Arts Center, 13 North Madison Street, Quincy 32351. Call 850-875-4866. Open Tues. through Sat. 10–5, Sun. 1–5 (closed Thanksgiving, Christmas, and New Year's Day). Web site: www.gadsden arts.org.

Hamaknockers Bar-B-Q, 3123 Crawfordville Highway, Crawfordville 32327. Call 850-926-4737. Open Mon. through Sat. 11–8:30.

H&H Antiques, 302 North Main Street, Havana 32333. Call 850-539-6886. Open Wed. through Sat. 10–6, Sun. noon–5.

Historic Pensacola Village, 205 East Zaragoza Street, Pensacola 32502. Call 850-595-5985. Open Mon. through Sat. 10–4. Web site: www .historicpensacola.org.

Indian Pass Raw Bar, 8391 Indian Pass Road, Port St. Joe 32456. Call 850-227-1670. Open Tues. through Sat. noon–9. Web site: www.indian passrawbar.com.

Indian Temple Mound, 139 Miracle Strip Parkway, Fort Walton 32548. Call 904-243-6521. Open Mon. through Sat. 10–4:30, Sun. noon–4:30 (in June and July).

Jackson's, 400 South Palafox Street, Pensacola 32503. Call 850-469-9898. Open Mon. through Sat. from 5:30 for dinner. Web site: www .jacksonsrestaurant.com.

Jamie's, 424 East Zaragoza Street, Pensacola 32502. Call 850-434-2911. Open daily for dinner 5:30–9.

Jerry's Drive In, 2815 East Cervantes Street, Pensacola 32503. Call 850-433-9910. Open Mon. through Fri. 10–10, Sat. 7–10. *Note:* No credit cards accepted.

Mirror Images Antiques and Little River General Store, 303 Northwest First Street, Havana 32333. Call 850-539-7422; 850-539-6900 for Little River General Store. Open Tues. through Sat. 10–5, Sun. 12:30–5.

Mission San Luis, 2021 West Mission Road, Tallahassee 32304. Call 850-487-3711. Open Tues. through Sun. 10–4 (closed Thanksgiving and Christmas Day). Web site: www.missionsanluis.org.

The Mockingbird Café, 211 Northwest First Street, Havana 32333. Call 850-539-2212. Open Wed. through Sat. for lunch 11–3, Fri. and Sat. for dinner 6–9, Sun. for champagne brunch 11–2.

National Museum of Naval Aviation, 1750 Radford Boulevard, NAS Pensacola 32508. Call 850-452-3604 or 1-800-327-5002. Open daily 9–5. Web site: www.navalaviationmuseum.org.

Orman House Museum, 177 Fifth Street, Apalachicola 32325. Call 850-653-1209. Open Thurs. through Mon. 9–5 (closed noon–1; closed Thanksgiving, Christmas, and New Year's Day).

Palacio, 13661 Perdido Key Drive, Pensacola 32502. Call 1-888-475-9055. Web site: www.resortquestnwfl.com.

Pensacola Cultural Center and Pensacola Little Theater, 400 Jefferson Street, Pensacola 32502. Call 850-432-2042. Web site: www.pensacolalittletheater.com.

Pensacola Museum of Art, 407 South Jefferson Street, Pensacola 32502. Call 850-432-6247. Open Tues. through Fri. 10–5, Sat. and Sun. noon–5. Web site: www.pensacolamuseumofart.org.

Pensacola Victorian Bed & Breakfast, 203 West Gregory Street, Pensacola 32501. Call 850-434-2818. Web site: www.pensacola victorian.com.

Planter's Exchange, 204 Northwest Second Street, Havana 32333. Call 850-539-6343. Open Wed. through Sat. 10–6, Sun. noon–5.

Red Barn Bar-B-Q, 5887 US 90, Milton 32583. Call 850-983-9771. Open daily 11–9.

T. T. Wentworth, Jr. Florida State Museum, 330 South Jefferson Street, Pensacola 32502. Call 850-595-5985. Open Mon. through Sat. 10–4. Web site: www.historicpensacola.org.

Wakulla Springs State Park, 550 Wakulla Park Drive, Wakulla Springs 32327. Call 850-224-5950. Open daily 8–sunset. Web site: www.florida stateparks.org/wakullasprings.

Wanderings, 312 Northwest First Street, Havana 32333. Call 850-539-7711. Open Wed. through Fri. 10–5, Sat. 10–6, Sun. noon–5.

From the Race Coast to the Space Coast

Speedways, Séances, Springs, and Shuttles

Overview: Getting from Daytona Beach to NASA's Kennedy Center is a short and easy trip down I-95. But why go the short way around if you have a long weekend, and an adventurous spirit, available to you? Instead, explore Daytona Beach's new family-centric attractions; make yourself a gourmet pancake and then jump in a crystal cool natural spring; climb a beautiful old lighthouse and visit a cottage inspired by a Disney movie; tour a pioneer settlement and get spiritual guidance from a medium. And all that's *before* you make it to the space shuttles.

Total length of trip: One-way from Daytona Beach to the Kennedy Space Center is approximately 174 miles, spread over a long weekend.

Getting there: From I-95's exit 261, you're only about 4 miles west from the heart of **Daytona Beach,** and International Speedway Boulevard (US 92 East) will get you there. To get to **Ponce Inlet,** take US 1 south for about 3 miles and turn left on FL A1A. Follow A1A for just over a mile and turn right on South Atlantic Avenue for less than 3 miles. Returning to Daytona Beach, take I-95 North for 6 miles to exit 268. Turn left on West Granada Boulevard (FL 40 West) and travel 20 miles to the intersection of FL 40 and US 17 to reach the **Pioneer Settlement** at **Barberville.** Then it's a straight shot down US 17 South for 14 miles to **DeLand.** From

DeLand, continue south on US 17 for just over 3 miles and then take the ramp to FL 472 East. In another 2.7 miles, turn left on Dr. Martin Luther King Belt (County Route 4101 [CR 4101]) and travel a half mile to reach Cassadaga Road (CR 4139). Follow this road for about 2 miles to reach **Cassadaga.**

On your next morning, return to US 17 South and drive 1.5 miles before turning right on French Avenue. In 2 miles you'll arrive at **Blue Springs State Park.** Returning to US 17, continue south for about 5 miles and turn left on Valencia Road for less than a half mile. Then turn right on DeBary Drive, and in another half mile right again at Margarita Road. In less than a half mile, turn right on Sunrise Boulevard to arrive at **DeBary Hall.** Then continue down (west) on Sunrise Boulevard to Clara Vista Street. Turn left here and travel 0.3 mile to Dirksen Drive. Turn right, and in about a mile you'll be back on US 17 South. In about 2 miles, take the ramp onto I-4 and drive 2.6 miles to exit 101B and FL 417 South (a toll road). Follow this road for 30 miles to exit 26, which will put you on FL 528 East, another toll road. Take exit 31 to get on FL 520 East toward Cocoa. In 25 miles, you'll come to North Atlantic Avenue (A1A). Turn right here and travel 2 miles to **Cocoa Beach.**

To get to your final destination, **The Kennedy Space Center,** travel back along A1A, heading north, for 7.5 miles. This will lead into FL 528 West, which you'll follow for 4 miles to exit 49/Merritt Island/Kennedy Space Center. Turn right onto Courtenay Parkway North (FL 3) and travel 10 miles before taking the ramp to NASA Parkway West (FL 405), which will lead you to the space center.

Highlights: Your journey begins on a Friday (typically, I've attached no importance to specific days for these trips, but on this occasion, it's important), exploring **Daytona Beach** and nearby Ponce Inlet. The city has made a concerted effort to become a more family-oriented destination. Long known for Bike Week, NASCAR, and as a spring break haven, it has largely phased out the college hordes and now focuses on providing a wholesome vacation experience with arts, culture, and entertainment options for all. But it still celebrates the two things that have carved its legacy: bikes and racing.

There's no more wholesome beginning than breakfast at the **Dancing Avocado Kitchen,** "where herbivores and carnivores eat in harmony." To get here, follow International Speedway Boulevard off I-95 for less than

5 miles to Beach Street and turn right. Fresh fruit juices and smoothies, breakfast burritos, and omelets are the morning specialties at this pleasant restaurant located in the heart of Daytona's historic district. After breakfast, check out **Daytona Magic** a few stores down; this store is well known to those in the business (David Copperfield is a customer), and it is a veritable supermarket of magical items and novelties. Then head next door to the **Angell & Phelps Chocolate Factory,** where you can take a free tour or sample and buy your choice of homemade confections that have been made here since 1925. There's a restaurant attached to the factory, which you'll be visiting later on.

From the downtown strip, take Beach Street back to International Speedway and turn left. In a few blocks, you'll hit US 1 (Ridgewood Avenue). Turn left again and drive about 5 miles before turning left on A1A (Dunlawton Avenue) and crossing the Halifax River. A1A will take you to Atlantic Avenue. Turn right and travel another 5.5 miles. Turn right again on Ocean Way Drive, and in less than a half mile turn left on South Peninsula Drive to arrive at the **Ponce de Leon Inlet Lighthouse.** The tallest lighthouse in Florida and the second tallest in the country, this beautiful redbrick tower rises 175 feet (or 203 steps) and offers unparalleled views of the area. What also sets it apart from most other lighthouses in the United States is that all the original keeper's dwellings still stand, and today they make up a series of exhibits and a museum that chronicles the tower's history. Also on display here is a wonderful Fresnel lens exhibit; the *Gay Wind*, a 1930s tugboat; and the remains of two ramshackle rafts used by Cuban refugees to sail to these shores.

From the lighthouse, turn left on Lighthouse Drive. A short distance away is **The Marine Science Center,** a tucked-away ecological treasure. The center has a series of exhibits focusing on local marine life, but the real treats here are their turtle and bird rehabilitation efforts. Visitors can view rescued, injured turtles from the "Turtle Terrace," and the center hosts an annual Turtle Day in April, when rehabilitated sea turtles are carried to the ocean and released.

For lunch, head back along Atlantic Avenue. In about a half mile, turn left on Inlet Harbor Road and follow it to **Ponce Inlet Harbor.** This marina offers boat trips, fishing charters, and other excursions on the water, and it also has a pleasant, tropical-themed restaurant that specializes in seafood (try their "angels on horseback"—oysters wrapped in bacon, breaded and fried, and served with béarnaise sauce—or one of their daily fish specials). This is a nice place to walk along the boardwalk after lunch, grab a drink at the adjacent bar (check out the funky-looking fish in the display outside), and watch some of the local birds.

Ponce Inlet Lighthouse

After, head back to US 1 and return to downtown Daytona Beach. In about 5 miles, turn left at International Speedway. In just under 2 miles, turn left on Bill France Boulevard to arrive at **Daytona USA,** the center of all things NASCAR. This is the hallowed home of the Daytona 500 (held each February) and the Pepsi 400 (held the first Saturday in July). I used to think this attraction would only interest racing fans, but then I visited Daytona USA. It is part museum, part memorial to the city's racing heritage, and part racecourse—there is much more to do than I expected. Visitors can take simulated rides and race against each other, enjoy a speedway tour out to Victory Lane and the track (where a car might be out for a practice run), or watch an IMAX movie of the Daytona 500. A very cool display here is a section of the track, showing a variety of current and past race cars, which gives you a greater appreciation of the steep angle at which these cars travel. All in all, Daytona USA is a destination with universal appeal.

From the speedway, head back along International Speedway Boulevard to Atlantic Avenue and turn left. In a half mile, you'll arrive at the

The Daytona USA racecourse

Hilton Daytona Beach Oceanfront Resort. With comfortable, newly renovated guest rooms and direct access to the beach, it's one of the better properties in Daytona. It's also steps away from the historic district, the pier, and boardwalk.

You'll want to relax in your room—or hit the world-famous, hard-packed sand beach—for an hour or two before stepping out in the evening. Where you go will depend on your interests. Motorcycle enthusiasts will want to spend some time exploring Beach Street down to Main Street, the main strip of bikedom in Daytona Beach. Here you'll find apparel, bars, bikes, bars, shops, and bars . . . everything a city needs to host **Bike Week** in February–March, the largest motorcycle event in the world. (Incidentally, unless you are serious about Bike Week, avoid Daytona Beach during this time.)

World-famous biker hangouts include **Ed Walden's**—the oldest individually owned and operated bar in the county (it's located in a converted gas station, which makes for a distinctive setting)—and the legendary **Boot Hill Saloon,** where customers' bras hang from the ceiling and a T-shirt is almost a mandatory purchase. At 290 Beach Street is one of several of Bruce Rossmeyer's **Harley-Davidson** dealers, a name synonymous with bikes in Daytona Beach and home of the world's largest inventory of Harleys.

Families will enjoy strolling along the boardwalk and **Ocean Walk Shoppes & Movies,** an open-air hangout steps away from the Hilton. Across the street is **Daytona Lagoon,** which is a kids'—and adult kids'—playground complete with laser tag, minigolf, go-carts, arcade, and water park. If you're looking for a more rustic, and fantastic bargain, activity (from May to August), check out a **Daytona Cubs** minor-league game at the historic Jackie Robinson Ballpark. Not only is the park a great memorial to one of baseball's legends, but the Cubs draw a loyal and vocal fan base and is one of the best-attended minor-league teams in the state.

If you're not at the ballpark, you'll want dinner. Return to Beach Street and **Angell & Phelps Café** for Continental fine dining (rack of lamb, filet mignon, and other classics), generous portions, and, of course, fantastic chocolate desserts.

Begin your second day with something light at the hotel, because you'll be indulging in a late breakfast feast in about two hours. Before you get there, stop by the underrated **Museum of Arts & Sciences** (MOAS). (To get here, take International Speedway Boulevard and in less than 3 miles

Daytona Lagoon

turn left on South Nova Road.) MOAS is a premier center of art, history, and heritage. Among its treasures are a 13-foot skeleton of a giant sloth; the Root Family Museum, which centers on an astounding collection of Coca-Cola memorabilia; and a Cuban Museum that houses a rare collection of Cuban art from the 18th to the 20th centuries.

If you're feeling ambitious, a short drive away (about 6 miles south on Nova Road, and then right on Dunlawton Avenue for 2.5 miles) is **Gamble Place,** the Cracker-style country home of James Gamble, of Proctor & Gamble. If you go, don't miss the log-cabin cottage modeled after Disney's 1937 *Snow White and the Seven Dwarves.* You can also take a pontoon boat ride or kayak down the calm, black waters of Spruce Creek at the adjacent **Cracker Creek Canoeing.**

From the museum, return to International Speedway Boulevard, or US 92, and head west (if you're coming from Gamble Place, hop on I-95 North for about 5 miles to exit 261) for about 15 miles to US 17. Turn right here and drive roughly 6 miles to Ponce de León Boulevard. Turn left and follow the road for 1 mile to get to **De Leon Springs State Park.** Legend has it that Ponce de León discovered the Fountain of Youth at this very spot (legend has him discovering the fountain all over the place, actually), and the waters of the spring are certainly invigorating enough to make anyone feel a bit more youthful.

But before you get to the spring, enjoy a well-deserved late breakfast at **The Old Spanish Sugar Mill Grill and Griddle House.** Housed in this rustic setting, you can order hot sandwiches, standard breakfast fare, or cook your own pancakes, made from stone-ground wheat and your choice of toppings. After your meal, head over to the park to walk among the beautiful Spanish moss–laden trees and then take a plunge in the water. Nature tours are also available.

After the springs, return to US 17 and travel north for roughly 6 miles until you get to FL 40. Turn right here, and you'll arrive at the **Pioneer Settlement** in Barberville. A living-history museum and center of education, the settlement is a collection of buildings and homes representative of Florida's Cracker past. Among the highlights of the tour are a 19th-century log cabin, a 1920s residence in the "shotgun" style typical of laborers working in the turpentine industry, an 1800s print shop, a rail depot with a large and impressive railroad diorama, and the only turpentine mill still open to the public in Florida. The place really comes alive in November for the annual **Fall Country Jamboree,** a huge festival of folk arts, music, crafts, and food.

When you leave the settlement, you might want to stop in at **Barberville Produce,** a rather odd, huge open-air market specializing in statues, figurines, and wrought-iron furniture. Then take US 17 back to **DeLand** (about 14 miles south) and enjoy a walk or drive through this picturesque town. Downtown DeLand, home to Stetson University, has many beautiful murals, mom-and-pop shops (check out **Dolls of DeLand,** which has quite a collection of "real-born," lifelike dolls, and **Quilt Shop of DeLand**), historic buildings (like the lovely **Athens Theater** on Florida Street), and quaint cafés and eateries. One of the best of these is **Boston Gourmet Coffeehouse,** on New York Avenue, a popular local meeting place for coffee, snacks, and sandwiches. While you're here, check out the **Museum of Florida Art** on North Woodland Avenue. A small museum, it still boasts a diverse collection of Florida art, with a special focus on emerging local artists.

Wander the town at your leisure and grab an early dinner. Two good choices downtown are **The Original Holiday House,** on US 17/92, for old-fashioned buffet-style dining with a series of carving stations (roast turkey, leg of lamb, roast beef, and pork are usual staples) along with help-yourself fresh vegetables, or, for a more youthful ambience, the **Brickhouse Grill** on Woodland Boulevard. Happy hour starts at 4 here and doesn't end until the place closes. A local hangout, it's a good choice for burgers, steaks, and barbecue.

One of DeLand's murals

Leave DeLand via New York Avenue, heading east for close to 4 miles before turning right on North Summit Avenue (CR 4139). In 2 miles, turn left on West Main Street and in a few blocks turn right on South High Street. In a half mile, you'll jog left on Ohio Street and then turn right on Macy Avenue (CR 4139) for a half mile. When you get to Kicklighter Road, turn left and you'll soon come to **The Ann Stevens House.** A country inn built in 1890, it has won a spate of awards, and it lives up to every one of them. Spread across a main building and a carriage house, the inn has immaculate rooms custom furnished to suit a theme or era (check out the Laredo room to get the feel of a log cabin, complete with ranch house bathtub), and beautiful gardens. Your hosts, Helene and Ed Gracy, are warm and friendly, and you'll be happy to check in and relax for the night, or head to **Sherlock's Pub,** located in the carriage house, for a nightcap.

At the beginning of this chapter, I mentioned starting this journey on a Friday. The reason is so that you'll be ready to start your Sunday morning with a visit to the nearby spiritualist camp of **Cassadaga** in time to join the Sunday service. Cassadaga is an incredible place, a community of mediums and spiritual healers that has thrived since 1895. As to their abilities and their beliefs, you can judge for yourself.

From the inn, it's a half mile to the camp: Turn left, heading west on Kicklighter Road, until you come to Marion Street (CR 4139). Turn right on Cassadaga Road and find a place to park. A block away is Stevens Street, which will take you down to the **Colby Memorial Temple.** The service starts at 10:30 and centers not on religious doctrine but rather spiritual enlightenment, empowerment, and understanding our own energies. At the end of the service, the medium who conducts the service will speak to audience members and share what he or she is hearing from the spirit world.

After the service, spend some time walking around, stopping at the visitors center at the **Cassadaga Spiritualist Camp Bookstore & Welcome Center** at the Andrew Jackson Davis Building (corner of Stevens Street and Cassadaga Road). It's not hard to find a medium here if you want a reading, and it's not hard to learn more about Cassadaga and its members. I spoke to two of the camp's members—**Joan Piper,** a medium, healer, and teacher, and Associate Pastor Rev. **Ben Cox**—who helped me learn more about the community, about spiritual readings and healings, and about what to expect during a consultation. In the middle of our conversation,

You won't lose your way in Cassadaga.

How to Prepare for a Session with a Medium

I spoke with mediums and teachers at Cassadaga about what steps visitors could take to get the most out of their session. The advice I received was simple, logical, and, well, spiritual:

- Come for the joy of the experience.
- Call ahead and make an appointment.
- Try to have specific questions in mind, and feel free to ask questions of the spirits who speak with you.
- Keep your mind open.
- Don't give the medium too much; let the medium give you the information he or she receives.
- Try to pray over a two-week period to the spirit whom you would like to meet.
- Don't know which medium to choose? See who's on the Web at www.cassadaga.org.

Cox (without any prompt from me) mentioned something that he couldn't possibly have known without talking to the spirit world.

When you're ready for lunch, step into the Cassadaga Hotel and head to the **Lost in Time Café** for sandwiches and other casual fare. Then it's time for a cleansing experience of a different sort. Head west on Cassadaga Road for just under 2 miles and then turn left on Dr. Martin Luther King Belt (CR 4101). In about a mile, you'll hit East Graves Avenue (County Route 4145). Turn right and drive about 2 miles to US 17/92. Turn right, and in a few blocks turn left on West French Avenue.

In about 2 miles, you'll reach **Blue Spring State Park.** A marked contrast from the concrete-lined basin at yesterday's De Leon Springs, this park has a more natural environment. The St. Johns River and the surrounding forests make this place special, as do the manatees that gather at the spring to enjoy its year-round 72-degree weather during the winter months (November to March). You can "adopt" a manatee here, and quite a few are regulars during the cold season; you can't swim with them (humans have a designated swimming area), but you can certainly see them up close. And during the summer, the cool, clear waters of the spring more than make up for their absence. River cruises and kayaks are available here, and the park is also home to the **Thursby House,** a two-story frame house built in 1872. The house isn't a must-see attraction, especially given where you go from Blue Spring.

You'll want to leave the park by about 2:30 if you want to see a grand Old Florida estate. Head back on US 17 and go south for 5 miles before turning left on Valencia Road. Over the next mile, turn right on DeBary Drive, right on Margarita Road, and right again on Sunrise Boulevard, to arrive at **DeBary Hall.** Hidden and often overlooked, this two-story hunting estate built during the 1870s by a New York wine importer has been beautifully preserved and restored. The visitors center has a brand-new movie theater that rotates and jiggles as it takes you out into the St. Johns River, and the docents are well informed about the DeBary family and the history of the place.

The longest drive of the trip begins after this stop and takes you down to Cocoa Beach. Get back on US 17 (take Sunrise to Clara Street, turn left, and then take another left at Dirksen Drive to reach the highway) and head south, winding around Lake Monroe, for about 8 miles. Then take the ramp onto FL 417 South (a toll road) for roughly 25 miles to exit 26 and FL 528 East (another toll road). In 16 miles, take exit 31 onto FL 520 for 10 miles to reach the **Lone Cabbage Fish Camp.**

At this point, you're not far from Cocoa Beach, which has plenty of oceanfront hangouts and restaurants. But if you want a rustic experience worthy of "backroads and byways" billing, look no farther than this place. If you leave DeBary Hall by 4, you should get here by 5, just in time for a half-hour, gator-filled airboat ride or a 60-minute airboat ecotour on the St. Johns River (advanced reservations required for the ecotours). Then, return to the main house and mingle with the locals while you sample crispy delicacies like fried catfish, gator tail, frog's legs, or other, less exotic, fare.

From Lone Cabbage, continue on FL 520 East for about 17 miles, crossing over Merritt Island and A1A until you get to Ocean Beach Boulevard. Turn right, and you'll arrive at **The Inn at Cocoa Beach.** With large rooms, an informal and friendly atmosphere, and a great pool steps away from the beach, the cozy inn is a welcome stop for the night after a long day. (You'll also appreciate the breakfast in the morning.) If you're up for it, take a drive along Atlantic Avenue (A1A) and check out the ocean and surf shops, some of which are open 24 hours a day. You can also take Atlantic to Meade Avenue, turn right, and follow it to the end

Airboats at Lone Cabbage Fish Camp

and the **Cocoa Beach Pier,** a long wooden pier stuffed with restaurants, bars, and shops that stay open late.

In the morning, you'll head out to your last stop. From the hotel, get back on A1A and turn right, heading north for less than 5 miles, and then continue on FL 528 West for another 4 miles before getting off at exit 49. Take a right on Courtenay Parkway (FL 3 North) and travel 10 miles to NASA Parkway. You've arrived at **The Kennedy Space Center.**

By all accounts, this is a blatant violation of the "backroads" theme, but I've included it not only as the final destination on this trip, but also because NASA offers so much to its visitors that a stop here is an all-day, must-do activity. Start with a guided tour of the facility (which is located on an island *six times* the size of Manhattan), watch the breathtaking IMAX movies narrated by Tom Cruise and Tom Hanks, meet an astronaut (you can even join him or her for a group lunch), and see your fill of shuttles and rockets. NASA's newest attraction, the Shuttle Launch Experience, is a thrilling ride and about the closest thing you'll get to actually piloting a shuttle into orbit.

Inside the Kennedy Space Center

So I cheated a bit by including the space center in this book. It's worth it.

Contacts:

Angell & Phelps Café, 156 South Beach Street, Daytona Beach 32114. Call 386-257-2677. Open for lunch Mon. through Sat. 11–3; for dinner Tues. through Thurs. 5–9, Fri. and Sat. 5–10. Web site: www.angelland phelpscafe.com.

Angell & Phelps Chocolate Factory, 154 South Beach Street, Daytona Beach 32114. Call 1-800-969-2634. Open Mon. through Fri. 10–5:30, Sat. 10–5. Web site: www.angellandphelps.com.

The Ann Stevens House, 201 East Kicklighter Road, Lake Helen 32744. Call 386-228-0310 or 1-800-220-0310. Web site: www.annstevens house.com.

Barberville Produce, Inc., P.O. Box 66, Barberville 32105. Call 386-749-3562. Open daily 8–6.

Blue Spring State Park, 2100 West French Avenue, Orange City 32763. Call 386-775-3663. Open daily 8–sunset. Web site: www.floridastate parks.org.

Boot Hill Saloon, 310 Main Street, Daytona Beach 32118. Call 386-258-9506. Open daily 11–2:30, extended hours during Bike Week. Web site: www.boothillsaloon.com.

Boston Gourmet Coffeehouse, 109 East New York Avenue, DeLand 32720. Call 386-738-BEAN. Open Mon. through Thurs. 7–7, Fri. 7–9, Sat. 8–9, Sun. 9–3.Web site: www.bostongourmet.com.

Brickhouse Grill, 142 North Woodland Boulevard, DeLand 32720. Call 386-785-1237. Open daily 11 AM–midnight. Web site: www.brick housegrill.com.

Cassadaga Spiritualist Camp Bookstore & Welcome Center, at the Andrew Jackson Davis Building (corner of Stevens Street and Cassadaga Road), Cassadaga 32706. Call 386-228-2880. Open Mon. through Sat. 10–5, Sun. 11:30–5. Web site: www.cassadaga.org.

Cracker Creek Canoeing, 1795 Taylor Road, Port Orange 32128. Call 386-304-0778. Open Thurs. through Sun. 8–5, pontoon boat tours at 11 and 2. Web site: www.oldfloridapioneer.com.

Dancing Avocado Kitchen, 110 South Beach Street, Daytona Beach 32114. Call 386-947-2022. Open Mon. through Sat. 8–4.

Daytona Cubs, Jackie Robinson Ballpark, 105 East Orange Avenue, Daytona Beach 32114. Call 386-257-3172. Web site: www.daytona cubs.com.

Daytona Lagoon, 601 Earl Street, Daytona Beach 32118. Call 386-254-5020. Open Sun. through Thurs. 10–10, Fri. and Sat. 10 AM–midnight (water park hours vary). Web site: www.daytonalagoon.com.

Daytona Magic, 136 South Beach Street, Daytona Beach 32114. Call 386-252-6767. Open Mon. through Sat. 9–5. Web site: www.daytona magic.com.

Daytona USA, 1801 West International Speedway Boulevard, Daytona Beach 32114. Call 386-947-6800. Open daily 9–7 (closed Thanksgiving and Christmas). Web site: www.daytonausa.com.

DeBary Hall, 210 Sunrise Boulevard, DeBary 32713. Call 386-668-3840. Open Tues. through Sat. 10–4, Sun. noon–4. Web site: www.debary hall.com.

De Leon Springs State Park, 601 Ponce de León Boulevard, De Leon Springs 32130. Call 386-985-4212. Open daily 8–sunset. Web site: www.floridastateparks.org.

Dolls of DeLand, 118 North Woodland Boulevard, DeLand 32720. Call 386-736-0004. Open Mon. through Sat. 10–6.

Ed Walden's, 745 South Beach Street, Daytona Beach 32114. Call 386-258-3935. Open from 9:30 AM until at least 11 PM daily. Web site: www.waldensbar.com.

Gamble Place, 1819 Taylor Road, Port Orange 32128. Call 386-255-0285. Open Thurs. through Sun. 8–5. Web site: www.moas.org.

Harley-Davidson, 290 North Beach Street and 510 Main Street, Daytona Beach 32114. Call 1-800-307-4464. Open Mon. through Sat. 8–8, Sun. 10–6. Web site: www.daytonaharleydavidson.com.

Hilton Daytona Beach Oceanfront Resort, 100 North Atlantic Avenue, Daytona Beach 32118. Call 386-254-8200. Web site: www .daytonahilton.com.

Inlet Harbor Marina & Restaurant, 133 Inlet Harbor Road, Ponce Inlet 32127. Call 386-767-3266. Open daily 11–9. Web site: www.inletharbor.com.

The Inn at Cocoa Beach, 4300 Ocean Beach Boulevard, Cocoa Beach 32931. Call 321-799-3460 or 1-800-343-5307. Web site: www.theinnat cocoabeach.com.

Joan Piper, medium, healer, and teacher, 1130 Stevens Street, Cassadaga 32706. Call 386-228-0435 for an appointment.

The Kennedy Space Center, DNPS Kennedy Space Center 32899. Call 321-449-4444. Open daily 9–5:30 (closing times may vary; closed Christmas). Web site: www.kennedyspacecenter.com.

Lone Cabbage Fish Camp, 8199 FL 520, Cocoa 32926. Call 321-623-4199. Open Sun. through Thurs. 10–9, Fri. and Sat. 10–10. Web site: www.twisterairboatrides.com.

Lost in Time Café, 355 Cassadaga Road, at the Cassadaga Hotel, Cassadaga 32706. Call 386-228-2323. Open daily 9–5.

The Marine Science Center, 100 Lighthouse Drive, Ponce Inlet 32127. Call 386-304-5545. Open Tues. through Sat. 10–4, Sun. noon–4 (closed Christmas). Web site: www.marinesciencecenter.com.

Museum of Arts & Sciences, 352 South Nova Road, Daytona Beach 32114. Call 386-255-0285 or 1-866-439-4769. Open Mon. through Sat. 9–5, Sun. 11–5. Web site: www.moas.org.

Museum of Florida Art, 600 North Woodland Boulevard, DeLand 32720. Call 386-734-4371. Open Tues. through Sat. 10–4, Sun. 1–4. Web site: www.delandmuseum.com.

The Old Spanish Sugar Mill Grill and Griddle House, at De Leon Springs State Park, De Leon Springs 32130. Call 386-985-5644. Open Mon. through Fri. 9–4; Sat., Sun., and holidays 8–4.

The Original Holiday House, 704 US 17/92 North, DeLand 32721. Call 386-734-6319. Open Tues. through Sat. 11:30–8:30, Sun. and holidays 11–8:30. Web site: www.holidayhouserestaurant.com.

Pioneer Settlement, 1776 Lightfoot Lane, Barberville 32105. Call 386-749-2959. Open Mon. through Fri. 9–4, Sat. 9–2, Sun. 11–4. Closed major holidays. Web site: www.pioneersettlement.org.

Ponce de Leon Inlet Lighthouse & Museum, 4931 South Peninsula Drive, Ponce Inlet 32127. Call 386-761-1821. Open daily 10–5, Memorial Day to Labor Day 10–9. Web site: www.ponceinlet.org.

Quilt Shop of DeLand, 115 West Rich Avenue, DeLand 32720. Call 1-866-734-8782. Open Mon. through Sat. 10–5. Web site: www.quiltshopofdeland.com.

Rev. Ben Cox, associate pastor, medium, healer, and teacher. Call 352-255-4873 for an appointment.

6

The Other Kingdom

Going beyond Disney

Overview: Look, I love the childlike wonder of Disney; I enjoy the adventure of Universal; I can scream throatily at Busch Gardens and clap along as the whale splashes the front row at SeaWorld. It's all happening in and around Orlando, and that's why more than 48 million tourists descended on the city in 2006. But there's more—far more—to this part of Florida than rides and fantasy.

In fact, one could argue that the range of activities, entertainment, and cultural highlights is so diverse that Orlando and its surrounding cities offer an exceptional vacation experience that have nothing to do with theme parks. Over the course of a week, I put this theory to the test and found out there's a whole other world out there for you to explore.

Total length of trip: About 100 miles over three nights and four days.

Getting there: To begin with, I'm going to assume a starting point of Disney World itself. After all, this is all about getting away from the theme parks, so what better place to start? From the Magic Kingdom, get onto Epcot Center Drive, which becomes World Center Parkway. Turn right onto FL 535, and left on US 192 (West Irlo Bronson Memorial Highway) into Kissimmee. The total trip is about 5 miles. It's another 30 miles going east and south on US 192 and US 441 to get to **Forever Florida** in St. Cloud. Day two will have you traveling about 10 miles on I-4 West to US

27 North for about 2 miles before taking a left on Deen Still Road and traveling less than 2 miles to get to **Wallaby Ranch** in Davenport. Returning to I-4, head east for roughly 30 miles to exit 87/Fairbanks Avenue. Turn right on Fairbanks and travel 2 miles to get to **Winter Park.** On day three, take Fairbanks Avenue for 3 miles and bear right on Edgewater Road for less than a mile. Turn left on Lee Road for less than a mile before turning right on US 441 for 19 miles, bearing left on Old US 441. Then take a left on County Route 500A (CR 500A) West for just over 5 miles to get to **Mount Dora.**

Highlights: We're going to begin this section in unique fashion, by discussing lodging. The reason is simple: I'm guessing you're in town for the parks and want to spend a few days discovering what lies beyond their boundaries. While everyone knows about the hotels that form part of the Magic Kingdom, it makes sense to stay outside the park if you want to hit the road. The **Radisson Resort Orlando-Celebration** in Kissimmee is less than 2 miles from Disney and offers exceptional value (outdoor free-form pools, family activities, and comfortable rooms) for the money. Just down the road on US 192, **Saratoga Resort Villas** is a fine option for families who want kitchens and plenty of space just minutes from the parks.

In Orlando, closer to the downtown arts district, the roller coasters, and the convention center is the **Rosen Shingle Creek,** one of a triumvirate built by hotelier Harris Rosen. (The other two, also located in Orlando, are the **Rosen Plaza** and **Rosen Centre Hotel.**) It might not have the publicized panache of a Westin or Ritz, but the Rosen Shingle Creek is a sprawling, polished hotel located at the headwaters of the Florida Everglades. Its elegantly furnished rooms, excellent amenities, and panoramic vistas for those on the higher floors make this a worthy stop. All the Rosen hotels also have an excellent restaurant on premises, but we'll get to that later.

Day One: Kissimmee

Now it's time to leave the rides behind. You can start by getting on Irlo Bronson Highway, or US 192, from I-4 and traveling east. This colorful stretch of your journey could very well carry the title of "home of the kitschiest gift shops in the nation." As you drive along (there are helpful guide markers to give you some idea of distance and directions to attractions) you'll see all manner of creative construction, architecture, and

Shell World's unique mascot

design. Among these are an enormous wizard, a huge orange, a building that looks like a camera, and a giant sculpture of an alligator chomping on a jeep (this was the site of a now-defunct attraction). There's also a seashell-covered Volkswagen Beetle representing **Shell World** and an updated, bright red VW Beetle with a massive lobster perched on its hood, advertising a local restaurant.

You'll get to see all of these visually stunning (or blinding, depending on your level of taste) monuments to over-the-top advertising as you travel down US 192, but your first stop comes less than a mile after you exit I-4 onto the road. Take a right at Celebration Avenue, and in about 1.5 miles you'll reach the town center of **Celebration.** As you drive past perfectly manicured front lawns, white-picket-fence dream homes, and quiet, tree-lined roads, feel free to start planning your relocation to this wondrous planned community that was built by Disney as a residential neighborhood unlike any other. Boy, did they ever succeed.

Celebration is an incredible place; established in 1994, it has quickly grown into a multicultural community. The town center is beautiful, with a retro-styled movie theater, shops, and restaurants forming a wide semicircle around a man-made lake. A water fountain in front of the theater draws laughing children on a hot day; people are pleasant and proud of their community; you see a full fleet of Neighborhood Electric Vehicles (NEVs) puttering around town—but that's not all that Celebration is known for. In winter, it "snows" here (bear in mind, this is Florida we're talking about). In the fall, "autumn leaves" carpet the road. Even the hospital has been designed not to feel like a hospital. There's a strong cinematic element to the place (think *Pleasantville* and Stepford), but its hypnotic draw is undeniable. I wanted to pack up and move after 10 minutes of wandering around. Fortunately, you can choose a shorter sojourn at the lovely boutique **Celebration Hotel,** which is decorated in grand old Southern plantation style.

A nice way to enjoy the morning is by getting tea (or coffee) and scones (or other pastries) at the British outpost **Sherlock's of Celebration,** located near the hotel. Leaving Celebration, return to US 192 and head east toward downtown Kissimmee. Roughly 6 miles down the road, turn right on North Bass Road and travel a short distance to the **Osceola County Historical Society and Pioneer Museum,** a tucked-away exhibit of

Celebration's quaint downtown

authentic Cracker homes; 19th-century businesses, including a citrus packinghouse and a general store; and back-then essentials like smokehouses and cow camps. A friendly guide will be happy to take you around.

Adventurers with a taste for military history and a thing for aviation (as well as the budget to splurge) will now have a chance to experience a one-of-a-kind treat: flying a World War II fighter plane. Back on US 192, head east and take the next right on North Hoagland Boulevard. Follow the road for a mile to reach **Warbird Adventures.**

Here, you can strap yourself into the cockpit of a North American T-6 Texan, also known as the SNJ or Harvard; these were the aircraft used to train more than 70 percent of Allied pilots during the war. This is the real deal, folks. Warbird puts you at the controls, with an experienced flight instructor in the back seat helping you along. No experience is necessary; as soon as you're in the air, you command the stick, and the experience is entirely up to you. If you want to cruise along and admire the view, you can. If you want something a bit more heart-pounding, your instructor will show you how to do 360-degree loops, rolls, you name it. It's not a cheap

One of the planes at Warbird Adventures

excursion, but it's unique and one of the most authentic experiences you can have. Warbird also has a MASH helicopter that you can navigate.

At this point on your journey along US 192, you have two different options in the wilder side of Florida. You can continue going east on US 192 for 23 miles before taking a right on Holopaw Road (US 441), which you will follow for about 8 miles to get to **Forever Florida.** It's hard to find a more touching monument to a parents' love for their son than this 4,700-acre natural preserve. Forever Florida was built by Dr. Broussard and his wife, Margaret, to meet the last wish of their son, Allan, a lifelong nature lover who succumbed to Hodgkin's Disease. Allan's dream to preserve Florida's ecosystem has been realized today in the form of a vast unspoiled tract of land that spans several ecosystems and habitats. Start your tour by watching an inspiring video about Allan's life and the work of the conservation. Then, swamp buggy tours through a cattle ranch and the preserve, along with horseback safaris and a petting zoo, allow you to experience this beautiful and charming retreat. After the two-hour ecosafari on the swamp buggy, grab lunch (sandwiches and burgers) at the lodge-style Cypress Restaurant located in the preserve's main building.

Your other choice is to take a left on North Orange Blossom Trail (US 441) and continue on US 441 for about 15 miles to **Gatorland.** The giant alligator mouth gaping open to mark the park's entrance has become an icon of this Old Florida roadside attraction that first opened its gate (or jaws) in 1949. Gatorland has come a long way since then and now offers a variety of shows featuring gator feeding, Gator Jumparoo (a crowd favorite), gator wrestling (your kids can sit on a gator and hold its mouth closed), and other scary or scaly critters. With a continuous entertainment program; thousands of alligators and crocodiles sharing the limelight with snakes, spiders, turtles, and birds; and a swamp walk with bird-watching stations, the park can keep you occupied for hours. And, when you're feeling peckish, stop by Pearl's Patio Smokehouse for some gator bites or, a more unique treat, gator ribs.

Whether you're returning from Forever Florida or Gatorland, you'll pass by Kissimmee's historic downtown, which begins as soon as you turn off US 192 onto Main Street. Dwarfed by Orlando, Kissimmee is a small town with a lot of history, and parts of it still seem to be clinging to a bygone era. The town was built on cattle, and it was here that I learned that Florida's cattlemen don't like to be called *cowboys*, a word they consider derogatory. Ironically, the men who tended the cattle in the old days earned

It's gators, gators everywhere at Gatorland!

another moniker—derived from the cracking sound their whips made—which today is considered derogatory by many people outside of Florida: Cracker. Kissimmee is Cracker town.

As you follow Main Street and bear right on Broadway, you'll realize this is not a tremendously prosperous downtown area; in many ways, it's a slice of Florida as far removed from Disney as you can get (and you won't see the Mouse anywhere). Still, its quaint, modest charm is what makes it special. Going down Broadway, you'll pass long-standing businesses like **Makinson's Hardware Store,** which has been here since 1884, and a smattering of antiques shops like **Lanier's Historic Downtown Marketplace.** You'll also see an assortment of colorful and nostalgic murals, especially if you take the time to drive or walk around town. At one end of the strip is the lovely Osceola County Courthouse, dedicated in 1890 and today the oldest in Florida that has seen daily use.

One of the odder cultural highlights here, located naturally on Monument Avenue, is the Monument of States, a funky 40-foot column composed of 1,500 stones, meteors, stalagmites, petrified wood, even teeth and bones. Every state and 20 countries are represented. Continuing down Monument Avenue, you arrive at another unexpected tribute, the

Bataan-Corregidor Memorial to Americans and Filipinos who served in World War II. At the intersection of Monument and Lakeshore Boulevard, turn right and drive by Lake Toho, which is world-famous for its large-mouth bass fishing (it's been featured on ESPN's *Bassmasters*). There's a fishing pier and public boat ramp on Kissimmee Lakefront Park at the edge of the water, and the small Kissimmee Lighthouse.

If you're with the family, you have one more chance to get up close with wildlife on your way back to your hotel. From US 192, turn left on Poinciana Boulevard (about a mile west of downtown Kissimmee) and travel for less than 3 miles to get to **Green Meadows Petting Farm,** where the kids can milk a cow, caress a water buffalo, and frolic with sheep and lambs, among other creatures.

By now, you might be ready for an early dinner. Since you're in an entertainment capital, consider a dinner show. There are several in Kissimmee, and they are fun ways to spend an evening. My money goes to **Medieval Times,** which is located right off US 192 between markers 14 and 15. There are a few of these throughout the country, but the one in Kissimmee is the original, and it has an attached medieval village staffed with helpful artisans that is worth checking out. As you chomp on your chicken and ribs, you'll see jousting tournaments, sword fights, plots to take over kingdoms, and expert horse riding. The crowd participates, throwing their support behind a different knight depending on where they sit. The costumes, pageantry, decent food, and talent of the swashbuckling knights make for a heck of a good time.

You can also return to Celebration for dinner. Not only is the atmosphere lovely in the evenings, but there are some good restaurants in town. My first choice is **Café D'Antonio** for classic, well-prepared Italian food (and a mean tiramisu). Next to D'Antonio's, **Seito Sushi** offers dependably tasty Japanese food highlighted by an extensive menu of typical and not-so-typical maki rolls.

After dinner, head east on US 192 for less than a mile to get to **Old Town.** This quirky strip is a true taste of Kissimmee, with bars, attractions (including a lively haunted house), rides (there's a human slingshot that launches you high into the air), shops (a very random collection), classic cars, and restaurants along a pedestrian brick-lined promenade. If you're here on a Saturday, don't miss the Saturday Nite Cruise at 8:30 PM, when hot rods, antique cars, and other vintage wheels ride down the main road to live music.

Day Two: Summer Sky and Winter Park

Your second day of exploration will have you leaving Kissimmee for other pastures. But, if you missed out on the Warbird experience, or if your pulse demands something less exciting, you have two other alternatives to take to the air. The first is to try your hand at hang gliding at **Wallaby Ranch** in Davenport, only 17 miles from Disney. To get here, take I-4 west to exit 58, turn right onto Champions Gate Boulevard, and follow the road until it ends at a T intersection; turn right here (you'll be on Ronald Reagan Parkway) and head west, crossing US 27, after which the road becomes Deen Still Road. Keep a sharp eye out on your left: There's no large sign, but the mailbox at 1805 Deen Still has the ranch's name on it.

It only took one tandem trip with Malcolm Jones, owner of Wallaby, to dispel many of the myths about this sport. For one, there was no sense of fear or discomfort. Because Florida is flat, you get towed up into the air, a more comfortable and easier—for the novice—approach to hang gliding. Once the cable was released, you coast along the wind currents in languid circles, admiring the marshy landscape below and picking out Disney landmarks from the air. It's a surprisingly tranquil, and breathtaking, way to spend the morning.

Couples looking for a more intimate aerial adventure should consider a hot-air balloon ride, an expensive but memorable activity. **Bob's Balloons** (call ahead for directions on where to meet Bob) is a good choice that will take you on an early (and I mean *early*) morning ride over mirror-smooth lakes, orange groves—in season, Bob will float down and let you pick an orange—and the green marshlands that dominate this part of the state. After a bumpy landing (all balloon rides have 'em), you'll celebrate your safe return with a champagne toast and the ballooner's blessing.

Returning to the land, you'll also return to the road and head north from Disney, where you'll soon discover two neighborhoods that are more reminiscent of a New England town than Florida. The closest is **Winter Park,** less than 25 miles away. With its tree-lined, redbrick streets and array of boutiques and fine restaurants, Winter Park is a hidden pocket of posh living just north of Orlando.

It makes sense to spend a night here, and the place to be is the **Park Plaza Hotel.** Built in the 1920s, the Park Plaza is an elegant throwback to the grand hotels of another era, before the big chains came along. With authenticity comes sacrifices, however, and the two major ones are the tiny

The view from one of Bob's Balloons

bathrooms and the sound of the early-morning train rumbling through and perhaps waking you up. (It didn't rouse me, but another guest complained of his stay at "Petticoat Junction.") From the balcony, you're in prime position to enjoy the sights and sounds of Park Avenue, and from its central location, all of Winter Park lies open to you.

Check in and then grab lunch at the hotel's restaurant: The **Park Plaza Gardens** happens to be one of the best spots in town, with a tough-to-beat combination of outdoor seating, modern interior, and a menu that ranges from gourmet salads to Kobe beef burgers to fine entrées (their crabcakes are plump and full of lump-meat goodness). After lunch, take a walk around town. Across the road from the hotel is Central Park, a wide green swathe adorned with fountains where you might find the local high school band giving free performances on a sunny weekend afternoon. A stroll along Park Avenue takes you past a shopping promenade with tiny alleys filled with upscale boutiques, cafés, and restaurants. If you're here on a Saturday morning, make sure to check out the excellent farmer's market at the corner of South Park and New England Avenues. Many local chefs buy their produce here.

For a truly old-fashioned experience, take a **Scenic Boat Tour** along a chain of lakes and beautiful, winding canals. These hour-long pontoon

One of Winter Park's scenic canals

boat trips, which have been a Winter Park tradition since 1938, are narrated excursions that let you see some of Winter Park's premier mansions, points of interest, and landscapes. The boats are located at the end of Morse Boulevard, which is off Park Avenue.

With three terrific cultural highlights, Winter Park has good reason to pride itself on its arts and culture: The first, located on Park Avenue, is the town's unique treasure: the **Charles Hosmer Morse Museum of American Art.** Known for the world's most extensive collection of Louis Comfort Tiffany works, the museum includes his famous lamps and leaded-glass masterpieces but also exhibits his lesser-known jewelry, pottery, and paintings. Also, don't miss the incredible Byzantine-inspired chapel that Tiffany designed for the 1893 World's Columbian Expo in Chicago.

The **Cornell Fine Arts Museum,** located on the beautiful campus of Rollins College, has recently opened in a polished new building and maintains a strong focus on fine-arts education. It has an extensive calendar of exhibits in addition to its permanent collection of Renaissance art, portraiture, and landscapes. On your way back from the Cornell, take a right on Fairbanks and follow it until it becomes Osceola Avenue. On the left, you'll find the **Polasek Sculpture Gardens,** an ideal place for a romantic stroll through manicured gardens where you can admire two hundred of Albin Polasek's works.

At night, Winter Park comes alive with the sounds of diners enjoying sidewalk table service at one of its many restaurants. There are many options to choose from, including a surprising diversity of ethnic food. One of the hippest and most popular eateries is **Luma on Park,** just across the street from the Park Plaza, where the eclectic menu changes daily, the wine cellar is stunning, and the decor is chic modern that would be at home in Soho. After your meal, walk a few feet down Park Avenue to **The Wine Room** for something a little different. A wine bar like no other, The Wine Room offers a tremendous variety of wines by the glass poured from state-of-the-art Enomatic wine dispensers.

Day Three: Mount Dora and the Return Trip

If you spend the night at the Park Plaza, you'll be halfway to your next destination when you leave Winter Park. Before you leave, stop by **Austin's Coffee & Film** on Fairbanks Avenue for a morning cup of joe. The quintessential college café (complete with grungy decor), Austin's uses organic coffee beans and has a selection of decent (and healthy) salads, sandwiches, and other light foods.

After, continue on Fairbanks, which turns into Edgewater Drive (FL 424) after about 3 miles, and turn left on Lee Road (FL 423). You'll be on Lee for a little more than half a mile before taking a right on North Orange Blossom Trail (US 441). This road will take you straight to **Mount Dora,** a quaint village known for its antiques shops and stuck-in-time serenity. Before you reach it, however, you'll take a slight detour in Apopka. Roughly 5 miles into your drive along 441, turn right at Piedmont Wekiwa Road and drive roughly 4 miles to get to **Wekiwa Springs State Park.** Locals and visitors alike flock to this pristine retreat for one main reason: to wade or snorkel in the deliciously cool (72 degrees year-round), clear spring waters. Canoe rentals are also available if you want a languid trip down the Wekiwa River.

Returning from Wekiwa to US 441 (you can take a slight shortcut by taking Wekiwa Springs Road to East Semoran Boulevard, or US 436, and turning right until it joins with US 441), you'll travel another 11 miles or so before the road splits into US 441 and Old Highway 441 South. Take the latter, which becomes Highland Street, for another few miles until you come to Fifth Avenue. Turn left and follow the road into the heart of the town.

Mount Dora is the destination of choice for couples who want a quiet weekend away from the hustle of the big city (or big park), and the best way to kick things off is by booking a room at one of Mount Dora's excellent bed & breakfasts. Two of my favorites are the **Mount Dora Historic Inn,** a small and adorable old house where charming hosts Jim and Ana Tuttle will spoil you rotten and feed you a gourmet breakfast "to live for," and **The Heron Cay Lakeview Bed & Breakfast,** a gorgeous Victorian property overlooking Lake Dora where the rooms are more spacious than most B&Bs and sumptuously decorated.

The historic downtown is an easy grid to navigate, with zero brand-name shops competing with the town's boutiques, art galleries, and numerous antiques shops. Mount Dora is known far and wide as an antiquing haven, and **Renninger's Antique Center** puts out the largest antiques fair in the state each weekend, with up to 1,200 dealers drawing tens of thousands of visitors. It's conveniently located right on US 441.

When you're ready for lunch, head to **5th Avenue Café & Market** for a savory, health-conscious light meal. Then, you can either continue to explore the town (be careful of heading down to the lakefront at dusk; alli-

Mount Dora Historic Inn

gators sometimes lurk around there) or, in keeping with the old-town atmosphere, enjoy a scenic train ride through and around Mount Dora with **Inland Lakes Railway** (you can do a lunch or dinner tour on the rails as well).

In the early afternoon, try to make it to **The Windsor Rose Old English Tea Room** or **The Garden Gate Tea Room** (both located on Fourth Avenue) for high tea and pastries, but save some appetite for the evening. Mount Dora has many fine restaurants, but in my opinion there is one that stands out from the crowd. Make sure to call ahead at **The Goblin Market** for outstanding eclectic cuisine in an intimate setting. A complete contrast from the sedate main dining hall downstairs is the funky lounge on the second floor. You'll love the story behind the name, too. After dinner, head to **The Frosty Mug,** an Icelandic restaurant and bar that is one of the town's main watering holes.

On your third day, you'll be ready to return to Orlando and end your "Disney and beyond" vacation. But before you return home, you might want to explore Orlando's downtown arts district and enjoy one final night on the town. If so, head back down US 441 for about 22 miles until you get to Princeton Street, and follow that a few miles until you get to **Loch Haven Park.** You're about 10 minutes north of the downtown arts district, but this park is a must-visit for museum lovers. Within its 45 acres is a trio of the city's best cultural highlights: the excellent and expansive **Orlando Museum of Art** (I especially love the Ancient Americas collection); the **Orlando Science Center,** which features a domed theater and planetarium in addition to its numerous interactive exhibits; and the **Mennello Museum of American Art,** best known for its permanent collection of Earl Cunningham paintings.

From Loch Haven Park, it's roughly 2 miles south on North Mills Avenue to East Robinson Street, where you'll turn right to head to the downtown arts district. Set away from the tourist-heavy parts of the city, this is a different side of Orlando, and one that keeps the Mouse at bay. It's the brisk and serious business center of the city, but nestled within the tall buildings is a thriving social and cultural scene with art galleries, parks, restaurants, bars, and clubs clustered in and around Orange Avenue. Just as you turn onto East Robinson Street, you'll come to **Lake Eola,** a pleasant urban oasis where you can stroll along a park and paddle around a floating fountain in a swan boat.

Orlando's nightlife is centered on nearby North Orange Avenue (just a few blocks east along Robinson Street), but before you indulge here, you have some decisions to make regarding dinner. At the beginning of this chapter, I mentioned the restaurants at the three Rosen properties. **Everglades Restaurant** in the Rosen Centre Hotel, and in Rosen Shingle Creek, **A Land Remembered,** named after Patrick Smith's book about Florida's history, celebrate Florida in menu and decor. (The former has oversized sculptures and colorful murals of local wildlife while the latter opts for a statelier plantation-style setting.) Both specialize in steaks and fine seafood. However, **Jack's Place,** at the Rosen Plaza, wins my vote for its character. The superb Continental fare is complemented nicely by caricatures of celebrities ranging from Albert Einstein to Queen Elizabeth. All are the work of owner Harris Rosen's father, Jack, who worked at the Waldorf Astoria for decades and became a celebrated caricaturist of the hotel's august guests.

Another "go where the locals go" destination is **Fusion 7,** a happy mélange of Mediterranean-inspired cuisine (featuring Orlando's first ceviche bar), lounge (with live acts several nights per week), and late-night club all rolled into one in a fancifully decorated space that is quite incon-

gruous in a strip mall. Finally, for a truly transporting meal, visit celebrated chef Norman Van Aiken's **Norman's.** Located in the Ritz-Carlton
Grande Lakes, this restaurant lives up to its lofty reputation as one of the
nation's best with astoundingly creative dishes (splurge for the "signature
dishes" menu—it's worth it).

Well fed, you can either head back to the downtown arts district or
catch a show on your last night. If it's a show you want, then I have to crum-
ble and, finally, tell you to head into theme park territory. Downtown
Disney is an adult playground where people can pick their club of choice
on Pleasure Island. I'd rather come here for **La Nouba,** a Cirque du Soleil
production that delivers all the pageantry, acrobatics, and visual spectacle
of its sister shows around the nation. Over at Universal's CityWalk, **Blue
Man Group** is more fun than you'd ever believe possible from three men
in blue paint who don't talk.

If a show isn't your cup of tea (or mug of beer), make your way back
to the downtown arts district, specifically to the corner of Orange and Wall
Streets. This is where the real action is for the locals who are as interested
in getting away from the amusement parks as you are. Wall Street Plaza, a
far cry from anything in New York, is crammed with pseudo dive bars,
kitschy martini bars, and totally incongruous tiki bars. The nightlife hot
spots along Orange and Church Streets each offer something different,
from chic lounges to rustic bars like **The Lodge,** which is named for and
designed after a ski lodge. Of some notoriety for its scantily clad patrons
is **Tabu,** the club with the largest dance floor and loudest music in the
downtown area.

Like I said, I'm not knocking the theme parks; they play their roles
expertly and are guaranteed to entertain. But the next time you're planning
your Disney vacation, you'll know that you have many alternatives to
explore should the costumes and long lines wear you down. If you want
to escape the Kingdom, it's good to know there's plenty of magic waiting
outside.

Contacts:

A Land Remembered, Rosen Shingle Creek, 9939 Universal Boulevard,
Orlando 32819. Call 1-866-996-9939. Open daily 5:30–10 for dinner.
Web site: www.landrememberedrestaurant.com.

Albin Polasek Museum & Sculpture Gardens, 633 Osceola Avenue, Winter Park 32789. Call 407-647-6294. Open September 1 through June 30, Tues. through Sat. 10–4, Sun. 1–4. Web site: www.polasek.org.

Austin's Coffee & Film, 929 West Fairbanks Avenue, Winter Park 32792. Call 407-975-3364. Open Mon. through Thurs. 7 AM–11 PM, Fri. and Sat. 7 AM–1 AM, Sun. 8 AM–midnight. Web site: www.austins coffee.com.

Blue Man Group, at Universal CityWalk, Orlando 32819. Call 1-888-340-5476. Performances usually run at 5 and 8 PM. Web site: www.universalorlando.com.

Bob's Balloons. Call 407-466-6380 or 1-877-824-4606 to reserve. Launches are generally at daybreak, but there are occasional afternoon flights as well. Web site: www.bobsballoons.com.

Café D'Antonio, 691 Front Street, Suite 110, Celebration 34747. Call 407-566-2233. Open Mon. through Fri. 11:30–3 and 5–10, Sat. 11:30–10, Sun. 11:30–9. Web site: www.antoniosonline.com.

Celebration Hotel, 700 Bloom Street, Celebration 34747. Call 407-566-6000 or 1-888-499-3800. Web site: www.celebrationhotel.com.

Charles Hosmer Morse Museum of American Art, 455 North Park Avenue, Winter Park 32789. Call 407-645-5311. Open Tues. through Thurs. and Sat. 9:30–4, Fri. 9:30–4 from June through August, Fri. 9:30–8 from September through May. Web site: www.morsemuseum.org.

Cornell Fine Arts Museum, 1000 Holt Avenue, Rollins College, Winter Park 32789. Call 407-646-2526. Open Tues. through Sat. 10–5, Sun. 1–5. Web site: www.rollins.edu/cfam.

Everglades Restaurant, Rosen Centre Hotel, 9840 International Drive, Orlando 32819. Call 407-996-2385 or 1-800-800-9840, ext. 3610. Open daily 5:30–10 PM. Web site: www.evergladesrestaurant.com.

5th Avenue Café & Market, 116 East Fifth Avenue, Mount Dora 32757. Call 352-383-0090. Open Tues. 11:30–3, Wed. and Thurs. 11:30–3 and 5–9, Fri. and Sat. 9–11 for breakfast and 5–9 for dinner, Sun. 10–3 and 5–9. Web site: www.5thavenuecafe.com.

Forever Florida, 4755 North Kenansville Road, St. Cloud 34773. Call 407-957-9794 or 1-886-854-EVER. Two-hour ecosafaris offered daily at 10 and 1. Horseback safaris need to be reserved in advance. Web site: www.foreverflorida.org.

The Frosty Mug, 100 East Fourth Street, Mount Dora 32757. Call 352-383-1696. Open weekdays 11–9, weekends 11–11. Web site: www.the frostymug.com.

Fusion 7, 13526 Village Park Drive, Orlando 32837. Call 407-582-9944. Open Tues. through Sun. 11 AM–2 AM. Web site: www.myfusion7.com.

The Garden Gate Tea Room, 142 East Fourth Avenue, Mount Dora 32757. Call 352-735-2158. Open Mon. through Sat. 11–3, Fri. and Sat. 5–8 for dinner.

Gatorland, 14501 South Orange Blossom Trail, Orlando 32837. Call 407-855-5496 or 1-800-393-JAWS. Open daily 9–5. Web site: www.gator land.com.

The Goblin Market, 331 North Donnelly Street, Mount Dora 32757. Call 352-735-0059. Open Tues. through Thurs. 11–3 and 5–9, Fri. and Sat. 11–3 and 5–10, Sun. noon–4. Web site: www.goblinmarket restaurant.com.

Green Meadows Petting Farm, 1368 South Poinciana Boulevard, Kissimmee 34746. Call 407-846-0770. Tours held between 9:30–4; farm remains open until 5:30. Web site: www.greeenmeadowsfarm.com.

The Heron Cay Lakeview Bed & Breakfast, 495 West Old Highway 441, Mount Dora 32757. Call 352-383-4050. Web site: www.heron cay.com.

Inland Lakes Railway, 150 West Third Avenue, Mount Dora 32757. Call 352-589-4300 for schedule and reservations. Web site: www.inland lakesrailway.com.

Jack's Place, 9700 International Drive, Rosen Plaza Hotel, Orlando 32819. Call 407-996-1787 or 1-800-366-9700. Open daily 5:30–10 PM. Web site: www.jacksplacerestaurant.com.

Lake Eola Café, Lake Eola Park, Orlando 32801 (for swan boat rentals). Call 407-232-0111. Open weekdays noon–6, weekends 10–8.

Lanier's Historic Downtown Marketplace, 108 Broadway, Kissimmee 34746. Call 407-933-5679. Open Mon. through Sat. 9–5:30. Web site: www.laniersantiques.com.

La Nouba, Downtown Disney Resort, Orlando 32830. Call 407-939-7600. Performances held Tues. through Sat. at 6 and 9 PM. Web site: www.cirquedusoleil.com.

The Lodge, 49 North Orange Avenue, Orlando 32801. Call 407-650-8786. Open daily 8 PM–2 AM.

Luma on Park, 290 South Park Avenue, Winter Park. Call 407-599-4111. Open for dinner Mon. through Thurs. 5:30–10, Fri. and Sat. 5:30–11, Sun. 5:30–9.

Medieval Times, 4510 West Irlo Bronson Highway, Kissimmee 34746. Call 1-888-WE-JOUST. Call ahead for showtimes. Web site: www .medievaltimes.com.

Mennello Museum of American Art, 900 East Princeton Street, Orlando 32803. Call 407-246-4278. Open Tues. through Sat. 10:30–4:30, Sun. noon–4:30. Web site: www.mennellomuseum.org.

Mount Dora Historic Inn, 221 East Fourth Avenue, Mount Dora 32757. Call 352-735-1212 or 1-800-927-6344. Web site: www.mount dorahistoricinn.com.

Norman's, 4012 Central Florida Parkway, Orlando 32837. Call 407-393-4333. Open for dinner Sun. through Thurs. 6–10:30, Fri. and Sat. 6–11. Web site: www.normans.com.

Old Town, 5770 West Irlo Bronson Memorial Highway, Kissimmee 34746. Call 407-396-4888 or 1-800-843-4204. Open daily 10–11; pubs open until later. Web site: www.old-town.com.

Orlando Museum of Art, 2416 North Mills Avenue, Orlando 32803. Call 407-896-4231. Open Tues. through Fri. 10–4, Sat. and Sun. noon–4. Web site: www.omart.org.

Orlando Science Center, 777 East Princeton Street, Orlando 32803. Call 407-514-2000 or 1-888-OSC-4FUN. Open Tues. through Thurs. 9–5, Fri. and Sat. 9–9, Sun. noon–5. Web site: www.osc.org

Osceola County Historical Society and Pioneer Museum, 750 North Bass Road, Kissimmee 34741. Call 407-396-8644. Open Thurs. through Sat. 10–4, Sun. 1–4.

Park Plaza Gardens, 319 Park Avenue South, Winter Park 32789. Call 407-645-2475. Open Mon. 11:30–2:30 and 6–9, Tues. through Sat. 11:30–2:30 and 6–10, Sun. 11–3 and 6–9. Web site: www.parkplaza gardens.com.

Park Plaza Hotel, 307 Park Avenue South, Winter Park 32789. Call 407-647-1072 or 1-800-228-7220. Web site: www.parkplazahotel.com.

Radisson Resort Orlando-Celebration, 2900 Parkway Boulevard, Kissimmee 34747. Call 407-396-7000 or 1-800-333-3333. Web site: www.radisson.com/orlando-celebration.

Renninger's Antique Center, 20651 US 441, Mount Dora 32757. Call 1-800-522-3555. Open weekends 9–5. Web site: www.renningers.com.

Rosen Shingle Creek, 9939 Universal Boulevard, Orlando 32819. Call 407-996-9939 or 1-866-996-9939. Web site: www.rosenshinglecreek.com.

Saratoga Resort Villas, 4787 West Irlo Bronson Highway, Kissimmee 34746. Call 407-397-0555 or 1-800-303-0427. Web site: www.saratogaresortvillas.com.

Scenic Boat Tours, 312 East Morse Boulevard, Winter Park 32789. Call 407-644-4056. Tours leave daily every hour from 10 to 4 (closed Christmas). Web site: www.scenicboattours.com.

Seito Sushi, 671 Front Street, Celebration 34747. Call 407-566-1889. Open Mon. through Thurs. 11:30–2:30 and 5–10, Fri. until 11, Sat. noon–11, Sun. noon–10. Web site: www.seitosushi.com.

Sherlock's of Celebration, 715 Bloom Street, Suite 130, Celebration 34747. Call 407-566-1866. Open daily 8:30–9. Web site: www.sherlocks group.com.

Tabu, 46 North Orange Avenue, Orlando 32801. Call 407-648-8363. Open Tues. through Sun. 10 PM–2 AM. Web site: www.tabunightclub.com.

Wallaby Ranch, 1805 Deen Still Road, Davenport 33897. Call 1-800-WALLABY for reservations. Web site: www.wallaby.com.

Warbird Adventures, 233 North Hoagland Boulevard, Kissimmee 34741. Call 407-870-7366 or 1-800-386-1593. Open Tues. through Sat. 9–5. Closed Sun. and Mon., Thanksgiving, Christmas, and New Year's Day. Web site: www.warbirdadventures.com.

Wekiwa Springs State Park, 1800 Wekiwa Circle, Apopka 32712. Call 407-884-2008. Open daily 8–sunset. Web site: www.floridastateparks .org/wekiwasprings.

The Windsor Rose Old English Tea Room, 142 West Fourth Avenue, Mount Dora 32757. Call 352-735-2551. Open Mon. through Fri. 11–4:30, Sat. and Sun. 11–5.

The Wine Room, 270 South Park Avenue, Winter Park 32789. Call 407-696-9463. Open Mon. through Wed. 10–10, Thurs. 10 AM–11 PM, Fri. and Sat. 10 AM–midnight, Sun. noon–7. Web site: www.thewineroom online.com.

CHAPTER

7

The Freshwater Frontier

A Weekend in the Heartland

Overview: These days, you see and hear a lot about discovering "The Real Florida," a statewide campaign to remember and honor Florida's roots. There are examples of "The Real Florida" throughout the state: mom-and-pop roadside attractions that have withstood the elements, the big theme parks, and beach-loving tourists; quaint towns that have maintained their character even through a fall from former glory; and vast, undeveloped regions where fishing villages cluster on the coast, continuing a cottage industry established hundreds of years ago. In the continuous ebb and flow of Florida's evolution, these stalwarts have survived—struggled, perhaps, but survived. And nowhere is this better represented than Florida's Freshwater Frontier.

A trip through the six counties that make up the Frontier is a journey into Florida's agricultural past and unchanged natural environment. This is a land of small towns, bounded by a vast community of lakes and rivers, nestled in a cultivated wilderness that includes an ancient and fragile ecosystem. Welcome to "The Real Florida."

Total length of trip: The round-trip is approximately 250 miles, spread over a weekend.

Getting there: The starting point for the journey is where I-75 intersects with US 27 roughly 25 miles west of Fort Lauderdale or 35 miles north of

Miami. From here, take US 27 north for 87 miles to get to **Gatorama,** which is right off the highway. It's another 27 miles on US 27 to **Lake Placid.** Continue on US 27 for just over 10 miles to reach FL 66. Turn left and follow the road for 25 miles. Make a quick right at US 17 (less than a mile) and then turn left on the Florida Cracker Trail (FL 64) for 15 miles, until you get to County Route 665 (CR 665). Take a left here and drive roughly 7 miles to get to **Solomon's Castle.**

From Solomon's Castle, take a left on CR 665, driving southeast, for about 7 miles until you come to CR 661. Turn right here and drive 10 miles, and then bear left on FL 70 Northwest. Continue to follow FL 70 for about 3 miles to reach **Arcadia.** From here, continue along FL 70 East for 2 miles and then turn right on FL 31, heading southeast. You'll be on this road for just over 36 miles, until it ends at Palm Beach Boulevard (FL 80). Turn left here and follow FL 80 east for about 21 miles. Then turn left on FL 29 and drive a half mile to get to **LaBelle.** To reach the final stop, **Clewiston,** get back on FL 80, heading east, for just over 21 miles, and then bear right on US 27. Follow the highway for roughly 9 miles to reach the town. Return along US 27 South for about 55 miles to get back to the starting point on I-75.

Highlights: To get to the Freshwater Frontier from I-75, you first have to travel along US 27 through the great open marshlands of the Everglades. It's an appropriate entry to the region; before the turnpikes and interstates, US 27 was a major artery through the state for commerce and tourism, and, at one point, the main route from Miami to Tampa. In an hour or so, you'll get to **Clewiston,** "America's Sweetest Town," but as this will be your last stop, you can drive on through. In another 30 miles or so, passing Moore Haven, you'll come to one of the most famous of Florida's roadside attractions: **Gatorama.**

Gatorama was the brainchild of Cecil Clemons, who opened the attraction in 1957. It was a regular stop for tourists until the 1970s, when I-75 and the Florida Turnpike plucked motorists off US 27 in favor of quicker roadways. Since 1986, it's been run continuously by a sixth-generation Florida Cracker family, and today it boasts the largest collection of big alligators and crocodiles in the country. Some of these guys are truly monstrous: "Mighty Mike" measures 14 feet, and to hear a jaw-snap from "Goliath" is like listening to a localized thunderclap. Other creatures call the park home, and as you walk along the covered walkway past the wooden bridge you'll come across panthers, a variety of birds, monkeys, and other creatures. There is also a habitat for baby alligators, one of which you can hold (once their mouths have been taped shut).

Whatever you do, don't miss the daily gator feedings, when owner Allen Register dangles raw chicken off a platform and the prehistoric predators launch themselves out of the water to grab their snack. Allen, who is fearless to the point of insanity, has been doing this for a long time, and he has the missing finger to prove it. He and his wife, Patty, are entertaining hosts who, along with their children, continue a half-century tradition that is easily worth the price of admission.

After this rather exhilarating introduction to the Freshwater Frontier, you'll continue on US 27 until you get to FL 70. Take a left here and drive to the **Archbold Biological Station.** This is a research center and not a tourist attraction, but it's a great place to learn more about the unique and rare geography of the area. Tourists can visit the main building for an informative video about this terrain, known as the Lake Wales Ridge. It's the highest territory in the state and has an ancient ecosystem that is home to one of the largest groups of endangered and threatened species in the country. The ridge is really a network of paleo-islands formed more than a million years ago, an arid sandbar that has evolved over time and today is a precious, and vanishing, natural treasure. After the video, take one of the short nature trails to complete your visit.

Leaving Archbold, head back on US 27 and continue north to **Lake Placid.** Not to be confused with Lake Placid, New York (although it was named after the New York town by Dr. Melvil Dewey, who came here to establish

One of the daily gator feedings at Gatorama

a resort destination), this town has an interesting story to tell. It begins in the early 1990s; Lake Placid had fallen on hard times, and its prospects for future growth were uncertain. Like many small towns in the United States, it was slowly dying. And then it learned about a small town in British Columbia called Chemainus, which had been in dire straits until it reinvented itself through art. Chemainus began a project to paint murals throughout the town, and the idea took off. It was a model that Lake Placid decided to emulate.

The result? Today, the town is an outdoor art gallery, with 40 murals (and counting) decorating the walls. The murals range in size (the largest being the massive *Cracker Trail Cattle Drive*, which comes with audio sam-

Outdoor art gallery

plings), but all pay homage to the town's history, the people who shaped it, and the surrounding nature. It's something of a scavenger hunt to find them all, and there are other works of art to accompany the murals. Here and there, plaques of native birds hang on the walls. More colorful and visible still are the garbage cans, many of which are shaped and painted to complement a nearby mural.

From US 27, take a left on Interlake Boulevard, and a right on Oak Avenue to arrive at the **Lake Placid Chamber of Commerce and Welcome Center,** where you can buy (for $3) a handy guide to the town's murals. Then head to **Chef Buddy's Italian American Deli** for a hearty sub, salad, or pasta lunch. After that, you're free to wander about, discovering these vibrant works and checking out Lake Placid's quaint shopping district. The **Caladium Arts & Craft Co-Op** is a good place to find handmade souvenirs and gifts. You'll notice there are no brand-name stores here; this is the result of stiff resistance by the chamber to retain its small-town charm and identity. For this reason alone, Lake Placid is a special place.

There is more to the town than murals. This is also the "Caladium Capital of the World." Highlands County produces 99 percent of these distinctive plants, so the title is well earned. Call **Happiness Farms** to see if there are any tours of their property, which will take you to their caladium fields. When in bloom, this is a beautiful, pastoral montage of red, green, and white.

Interestingly, Lake Placid also has the most resident clowns of any town in Florida. This is due to Toby's Clown School, which has graduated more than eight hundred clowns since 1990. One of the murals on Main Avenue shows three of its graduates—Keith Stokes, Ora Mae Meggitt, and Dick Meggitt—who are current residents.

For dinner, head north along US 27 to nearby Sebring. Just off the highway to your left is **The Watering Hole,** an absolute must both for its food and ambience. The restaurant is pure Florida Cracker in its decor, with rich wood paneling and furniture giving it the feel of a lodge (I also love the mounted alligator skull with bull horns). Your food is served on metal platters, but don't be deceived by the down-home look and feel of the place; it serves up some of the best steaks in the area (some say the state). In fact, The Watering Hole has won Highland County's award for best steaks, seafood, restaurant, and live entertainment *for ten years straight!* Oh, and in case you need another reason to go, there's "Bully," the restaurant's resident live 14-foot alligator.

Solomon's Castle

Spend your first night at Lake Placid. **Lake Grassy Suites** is nothing fancy but a clean and comfortable, all-suite hotel with kitchen, a small private beach area, and lovely lake views in the morning. It's located right off US 27, just south of the downtown area.

On day two, leave Lake Placid early and head north on US 27, crossing into Sebring again. When you get to the Hammock Road intersection, take a left to arrive at **Highlands Hammock State Park.** One of the first state parks in Florida, it remains a large, deeply lush forest of broad-leaf trees, pinelands, and marshes. Its nine nature trails include an elevated boardwalk through a cypress swamp. Keep your eyes open for deer, otter, fox, and even a rare black bear. (For the record, I saw a family of deer on my last trip into the park.)

When you leave the park, take CR 635 South to FL 66 and turn right. You'll head west for about 35 miles on 66 and then on the Florida Cracker Trail (US 17 and FL 64), until you get to CR 665. Turn left here and follow the signs for **Solomon's Castle.** You're now leaving Old Florida behind and entering a world of whimsy and fantasy inspired by one man's inspiration and another man's used car parts.

Howard Solomon is a magician with junk. An internationally known sculptor, he decided to realize his dream in the near-total obscurity of Ona, Florida. His dream, as it turns out, was to build a bona fide castle out of recycled odds and ends, complete with turrets and towers, stained-glass windows, and galleries of his sculptures, most of which are made out of used auto parts. Howard will be your guide through this wacky and wonderful realm, which includes the castle interior, the Boat in the Moat restaurant, and the lighthouse. Everything here is handmade (Howard's workshop is out behind the castle) and family run. After the tour, step inside the boat for lunch and check out the gift shop for a unique souvenir.

Leaving Solomon's Castle, you head southeast on CR 665, CR 661, and then FL 70 to arrive at **Arcadia,** a historic railroad town. Arcadia's main street has some lovely old architecture (check out the Opera House and the

Arcadia Opera House

Arbor Reception Hall) and a cluster of antiques shops. If you're here early enough, or if you skipped the Boat in the Moat, stop by **Wheeler's Café** for old-fashioned, no-frills Southern cooking and a slice of their out-of-this-world peanut butter pie.

If you can budget three nights for this trip (i.e., over a long weekend), you can spend one night either in Solomon's Castle or in Arcadia. At Solomon's, you have a choice of the Blue Moon Room, located inside the castle, and the Lily Life House Bed & Breakfast, located in an adjacent building; in Arcadia, **The Historic Parker House** is the epitome of a bed & breakfast inn that captures—in every detail—Southern charm, comfort, and hospitality.

If this is a weekend trip, depart from Arcadia and continue on FL 70 until you hit FL 31. Head south on this road for 36 miles until it ends at Palm Beach Boulevard (FL 80). When this road intersects with FL 29 (Hickpochee Avenue), you've arrived at the center of **LaBelle.** Known for picturesque oak-lined streets, the stately redbrick Hendry County Courthouse (LaBelle has been the county seat since 1923), and strong agricultural roots (Hendry County is the second-largest citrus producer in the state), this is among the larger of the small towns that make up the Freshwater Frontier.

LaBelle hugs the banks of the winding Caloosahatchee River, and its historic district runs from Bridge Street to Hickpochee Avenue. It's a small strip that has fallen from its former glory but still has a few interesting shops and buildings. One of these is the **Harold P. Curtis Honey Company.** A family-owned business since 1954, this is a working beehive and honey-producing plant. You can take a tour of the property, learn about beekeeping, visit a live working hive, and sample or buy one of the four varieties of honey made here: Orange Blossom (the local favorite), Palmetto, Wild Flower, and Mangrove.

Bridge enthusiasts may want to see **Fort Denaud Bridge,** one of the last remaining swing bridges in the state. To get here, drive along Fort Denaud Road until a right turn at FL 78 takes you to the bridge. Along the way are some beautiful old homes and views of the river. Head back to FL 80 for an early dinner (or supper, if you will) at **Flora & Ella's Restaurant & Country Store.** Set in a bright yellow, Florida-style home, this dining institution has been serving Southern specialties like Hoppin' John, fried green tomatoes, and chicken 'n dumplings since 1933. But they are most famous for their fantastic pies, which are made fresh.

From here, it's a straight shot east on FL 80 for about 30 miles to **Clewiston,** the last stop on the Frontier. Clewiston, dubbed "America's Sweetest Town," is so named for its long association with the sugar industry. Since 1929, the Southern Sugar Company, which was later renamed the U.S. Sugar Corporation, has dominated Clewiston's economy and society.

As you'll likely be arriving in the evening, make your first stop **The Clewiston Inn,** at the corner of US 27 and Royal Palm Avenue. This is a grand old hotel in the typical Southern style, a beautifully furnished landmark and a worthy place to spend your last night on the Frontier. After you've settled in, head down to **The Everglades Lounge** for a drink and a glimpse at the vivid Everglades mural, which was painted by J. Clinton Shepherd and wraps around all four walls.

The Clewiston Inn

Before you head home, enjoy the day in Clewiston. In the morning, go fishing and/or catch an airboat ride on Lake Okeechobee, the second-largest freshwater lake in the United States. Alligators, largemouth bass, and a variety of birds draw hordes of anglers and tourists to the lake each year. To get on the water, head to **Roland & Mary Ann Martin's Marina &**

Big O Airboat Tours

Resort, which is right on the lake. Here, you can book a fishing or scenic trip with **Big O Airboat Tours.** It's a noisy (don't worry, you get earplugs) but fun ride with ample opportunity to see the local wildlife (including one odd alligator who was convinced our airboat was a potential mate). After the ride, the somewhat out-of-place Tiki Bar at the marina is a nice place to grab a drink or a quick lunch.

If the airboat is not your thing, take a closer look at Clewiston's biggest industry with **Sugarland Tours,** offered by the chamber of commerce. This bus tour takes you to sugarcane fields and a sugar mill, and culminates with lunch at The Clewiston Inn. Also visit the **Clewiston Museum** for a glimpse into the town's history, which not only covers the sugar industry but also the people who settled here before the 1920s. This includes, as one would expect, the Seminole Indians, and, quite unexpectedly, Japanese farmers who arrived in 1915 (in fact, the first business in Clewiston was the Watanabe Hotel) and struggled due to Lake Okeechobee's unpredictable flooding.

THE FAIRS AND FESTIVALS OF THE FRESHWATER FRONTIER

The towns and communities that make up this part of southcentral Florida are a throwback to an older, quieter lifestyle, and their annual celebrations center on what the land provides. The biggest bashes along the Frontier are:

The Caladium Festival, held in Lake Placid at the end of August, features caladiums galore, food, live music, clowns, face painting, arts and crafts, mural renderings, a car show, and a dance.

The Swamp Cabbage Festival, held in LaBelle over the last weekend of February, is a huge event, with a carnival, Swamp Cabbage King and Queen crowning, rodeos, parade, lawnmower racing competition, car show, bass tournament, live music, dancing, and food.

The Sugar Festival, held in Clewiston in April, features entertainment, food, arts and crafts, and old-fashioned cane grinding to mark the end of the sugarcane harvest.

Contacts:

Archbold Biological Station, P.O. Box 2057, Lake Placid 33862. Call 863-465-2571. Main office open Mon. through Fri. 8–5. Web site: www.archbold-station.org.

Big O Airboat Tours, 920 East Del Monte, at Roland & Mary Ann Martin's Marina, Clewiston 33440. Call 863-983-2037. Web site: www.bigofishing.com.

Caladium Arts & Craft Co-Op, 132 East Interlake Boulevard, Lake Placid 33852. Call 863-699-5940. Open Mon. through Fri. 9–4.

Chef Buddy's Italian American Deli, 204 North Main Avenue, Lake Placid 33852. Call 863-465-6800. Open Mon. through Fri. 10–5, Sat. 10–2.

The Clewiston Inn, 108 Royal Palm Avenue, Clewiston 33440. Call 863-983-8151 or 1-800-749-4466. Web site: www.clewistoninn.com.

Clewiston Museum, 109 Central Avenue, Clewiston 33440. Call 863-983-2870. Open Mon. through Fri. 1–5. Web site: www.clewiston.org/museum.htm.

Flora & Ella's Restaurant & Country Store, 550 FL 80, LaBelle 33935. Call 863-675-2891. Open Mon. through Sat. 6 AM–8 PM.

Gatorama, 6180 US 27, Palmdale 33944. Call 863-675-0623. Open daily 10–5. Web site: www.gatorama.com.

Happiness Farms, 704 County Route 621 East, Lake Placid 33852. Call 863-465-2313 or 1-866-892-0396. Web site: www.happinessfarms.com.

Harold P. Curtis Honey Company, 335 North Bridge Street, LaBelle 33975. Call 863-675-2187. Open Mon. through Fri. 9–5, Sat. 10–4. Web site: www.curtishoney.hypermart.net.

Highlands Hammock State Park, 5931 Hammock Road, Sebring 33872. Call 863-386-6094. Open daily 8–sunset. Web site: www.florida stateparks.org.

The Historic Parker House, 427 West Hickory Street, Arcadia 34266. Call 863-494-1060. Web site: www.historicparkerhouse.com.

Lake Grassy Suites, 1865 US 27 South, Lake Placid 33852. Call 863-465-9200.

Lake Placid Chamber of Commerce and Welcome Center, 18 North Oak Avenue, Lake Placid 33852. Call 863-465-4331. Open Mon. through Fri. 9–4.

Roland & Mary Ann Martin's Marina & Resort, 920 East Del Monte, Clewiston 33440. Call 863-983-3151 or 1-800-473-6766. Tiki bar and Galley open daily 5:30 AM–9 PM. Web site: www.rolandmartin marina.com.

Solomon's Castle and the Boat in the Moat Restaurant, 4533 Solomon Road, Ona 33865. Call 863-494-6077. Open Tues. through Sun. 11–4. Closed July–September. Web site: www.solomonscastle.com.

Sugarland Tours, 109 Central Avenue, at the chamber of commerce, Clewiston 33440. Call 863-983-7979. Tours leave weekdays at 10. No children under 12 permitted. Web site: www.clewiston.org/sugarland tours.htm.

The Watering Hole, 6813 US 27, Sebring 33872. Call 863-382-4554. Open Mon. through Sat. for dinner 4–10, bar and lounge open daily, with live music Fri. and Sat. 9:30 PM–2 AM. Web site: www.wateringhole sebring.com. *Note:* No credit cards accepted.

Wheeler's Café, 13 South Monroe Street, Arcadia 34266. Call 863-993-1555. Open daily 6 AM–2:30 PM.

CHAPTER

8

The Center of It All

All-American Polk County

Overview: In 2007, Polk County was named an "All-American County" by the National Civic League. This recognition of one community's efforts to strive for civic excellence meant a lot to Polk's citizens, not just because it was a prestigious national award, but because of what it represented and how it highlighted—in red, white, and blue—what Polk County is all about.

Why did Polk get the nod over so many other applicants? Perhaps it was due to the town's commitment and collective interest in establishing a flourishing arts community; maybe it was because of its preservation of cultural landmarks and its Old Florida heritage; and surely, part of the reason was the recognition of its open, friendly character. And that's exactly what you get when you visit this part of Florida: amiable people, time-honored traditions, quaint attractions and destinations, and, above all, a sense of community.

Total length of trip: About 190 miles over three days.

Getting there: From Orlando, take I-4 West toward Tampa. Drive roughly 38 miles to exit 44. Take the exit and turn left at FL 599. Follow this road for less than a half mile to get to **Fantasy of Flight** in **Polk City.** From here, continue on I-4 for another 11 miles before you come to exit 32 onto US 98 South. In another 4 miles, turn right at Main Street to arrive at the heart of **Lakeland.** Then take US 92 East for about 9 miles, bearing right on Havendale Boulevard (FL 544 East) for just over 3 miles until you come to Eighth Street/US 17. Turn right here and follow US 17 South for about 2.5 miles, before turning left on Cypress Gardens Boulevard (FL 540 East), which will take you to **Cypress Gardens.** To get to **Lake Wales,** follow FL 540 East for about 6.5 miles. When you get to US 27, turn right and head south for roughly 6 miles to arrive at Central Avenue. From here, take US 17 South for about a half mile to FL 60. Turn left here and head east for 25 miles to **River Ranch.** Returning to Orlando, take FL 60 back to US 27 and head north for roughly 23 miles to I-4. Head east on I-4 for another 28 miles to return to Orlando.

Highlights: It's not like Polk County needed the All-American designation to be a viable destination for tourists who were looking for something different. Straddling Tampa and Orlando, this part of central Florida has held its own in the attractions arena long before either Busch Gardens or Disney showed up. In fact, Florida's oldest theme park is in Polk County—but we'll get to that in a bit.

Heading west on I-4, your first stop will be off exit 55, at the relatively new **Polk Outpost 27.** Located on US 27, this is a better-than-average welcome center. You'll note that aviation dominates the decor, from the biplane protruding from the wall in the entrance, to the children's simulator ride. Along with the standard collection of flyers and brochures, there's a putting green, a theater, and a cool little kiosk where you can have your picture taken and e-mailed instantly to friends and family. And just out back is an orange grove, a fitting background: Polk County is the state's largest citrus producer.

LAKES AND GREENS

In addition to its many attractions, Polk County is famous for its lakes and golf courses—more than 550 lakes and more than 500 holes of golf, to be precise. Waterskiing, airboats, fishing trips, and championship nine- and 18-hole courses abound in this region. There are far too many to list here, but if you're interested, check out the Polk Outpost 27 for more information on these activities.

If you're traveling with the family, you might want to book a vacation home. **Imagine Vacation Homes** offers spacious, well-appointed homes in nearby Davenport (from I-4, take US 27 North to Lake Davenport Road). For less than a hotel, you can get a multiple-bedroom house with a pool, kitchen, and plenty of privacy, a short ride from Disney and everything Polk has to offer. For single travelers and couples, keep going. You'll be staying in Lakeland.

It's not quite a back road, but your next destination will have you hopping back on I-4 and continuing west to exit 44. Turn left on Broadway Boulevard and you'll arrive at **Fantasy of Flight,** one of the best aviation attractions in the nation. Fantasy of Flight was the brainchild of one man, Kermit Weeks, and showcases the largest private aircraft collection in the world; but more than that, it echoes Weeks's own love of flying and humanity's exploration of the skies. Opened in 1995, it has grown to include a variety of experiences and attractions. A self-guided three-hour tour takes visitors from the earliest attempts at flight through vintage aircraft from both World Wars (and a chance to enter a B-17 Flying Fortress). The displays and exhibit halls are very well designed and vividly re-create the different environments.

Other tours give you a behind-the-scenes look at the meticulous restoration work that goes into these historical aircraft. There are daily aircraft exhibitions, and a chance to peruse Weeks's vintage collection at your leisure. If you want to get a little more interactive, try one of the state-of-the-art flight simulators, complete with preflight briefing, and participate in a mock battle over the Pacific Ocean. For those who want to go beyond that, you can even get in a hot-air balloon or fly one of two vintage open-cockpit biplanes—the Boeing Stearman PT-17 or the 1929 D-25. The basic diner food at the **Compass Rose Diner** here isn't the best, but the setting matches the aviation theme and old-time style of this unique attraction.

After Fantasy of Flight, head back on I-4 (flaunting the "back roads" rule book for the last time) and continue west to exit 32, which will put you on US 98 South. Follow the road for 4 miles to reach Main Street. Take a right here, and you'll come to downtown **Lakeland** and **The Terrace Hotel.** There is a lot to recommend about the Terrace: A beautiful, stately old building overlooking Lake Mirror, the hotel—built in 1924—is a slice of Old Florida luxury, and it has one of the best restaurants in the region. You'll be dining there tonight.

Fantasy of Flight

You should be in Lakeland by the early afternoon. For lunch, try **Harry's Seafood Bar & Grille,** just around the corner from the Terrace and across from Munn Park, for Cajun cooking in a relaxed pub environment. The historic district at Munn Park has many examples of vernacular architecture (if you're interested, pick up a *Lakeland Walking Tour* pamphlet at your hotel).

After lunch, drive south down Massachusetts Avenue to Lake Morton Drive. Turn left and circle the lake until you arrive at East Palmetto Street and the **Polk Museum of Art.** The museum is a robust addition to the local arts scene, with a permanent collection focusing on modern and contemporary works, an Asian hall, European and American decorative arts, a pre-Columbian collection, and African art.

Visiting the Polk Museum is a good primer for the next stop, an equally unexpected and incredibly significant destination for art lovers. Continue east on Palmetto Street for a few blocks to South Ingraham Avenue, which will lead you to **Florida Southern College.** Ordinarily, a small college of only two thousand students would not be listed in a guidebook, but this place boasts an architectural treasure trove that makes it one of the most fascinating campuses in the country: Its buildings and esplanades make up the only university structures designed and built by the legendary Frank Lloyd Wright.

Wright had been instrumental in the establishment of the university since the late 1930s, when then-president Ludd Spivey convinced him to help erect a "great education temple" in Florida. So began an unusual marriage of one of the world's noted masters of his art and a relatively unknown educational mission in a remote area. But the 18 structures designed by Wright—while suffering over the years from lack of upkeep (due to lack of funding)—still stand on this amazing campus, and a new effort is under way to restore them to their full glory.

Stop by the visitors center to begin your tour of the campus. After, return to Lake Mirror. On the south side of the lake is **Hollis Gardens,** a small but lovely botanical garden with color-coordinated collections of plants and flowers, a limestone grotto, two ponds, and a variety of local and exotic flora, herbs, and vegetables. A walk here and around the lake should prime you for a gourmet dinner at **The Terrace Grill.** Enjoy the traditional, well-prepared Continental menu (wood-grilled filet mignon, herb-crusted rack of lamb, and other well-known favorites) in an elegant, high-ceilinged dining room.

If you're a baseball fan and you're here in the spring, you might want to forego the gardens to catch a Detroit Tigers game at **Joker Marchant Stadium,** or a Cleveland Indians game in nearby Winter Haven at **Chain of Lakes Park.**

Get an early start on your next day with breakfast at The Terrace Grill, and then check out of the hotel, heading south on Massachusetts Avenue for about a half mile. Bear right on US 98 and travel 4 miles to take the ramp onto Polk Parkway East (FL 570). (Bring change for the toll.) In less than 3 miles, take exit 14 and get on Winter Lake Road. You'll head east on this road for about 8 miles (it turns into FL 540) until you get to US 17. Turn left, heading north, and in less than 2 miles turn right onto Cypress Gardens Boulevard, which will bring you to **Cypress Gardens.**

Florida's original theme park is worth the trip, not for its roller coasters—it can hardly be expected to compete with the bigger parks—but for its other virtues. (It's also a fraction of the price.) Sure, there are some fun rides here (with a new addition, the Starliner, which opened in June 2007), but more than that, you're coming for the quaint, wholesome Southern charm of the place, exemplified by the costumed Southern belles who greet you at the entrance and can be seen wandering around the park. You're here for the lush and lovely landscapes, with sculpted gardens and huge, colorful topiaries; a canopied forest with awesome, ancient banyan trees; and waterfalls

Southern belles at Cypress Gardens

and fountains in abundance. And you've come for its star attraction: the waterskiing show. Cypress Gardens is the granddaddy of the sport and home to many of its innovations. Shows run throughout the day and are made all the more fun by an enthusiastic staff, an element of comedy, and impressive acrobatics.

Enjoy the park, catch a show, and be ready to leave for a late lunch. You can eat here, of course, but then you'd be missing out on a fantastic experience that continues the quaint cultural legacy of this part of Florida. Continue east on Cypress Gardens Boulevard (FL 540) for 6.5 miles, and then turn right on US 27, heading south. In less than 2 miles, you'll come to Chalet Suzanne Road (County Route 17A [CR 17A]). Turn left and follow this road (which turns into Chalet Suzanne Lane) for 2 miles to arrive at **Chalet Suzanne.**

Since 1931, this family-owned restaurant and inn has been an old-fashioned, romantic, and hidden treasure in central Florida. The pink Swiss chalet, nestled in a manicured garden adorned with sculptures and fountains, gives you the impression of entering a fairy tale. It's so well loved that the Hinshaw family even installed an airstrip nearby so their clients could fly in for a meal or a weekend stay. A traditional lunch at the chalet is a multiple-course feast of generations-old family recipes that includes a delicious broiled grapefruit appetizer, the famous Soup Romaine (also known as Moon Soup because it was a favorite among the astronauts of the Apollo missions), and your choice of entrée.

After lunch, check in for the night at one of the quaint rooms in either the main chalet or the attached "village." Then head back out along Chalet Suzanne Road to North Scenic Highway (US 27 Alt.). Turn right here and, in about 3.5 miles, bear left on Burns Avenue (CR 17A). Follow this road for about 1.5 miles, and then turn left at Tower Boulevard to arrive at the **Historic Bok Sanctuary.**

The sanctuary makes for a peaceful, meditative interlude in your journey. Bok's lush gardens slope up to the highest point in Florida and culminate in a soaring art deco and neo-Gothic "singing tower," so named for its famous carillon. The music of the carillon is produced through 60 bronze bells weighing between 16 pounds and 12 tons. Recorded selections can be heard throughout the day, and live recitals are sometimes performed at 1 and 3 PM. In front of the tower is a lovely reflecting pool, and completing the idyllic view are the swans floating along the surface. This is a place of quiet reflection.

While you're here, don't miss the **Pinewood Estate,** a 1930s home adjacent to the sanctuary that now houses European antiques from the 17th to the 19th centuries. The home follows a Mediterranean design, with tiled floors and staircases, elegant Tuscan gardens, wrought-iron fixtures, and Moorish doors.

For dinner, you have one of two fine-dining options to round out a busy day. Either return to Chalet Suzanne (jackets are required for dinner) or head to **Antonio's,** at the Best Western opposite Cypress Gardens, for sophisticated Italian cuisine with all the trimmings—live piano music, tableside cooking, roses for the ladies, soft candlelight ambience, and a well-heeled clientele.

If you're here on a Saturday, then another—and not quite so formal— way to spend your night is by checking out the weekly rodeo at **Westgate River Ranch.** To get here from the Bok Sanctuary, turn left on CR 17A (Burns Road) and right on County Route 17B (North Buck Moore Road) for about 1.5 miles until you hit FL 60. Turn left and head east for roughly

Florida's Natural Grove House

22 miles to reach the ranch. After the rodeo, head to the Smokehouse Grill at the marina for barbecued chicken 'n ribs, burgers, and steaks.

Westgate is a nostalgia of a different variety—the Florida of the cattlemen. In addition to the rodeo, this bona fide dude ranch features horseback riding, hay rides, a Western-style saloon, and a re-created mini village with country store, post office, and Western store. It also offers skeet shooting, a nine-hole golf course, and water excursions including sunset cruises, airboat rides, and fishing trips out on Lake Kissimmee. The ranch will appeal to the outdoorsperson in you, and if it's not your thing on a Saturday night, I would recommend a visit on your last day in Polk County.

Before you hit the ranch, take a quick morning tour of historic downtown Lake Wales, roughly 6 miles south of Chalet Suzanne on US 17 (turn left on Park Street to reach the shopping arcade that runs between Park and Stuart Streets). Inside the arcade is **Très Jolie,** a small café where you can check out a funky collection of hats and curios while you munch on authentic Parisian pastries. The arcade and its surrounding area is an antiques district with art galleries, murals, and some interesting gift shops.

To get from downtown Lake Wales to Westgate, take Stuart Avenue to North Scenic Highway (US 27 Alt.). Turn right and follow the road for about a half mile. The road jogs left on Polk Avenue and then right on Hesperides Road, which turns into FL 60. You'll follow FL 60 for just over 24 miles to reach Westgate. The ranch has so many activities that you might want to spend a night in one of their cozy log-cabin-style rooms if you have the time.

The ranch is your last stop, save one: Return along FL 60 to US 27, which will reconnect with I-4. Roughly a half mile north of FL 60 on US 27, stop by **Florida's Natural Grove House.** A farmer's cooperative since 1933, Florida's Natural is the only major citrus company that's 100 percent owned by its growers. The visitors center across the street from the main plant has an excellent in-house theater with a movie about the orange industry in Florida and the story of Florida's Natural. You get a free sample of Florida orange juice—a fitting end of your journey into All-American Polk County.

Contacts:

Antonio's, 5665 Cypress Gardens Boulevard, at the Best Western Admiral's Inn, Winter Haven 33884. Call 863-324-5950. Open for dinner Tues. through Sat. 5:30–10 (last seating at 9).

Chalet Suzanne, 3800 Chalet Suzanne Drive, Lake Wales 33859. Call 863-676-6011 or 1-800-433-6011. Open daily 8 AM–9 PM. Web site: www.chaletsuzanne.com.

Chain of Lakes Park (Cleveland Indians Spring Training), 500 Cletus Allen Road, Winter Haven 33884. Call 863-293-3900. Web site: www.indians.com.

Cypress Gardens, 6000 Cypress Gardens Boulevard, Winter Haven 33884. Call 863-324-2111. Open daily at 10; closing times vary (closed Thanksgiving and Christmas). Web site: www.cypressgardens.com.

Fantasy of Flight, 1400 Broadway Boulevard Southeast, Polk City 33868. Call 863-984-3500. Open daily 10–5; hours may vary (closed Thanksgiving and Christmas). Web site: www.fantasyofflight.com.

Florida Southern College, 111 Lake Hollingsworth Drive, Lakeland 33801. Call 863-680-4111. Visitors center open Mon. through Fri. 10–4. Web site: www.flsouthern.edu.

Florida's Natural Grove House, 20160 US 27, Lake Wales 33853. Call 863-676-1411. Open Mon. through Fri. 10–5, Sat. 10–2; closed June–September. Web site: www.floridasnatural.com.

Harry's Seafood Bar & Grille, 101 North Kentucky Avenue, Lakeland 33801. Call 863-686-2228. Open Sun. through Thurs. 11–10, Fri. and Sat. 11–11. Web site: www.hookedonharrys.com.

Historic Bok Sanctuary, 1151 Tower Boulevard, Lake Wales 33853. Call 863-676-1408. Open daily 8–6 (last admission at 5). Web site: www.boksanctuary.org.

Hollis Gardens, 702 East Orange Street, Lakeland 33801. Call 863-834-6035. Open Tues. through Sun. 10–dusk.

Imagine Vacation Homes, 115 Lake Davenport Boulevard, Davenport 33897 (rental office). Call 863-424-7566 or 1-888-489-2488. Web site: www.imaginevacationhomes.com.

Joker Marchant Stadium (Detroit Tigers Spring Training), 2301 Lakeland Hills Boulevard, Lakeland 33805. Call 863-834-6035.

Polk Museum of Art, 800 East Palmetto Street, Lakeland 33801. Call 863-688-7743. Open Tues. through Sat. 10–5, Sun. 1–5 (closed major holidays). Web site: www.polkmuseumofart.org.

Polk Outpost 27, US 27 and I-4. Call 1-800-828-7655. Open daily 9–6. Web site: www.visitcentralflorida.org/polkoutpost27.

The Terrace Hotel and The Terrace Grill, 329 Main Street, Lakeland 33801. Call 863-688-0800 or 1-888-713-2123. Web site: http://terrace hotel.com.

Très Jolie, 229 East Stuart Avenue, Lake Wales 33853. Call 863-676-4142. Open Tues. through Fri. 9–4, Sat. 9–3.

Westgate River Ranch, 3200 River Ranch Boulevard, River Ranch 33867. Call 1-888-808-7410. Rodeo every Sat. at 7:30; hours vary for other activities. Call for reservations/information. Web site: www.westgatedestinations.com.

9

The Nature Coast

Discover the Undiscovered

Overview: If there is one stretch of tourist-happy Florida that doesn't get marquee billing, it's the rugged coastline that stretches from Tampa up to the "Big Bend" that curves around the Gulf of Mexico before forming the southern shores of the Panhandle. It's not that there's nothing to do here; one of Florida's lasting original tourist attractions lies along this route, along with some of its most beautiful parks and a cluster of interesting communities. But this part of the state also has a largely untouched feel to it. There is a (relative) dearth of sun-dappled beach and a comparative excess of marshy flats that exhibit a wilder beauty. Fishing villages dot the coast, nature still holds sway over much of the land, Florida's Cracker history is preserved, and some roads lead nowhere. As you travel through this part of the state, you might get the feeling that you could come back in 20 years and find that not much has changed.

What a pleasant thought.

Total length of trip: The round-trip from Tampa is roughly 400 miles, spread over three nights and four days.

Getting there: It would be to your advantage to take this trip in July or August. From Tampa International Airport, take FL 589 for 46 miles to exit 46. Turn left on Cortez Boulevard (FL 50 West) and travel 6 miles to

US 19 and **Weeki Wachee Springs Park.** From here, you'll be on US 19 for much of this journey. Head north on this road for 73 miles to **Dakotah Winery** in Chiefland. After another mile on US 19, bear right on FL 26 and travel 8 miles to reach **Trenton.** Continue east for 17 miles on FL 26 to get to **Dudley Farm Historic State Park,** and then head back on US 19 and continue north for 30 miles before turning left onto FL 51. In 8 miles, you'll arrive at the **Steinhatchee Landing Resort.**

On your return trip, take County Route 358 (CR 358) east for about 7 miles to US 19, and then head south for 22 miles before turning right on 19th Avenue (FL 320). In 5 miles, you'll reach **Manatee Springs State Park.** Return to US 19 and continue south for roughly 12 miles before turning right on FL 24. Follow this road for about 21 miles to **Cedar Key.** From Cedar Key, return to US 19 and continue 41 miles south to **Homosassa Springs State Wildlife Park.** Then continue on US 19 for roughly 39 miles before bearing right on US 19 Alt. Follow this road into **Tarpon Springs.** At Tarpon Avenue, turn left and drive 1 mile to reconnect with US 19. In 7 miles, turn left on Curlew Road (FL 586 East) and follow the road for about 13 miles to return to Tampa International Airport.

Highlights: This tour will have you visiting two of the ocean's cutest residents (one real, the other contrived), three of Florida's award-winning state parks, and two forgotten fishing villages, among other highlights. From Tampa's airport, you're only about 50 miles away from your first stop, and your first "marine" encounter: **Weeki Wachee Springs Park,** an appropriate introduction to this area.

Weeki Wachee is home to a bevy of real-life, bona fide mermaids . . . well, okay, not quite bona fide, but the effect of staring at these underwater belles is still quite remarkable. You can even catch the mermaids eating and drinking underwater, take a riverboat cruise, or check out **Buccaneer Bay,** a water park fed by springwater. But make sure you call ahead; as of this writing, Weeki Wachee is in the middle of a "Save Our Tails!" campaign to rescue the park from permanently closing its doors. I hope it's open when you go, because it's part of Florida's tourist lore.

The park is located at the intersection of FL 50 and US 19, and you'll follow US 19 north for most of this journey. After Weeki Wachee, the road takes you into Levy County, known as "Florida's Natural Paradise." (Just about every part of this state has a catchy moniker, but you'll soon find that this one is well named.) You'll be on US 19 for roughly 73 miles before you drive through Chiefland. As you leave the town, keep an eye out on the right for the **Dakotah Winery.**

A family business specializing in wine made from Florida-native muscadine grapes, the winery is a labor of grape and love. Owners Max and Rob Rittgers are charismatic hosts who have produced award-winning wines (sample a few in their tasting room) and built a pleasant haven for visitors and friends. You can tour the property, which includes a wine cellar, a pond that serves as a mini bird sanctuary, and the grounds, where you'll find antique vehicles, arbors, and a general aura of calm and peace. The winery adheres to a nature-loving philosophy: No pesticides are used, the facility employs solar power, and the vines are pruned by sheep. This is a special place, run by wonderful people.

After Dakotah, you'll be ready for a late lunch. Fortunately, you're only about 10 miles from a terrific place that you wouldn't expect in these parts. Continue north on US 19 for just over a mile and then bear right on FL 26. Travel roughly 8 miles to reach the old railroad town of Trenton, and turn left on Northwest First Street. You'll see **Petrello's** on the left. The restaurant is located in the "Olde Boarding House," a classic example of Cracker-style architecture, but inside it's a whole new world, with Tuscan accents and the warm, friendly atmosphere of an authentic Italian eatery that could easily be found in Brooklyn. The menu is indicative of two generations of Italian chefs, who blend their family recipes with traditional Italian specialties (the Rotini Petrello is one of their signature dishes).

After lunch, turn left on FL 26 and take the first left on Main Street. A few blocks down the road is the **Suwannee Valley Quilt Shoppe.** Housed in a 1920s Coca-Cola bottling plant, this homage to a long-established American family tradition stocks a huge selection and variety of fabrics, conducts quilting workshops, and has a tearoom where you can enjoy cakes and pastries. A block away, in a restored 1910 dry goods store, there are stained-glass, custom framing, and other arts and crafts shops.

From the quilt shop, return to FL 26 and drive roughly 17 miles to reach a local cultural gem: the **Dudley Farm Historic State Park** (the park will be on your left, so you'll need to make a U-turn on FL 26 to reach it). Dudley Farm is a working 19th-century farm and a unique chance to see how life was in the mid-1800s. Among the 18 restored buildings are a general store, stables, farmhouse, sweet potato cellar, kitchen, and tobacco barn. Horses, cows, chickens, and other animals are on the premises, along with a staff—duly attired in the clothing of the era—that can be found

Dudley Farm Historic State Park

cracking sugar cane, grinding grain, tending the flower garden, and performing all the tasks that a 19th-century family would face in the day-to-day running of their farm.

From Dudley Farm, retrace your steps to US 19, about 25 miles away (it's also US 27 Alt. and US 98). Turn right and travel 30 miles to the almost nonexistent town of Tenille. At the blinking yellow light, turn left onto FL 51. In 8 miles, you'll see the entrance to the **Steinhatchee Landing Resort** on your left. There are some places that you fall in love with as soon as you see them, and Steinhatchee Landing was one such place for me.

Tucked away by a sleepy fishing village along the banks of the Steinhatchee River, this one-of-a-kind resort—brainchild of Dean Fowler, developer, Southern gentleman, and charming host—is a well-planned cluster of homes and cottages built in Florida Cracker and Victorian styles, equipped with luxurious amenities (working gas fireplaces, oversized whirlpool bathtubs, TVs in the bathrooms), and furnished in a rich yet comfortable and homey style. Accommodations at Steinhatchee can range from one-bedroom honeymoon cottages to large homes capable of hosting a family (one of these homes has often welcomed President Carter and his family). Amid manicured grounds, which include herb and spice gardens, a chapel fit for an unforgettable wedding, pool, conference center, tennis courts, petting zoo, and docks from where a kayak or a pontoon boat will put you on the river, the resort is a retreat in the truest sense. You can't help but feel a sense of welcome respite and back-to-the-land tranquility as soon as you arrive.

But that doesn't mean your time at Steinhatchee will be uneventful; there is plenty to do, which is why I'd recommend at least a two-night stay. Take an hour or two in the late afternoon to enjoy the place, acclimate yourself, and relax after your journey. Before you head out to dinner, you might want to drive around (it won't be a long drive!) and take in the town.

Continue on FL 51 to Riverside Drive and follow this road as it hugs the riverbanks. There is one curious road in Steinhatchee called the **Road to Nowhere.** To get here, cross over the bridge at 10th Street from Riverside Drive and turn left on CR 358. In less than 2 miles, turn right on CR 361 and follow it all the way down to . . . well, nowhere.

The story goes that, back in Steinhatchee's more disreputable days, this road served as a landing strip for small airplanes whose main cargo was drugs. These days, it's a local curiosity, an unlit, paved road that just kind of stops in the middle of nothing. But there are trails from here that take you down to the coast, and some beautiful salt marshes. Be careful of the roads here; even seasoned residents can get their vehicles caught in the wet

Steinhatchee Landing Resort

earth, but if you can negotiate the trails, the majestic views show you a different side of Florida.

Return to Riverside Drive for dinner, following it west until it merges with First Avenue. In less than a half mile you'll come to **Roy's Restaurant,** a Steinhatchee institution. Located at the mouth of the river, Roy's is a casual, family-friendly spot best known for its seafood dinners, such as breaded and fried grouper fingers, mullet (a Southern delicacy), and bay scallops. Then, it's back to your cozy accommodations and a quiet, peaceful sleep.

Hopefully you've planned your visit in July or August, because this is scalloping season, and Steinhatchee is the state's unofficial scalloping capital. This is a tremendously fun activity, and all you need is snorkeling gear, fins, and a mesh bag (your boat captain can provide what's missing if you call ahead). After breakfast at the resort, we went out with **Capt. Jim Henley,** who runs fishing and scalloping charters. Donning our gear, we jumped into the temperate waters of the Gulf (at depths of about 5 feet) and began to hunt for scallops. Once you know what you're looking for (look out for the scallops' blue "eyes"), it's simply a matter of diving down and grabbing the little guys before they scuttle off (yes, they *do* move). Load up your bag and return triumphant to the resort, where you can clean and cook your catch for lunch.

If you're not here during scalloping season, you can go fishing with Captain Henley or hop in a kayak. The resort has several kayaks; you can take one out on the river or let the staff at the Landing take you up to Steinhatchee Falls, from where you'll have a meandering, just-you-and-nature journey down to the resort. Another option is to take a kayak eco-tour or fishing trip with Mark Fisher of **Steinhatchee Kayak Tours,** out on Dallus Creek. The creek winds through pristine, untouched marshlands and is an official part of the Great Florida Birding Trail.

For the less active, the Landing has pontoon boats ready to take you on a cruise along the winding, tannin-browned Steinhatchee River. You can tie up at **Hungry Howie's,** a regional chain famous for their flavored-crust pizzas, for lunch. Your day out on the water can stretch from a half day to a full day, depending on the activity. Once you return to the resort, you'll probably want to rest and spoil yourself with a bath before dinner. When you're ready, head back down FL 51 toward Riverside Drive. In about a half mile, you'll come to **Fiddler's Restaurant,** the town's fine-dining establishment. Two of the highlights of the seafood-heavy menu are the grilled grouper specials (served either with a caper sauce or a lime-and-dill sauce).

The next morning, following breakfast at the main house, you'll bid farewell to Steinhatchee Landing and begin the journey home. But there are still a few stops along the way before you return to Tampa, and the first of these is in Chiefland. Take CR 358 east for roughly 7 miles to US 19, and then head south for 22 miles before turning right on 19th Avenue (FL 320). This turns into 115th Street, and in 5 miles you'll arrive at **Manatee Springs State Park.**

On a summer day, you'll appreciate the park's natural beauty and a deliciously cool dip, snorkel, or dive in its crystal clear spring-fed waters. The park is home to the largest of the springs that feed into the Suwannee River. Chiefland is blessed with another park nearby, Fanning Springs, but I prefer Manatee Springs for its more natural setting. In summer, walk along the boardwalk to the river's edge and you'll see huge, prehistoric-looking sturgeon leaping fully out of the water before landing again with a large splash. In winter, there is always a chance to encounter manatee here.

From Manatee Springs, you're only a short distance from another quiet fishing village, but one with a very different atmosphere. Travel back along 115th Street to US 19, and continue south for roughly 12 miles before turning right on FL 24. Follow this road for about 21 miles to **Cedar Key.**

Located 3 miles (and four bridges) out into the Gulf of Mexico, Cedar Key bills itself as Florida's second-oldest city. (Native Americans have been recorded as living here for more than five thousand years, and various shell mounds still stand.) It's also a community that has had to reinvent itself over the years. Named for the cedar trees that once grew in abundance here, the island thrived in the 1800s thanks to its valuable timber, which the Faber and Eagle companies turned into pencils. Just as the Civil War erupted, the Florida Railroad's first coast-to-coast train reached its terminus at Cedar Key (then called Way Key).

The town was incorporated in 1869 and prospered until the turn of the century, when its depleted timber and hurricanes combined to cripple the economy. In the 1900s, Cedar Key switched to fishing and oyster harvesting as its mainstay. The 1960s saw the emergence of an artists' community on the island, but in the 1990s, Cedar Key was transformed again. A state-imposed ban on gill net fishing decimated the local fishing industry, and the townspeople were forced to switch gears again. The state stepped in, introducing job retraining programs to acclimate local anglers to a new industry: clam farming. The results were so successful that today, less than 20 years later, Cedar Key is the country's top producer of farm-raised clams.

This is a resilient town, and one that has retained its essence of a remote outpost on the very edge of an untamed land. You can walk around Cedar Key's downtown strip (or rent a handy golf cart to putter around town) and feel its small-town roots, its storied history, and its close affinity to the water. For tourists, this is a very different kind of island escape: most cell phones don't work; getting out on the water is the primary activity; the local arts scene is justly well known.

If you spend a happy hour or two at Manatee Springs, you should arrive at Cedar Key by lunchtime. Follow FL 24 to its end at First Street, and then find a place to park. From here, it's a short walk to Dock Street, which curves around a cluster of restaurants and shops that forms the most happening area of town. Stop in at the **Seabreeze Restaurant and Lounge** for lunch. Seabreeze is a quirky place; on the lower level, a life-sized poster of an attractive lady waits at a table for a companion, while at the end of the bar, you might catch the fixed eye of the resident mannequin barfly. The upstairs seating room has a nice maritime-inspired mural, and both levels offer lovely views of the water. Seabreeze is a good place to try a Cedar Key specialty: hearts of palm salad served with a dollop of green-colored ice cream dressing. I know, it sounds weird, but it's delicious and wonderfully refreshing. The restaurant stays open late, offering live music on Friday and Saturday.

After lunch, tour the island by boat with **Captain Doug's Tidewater Tours.** This is a terrific way to see some of the local sights around Cedar Key, including the outer islands that form part of the Cedar Key National Wildlife Refuge. You might spot dolphins, turtles, manatee, and rays in the water, along with an amazing variety of birds. Bald eagles, brown and white pelicans, herons, roseate spoonbills, wood storks, and egrets are just a sampling of the birds who claim full- or part-time residence at the refuge. The tour also takes you around Seahorse Key, where you can see the Lighthouse at Seahorse Key (closed to the public) and, in summer, hundreds of spectacular frigate birds. Beautiful in flight, they are stunning when they land and when the males puff out their red throats in a mating ritual.

Returning to shore, you'll want to check in for the night. If you want to stay at a historic landmark, head straight to **The Island Hotel** on the corner of Second and B Streets. Built in 1859 as a general store, the bed & breakfast has an Old Florida feel well captured in the hand-cut wooden walls and rustic furnishings of its 10 guest rooms and second-floor parlor. To complete the back-in-time picture, there are no phones or TVs in the

Cedar Key "Honeymoon Cottage"

rooms. For more modern accommodations, check out **The Island Place at Cedar Key,** where oceanfront one- and two-bedroom condominiums can be rented on a daily, weekly, or monthly basis. The views are lovely and the apartments quite comfortable.

In the afternoon, check out some of the local artists' shops along Second Street, like **The Cedar Keyhole Art Gallery** and **Island Arts.** Also on this street is **The Cedar Key Historical Museum,** a small place that chronicles the island's past from prehistoric times to the modern era. Cedar Key is a photo-friendly destination: The beach beneath the dock is a good place to spot horseshoe crabs in the summer; west of the Dock Street promenade and the Island Place hotel, you can make out a crumbling, dilapidated structure barely standing on wooden pilings in the middle of the bay, locally known as "The Honeymoon Cottage"; and the sunsets visible from Dock Street are spectacular.

For dinner, you'll have a hard time choosing from these two options: The Island Hotel has an excellent restaurant that serves up a mean crab bisque and, of course, heart of palm salad with ice cream dressing. For your entrée, try the delicious local clams, stuffed grouper, or steak au poivre. Down the road on Second Street is **Tony's Seafood Restaurant,** which is known on-

and off-island for its fresh local seafood. Start off with a bowl of clam chowder as good as anything you'll get in Boston, but save room for the almost ridiculous Tony's Platter, a veritable cornucopia of delicious goodies from the sea. (*Note:* You can also do Tony's for lunch the next day.)

In the morning, enjoy kayaking along the Gulf or out to one of the many surrounding islets; **Kayak Cedar Keys** are the people to call. Of course, Cedar Key remains a fishing haven, and fishing charters are available from the dock. When you're ready for lunch, you can head to **Ann's Other Place** on Dock Street, a casual local eatery with a rustic nautical setting and fresh daily specials.

Finally, before you leave Cedar Key, call ahead and see if you can stop by **Southern Cross Sea Farms, Inc.,** one of the largest hard-shell clam farms in the United States. Owner Bill Leeming and biologist Scotty encourage visitors and are happy to explain the remarkable and meticulous process of clam farming as they take you around their facility. A visit to Southern Cross will give you new respect for clams, clam farming, and Cedar Key—or "Clamelot."

Returning to US 19, you'll be heading back to Tampa, but, in a case of karmic balance, your last attraction in this part of Florida will have you repeating your first activity on the tour: visiting an aquatic star. This one, however, is real and far more solid. Follow US 19 for about 41 miles to reach **Homosassa Springs State Wildlife Park,** the only place in Florida to *guarantee* a manatee sighting.

The park has a variety of activities and attractions, including all manner of local wildlife and birds (alligators, bears, cougars, key deer, flamingoes, and whooping cranes headline the list), but the main draw are the underwater gentle giants, and Homosassa has found a unique way to showcase them. Their floating underwater observatory, known as "The Fish Bowl," brings you up close and personal with the park's resident manatees. If you're really lucky, one of them will press its face up against the glass and stare right at you. The Fish Bowl, logically, is also a great place to see fish, in an ironic role reversal (after all, you're the one in the bowl).

If you can stretch your Nature Coast trip by a day, you'll get to visit the top-rated beach in the United States: **Caladesi Island State Park.** Voted #1 in 2008 by Dr. Stephen P. Leatherman (better known as Dr. Beach), Caladesi's unspoiled beauty won out over 100 other beaches around the nation. What makes it so special? For starters, it's one of Florida's last remaining completely natural islands along the Gulf Coast. Caladesi boasts pristine white sands, nature trails and kayak trails, and excellent fishing. Nesting turtles and other wildlife can be spotted on the island. Finally, the park is only accessible by private boat or the Caladesi Connection ferry service from nearby Honeymoon Island State Park, making it more isolated than most beaches. Caladesi Island is open every day from 8 AM to sundown, with ferry service beginning at 10. To get here from Tampa, take I-75 South to I-275 South. Exit at Hillsborough Avenue. Take a slight left at Curlew Road (SR 586), and continue on SR-586 to Honeymoon Island State Park and the Caladesi ferry.

Rather than take the toll road home from Homosassa (which is the way you came), continue to follow US 19 South, which is more scenic and has the distinct advantage of taking you through **Tarpon Springs,** a quaint Greek community and the unofficial sponge capital of the state. If you've timed your trip right, you'll be getting to Tarpon Springs in time for dinner at a terrific Greek restaurant.

Follow US 19 for roughly 39 miles, and then bear right on US 19 Alt. Continue on this road for just over 2 miles, and then turn right on Dodecanese Boulevard. Then turn left at Athens Street and look out for the blue awning of **Costa's.** A local favorite for their mountainous Greek salad and other specialties, Costa's is known for delicious food, hearty portions, and casual, friendly service. If you can't figure out what you want, go whole hog and order the large sampler platter.

Return to US 19 Alt. and continue south for a half mile to Tarpon Avenue. Turn left here and, in a mile, turn right on US 19. In just under 7 miles, turn left on Curlew Road (FL 586 East) and follow the road for about 13 miles to return to Tampa International Airport, and the end of your journey.

Contacts:

Ann's Other Place, 360 Dock Street, Cedar Key 32625. Call 352-543-5494. Open Tues. through Fri. 11–9:30, Sat. 7 AM–9:30 PM, Sun. 7–4.

Caladesi Island State Park, #1 Causeway Boulevard, Dunedin 34698. Call 727-469-5918. Open daily 8 AM–sundown. Web site: www.florida stateparks.org/caladesiisland/default.cfm.

Captain Doug's Tidewater Tours, on the dock at Cedar Key. Call 352-543-9523. Closed Sunday. Web site: www.tidewatertours.com.

Capt. Jim Henley, P.O. Box 565, Steinhatchee 32359. Call 352-498-0792. Web site: www.saltwaterfishn.com.

The Cedar Key Historical Museum, corner of Second Street and FL 24, P.O. Box 222, Cedar Key 32625. Call 352-543-5549. Open Sun. through Fri. 1–4, Sat. 11–5. Web site: www.cedarkeymuseum.org.

The Cedar Keyhole Art Gallery, 457 Second Street, Cedar Key 32625. Call 352-543-5801. Open daily 10–5. Web site: www.cedarkeyhole.com.

Costa's Restaurant, 521 Athens Street, Tarpon Springs 34689. Call 727-938-6890. Open daily 11–10.

Dakotah Winery, 14365 Northwest US 19, Chiefland 32626. Call 352-493-9309. Open Mon. through Sat. 10–5. Web site: www.dakotah winery.com.

Dudley Farm Historic State Park, 18730 West Newberry Street, Newberry 32669. Call 352-472-1142. Open Wed. through Sun. 9–5 (farmstead closes at 4). Web site: www.floridastateparks.org.

Fiddler's Restaurant, 1306 Southeast Riverside Drive, Steinhatchee 32359. Call 352-498-7427. Open for dinner Mon. through Thurs. 4–10, for lunch and dinner Fri. through Sun. 11–10. Web site: http://fiddlers restaurant.com.

Homosassa Springs State Wildlife Park, 4150 Suncoast Boulevard, Homosassa 34446. Call 352-628-5343. Open daily 9–5:30. Web site: www.floridastateparks.org/homosassasprings.

Hungry Howie's, 806 Riverside Drive, Steinhatchee 32359. Call 352-498-7100. Open Sun. through Thurs. 11–8, Fri and Sat. 11–9. Web site: www.hungryhowies.com.

Island Arts, 509 Second Street, Cedar Key 32625. Call 352-543-6677. Open daily 10–5. Web site: www.artbycarolmay.com/islandarts.html.

The Island Hotel & Restaurant, 373 Second Street, Cedar Key 32625. Call 352-543-5111 or 1-800-432-4640. Web site: www.islandhotel-cedar key.com.

The Island Place at Cedar Key, 550 First Street, Cedar Key 32625. Call 352-543-5306 or 1-800-780-6522. Web site: www.islandplace-ck.com.

Kayak Cedar Keys. Call 352-543-9447. Web site: www.kayakcedar keys.com.

Manatee Springs State Park, 11650 Northwest 115th Street, Chiefland 32626. Call 352-493-6072. Open daily 8–sunset. Web site: www.florida stateparks.org.

Petrello's at the Olde Boarding House, 115 Northwest First Street, Trenton 32693. Call 352-463-8494. Open Tues. through Thurs. 11–2:30 and 5–9, Fri. and Sat. 11–10.

Roy's Restaurant, 100 First Avenue Southwest, Steinhatchee 32359. Call 352-498-5000. Open daily 11–9. Web site: www.roys-restaurant.com.

Seabreeze Restaurant and Lounge, 310 Dock Street, Cedar Key 32625. Call 352-543-5738. Open Sun. through Wed. 11–9, Thurs 4:30–9, Fri. and Sat. 11–10. Web site: www.seabreezeonthedock.com.

Southern Cross Sea Farms, Inc., 12170 FL 24, Cedar Key 32625. Call 352-543-5980 or 1-866-CLAMBIZ. Web site: www.clambiz.com.

Steinhatchee Kayak Tours. Call 352-213-7057. Web site: www.stein hatcheekayaktours.com.

Steinhatchee Landing Resort, 203 Ryland Circle, Steinhatchee 32359. Call 352-498-3513 or 1-800-584-1709. Web site: www.steinhatchee landing.com.

Suwannee Valley Quilt Shoppe, 517 North Main Street, Trenton 32693. Call 352-463-3842. Open Tues. through Sat. 10–5. Web site: www.suwanneeshops.com.

Tony's Seafood Restaurant, 597 Second Street, Cedar Key 32625. Call 352-543-0022. Open Mon. through Thurs. 11:30–8, Fri. and Sat. 11:30–9, Sun. noon–8.

Weeki Wachee Springs Park, 6131 Commercial Way, Spring Hill 34606. Call 352-596-2062. Open in winter Thurs. through Sun. 10–3 (closed December 24–25, New Year's Eve, and New Year's Day); open in summer daily 10–4. Hours are subject to change. Web site: www.weeki wachee.com.

CHAPTER

10

The Deep North

From Blue Springs to Silver Spurs

Overview: Florida is a large state divided into no less than eight regions. Between Jacksonville and the Panhandle lies the great expanse of north-central Florida, a green and blue space, an old and new place. There is heritage here: estates and farms more than a century old; the cultural bounty of the University of Florida at Gainesville; and the historic, unforgettable forgotten town of Micanopy. There is great natural beauty: majestic oaks draped with Spanish moss, magnolia trees, rolling hills, the winding Suwannee River, and the region's sparkling blue treasure, its numerous natural springs. There is romance, as evidenced by the caliber and number of charming bed & breakfasts along this tour. And, finally, just below in Marion County, there is the rural, pastoral charm of Florida's horse country.

Total length of trip: The one-way trip, from Tallahassee to Ocala, is about 210 miles if you avoid I-75 and take the more scenic route. There is enough to see and do to make this a three-night/four-day journey (the B&Bs along the way make it worth your while to take it slow).

Getting there: Your starting point for this trip can be Tallahassee or, to do it in reverse, Orlando; I chose the road from Tallahassee. From Florida's capital, hop on US 90 (also FL 10) East, a scenic road that takes you through

Monticello, roughly 25 miles from Tallahassee, and **Madison,** in another 30 miles. When you leave Madison, stay on US 90 East for about 29 miles to get to the town of **Live Oak.** Here, turn left at Ohio Avenue (US 129), and in a few blocks turn right at Duval Street (County Route 136 [CR 136]). Follow this road for about 15 miles to arrive at White Springs.

At this point, US 41/441 will take over from US 90. From White Springs, head east on Springs Street (US 41) and follow the road for about 22 miles until you reach CR 240. Turn right here and drive 10 miles before turning left at Southwest Ichetucknee Avenue. In another 5 miles, turn left at Elim Church Road (CR 238) to reach **Ichetucknee Springs State Park.** From here, continue on CR 238 for roughly 3 miles before turning right on FL 47. In 2 miles, turn left on US 27 (also FL 20) and drive 10 miles to get to **High Springs.** After, continue southeast on US 27 (FL 20), which will turn into US 441 (FL 25). In 22 miles, turn left on FL 26 to reach downtown **Gainesville.** From here, head back to US 441 and drive roughly 11 miles, bearing right to get to Northeast Cholokka Boulevard and **Micanopy.**

To get to the **Marjorie Kinnan Rawlings Historic State Park** from Micanopy, return to US 441 and drive 1 mile before turning left at CR 346. Travel 5 miles, and then turn right at CR 325. In another 4 miles you'll reach the park. Continue south on CR 325 for 4 miles, and then turn right on US 301. In 19 miles, you'll reach **Ocala.**

Highlights: The drive from Tallahassee to White Springs along US 90 is not only pleasantly green, but it also takes you through some interesting small towns. If you don't mind the detour, start your trip by taking Miccosukee Road, a lovely, Spanish-moss-laden canopy road, and then turn right to join with US 90.

The first small town you come to, roughly a half hour away, is picturesque **Monticello.** This town is known as much for its lovely antebellum homes as it is for its past residents; specifically, its ghosts. Ghosts (or tales of them) are everywhere; in the old opera house across from the lovely, centrally placed Jefferson County Courthouse; by the old hanging tree; at the Palmer House on 325 South Jefferson Street; and at the gorgeous **John Denham House,** an 1872 mansion and bed & breakfast that serves as a perfect final stop if you're making this trip up from Orlando instead of Tallahassee. (Ironically enough, whichever starting point you choose, you'll end up at a B&B known for its ghosts. Weird.) *ABC News* once called

John Denham House

Monticello the "South's most haunted town," and in October, you can find out why on one of the ghost tours organized by the chamber of commerce and **Big Bend Ghost Trackers.**

US 90 takes you around the courthouse and continues on eastward toward **Madison,** 30 miles away. About halfway to Madison, the road runs through a small town by the name of Greenville, where Ray Charles spent his childhood years. There is a bronze statue of him playing the piano in the town's park. Follow US 90 into Madison until you reach Range Street. Stop here and check out the **Four Freedoms Park,** named after Franklin D. Roosevelt's stated four freedoms: freedom of speech and expression, freedom of worship, freedom from want, and freedom from fear. (Check out the beautiful white sculpture symbolizing the freedoms.) The park is a tribute to Capt. Colin P. Kelley, Madison native and the first U.S. war hero of World War II. Across from the park is the county courthouse, which is very similar in design to that of Monticello and several others in north Florida.

Continue down Range Street, and you'll arrive at **Madison Antiques Market and Interiors,** a large shop with an impressive collection of

Victorian jewelry, clothing, period American furniture, and some fabulous vintage pieces. Also on Range Street is the lovely **Four Freedoms** wedding chapel and adjacent bed & breakfast. Another good stop for those making the trip up from Orlando, this place is perfect for honeymooners and couples looking for a romantic escape. The bed & breakfast has warm, intimately decorated rooms (one with a heart-shaped tub), and hosts Stephen and Rae Pike are just as charming.

There are a number of stately 19th-century mansions in Madison, and a drive or stroll around will give you a glimpse of these historic homes. Then, as you've only traveled 50 miles from Tallahassee, you'll head back to US 90 and soldier on toward White Springs, which—thanks to its springs, believed to have healing powers—was Florida's first tourist destination.

In roughly 19 miles, you'll come to the town of Live Oak. Turn left on Ohio Avenue and in a few blocks make a right on CR 136. You'll be on this road for about 15 miles before you get to US 41. Take a right and look for the colorful **Suwannee River Diner.** Stop in and gorge on a gut-busting cafeteria-style Southern buffet, starring a crispy fried chicken and featuring lima beans, black-eyed peas, and daily specials. The decor is dominated by a busy mural that wraps around the interior and memorializes the river and the local area.

When you're ready to be carried out, head to US 41 and go back the way you came, continuing past the intersection of CR 136 and US 41. Look out on your left for the entrance to the **Stephen Foster Folk Culture Center State Park.** Located on the banks of the Suwannee, this sprawling park can easily occupy you for a day or two, especially if there is an event going on, which there often is. Folk festivals (the annual Florida Folk Festival has been held here each Memorial Day for more than 50 years), quilt shows, musical events, and, now there is an annual Healing Arts Festival and Workshop are just a few of the regulars on the calendar.

But there is much more to this place than its events. The park is named after Stephen Foster, considered America's first great composer and songwriter, and the master who penned Florida's state song, "Old Folks at Home." Ironically, Foster never visited the Suwannee River, which he immortalized with his music. Begin your visit at the antebellum mansion that marks the Stephen Foster Museum. Here, a docent in period dress will guide you through the main hall and the superb collection of moving and musical dioramas that depict some of Foster's most well-known songs.

After, walk to the Carillon Tower, which houses the Stephen Foster Carillon—the world's largest tubular bell instrument—inside a campanile that stands 200 feet above the ground. There are daily concerts. Also, don't miss a visit to the Craft Square, where you can watch various artists at work and buy their goods, before making your way down to the gazebo and the banks of the Suwannee.

You might actually want to get *on* the Suwannee River and see what all the fuss is about while you're in White Springs; if so, head to **American Canoes Adventures, Inc.,** on Bridge Street (CR 136). There's a menu of trips you can reserve, from a 3-mile journey to a 12-mile trek. All prices include admission to the Stephen Foster Folk Culture Center State Park, so make this your first stop if you're into kayaking or canoeing.

After the park, retrace your steps to Bridge Street and turn right. Take your first left at River Street and look out for a beautiful old house fronted by Spanish-moss-draped trees. This is the **Sophia Jane Adams House,** a family-owned B&B that has been passed down from Sophia Jane in 1893 to her great-grandson Watkins Saunders. The place certainly has the feel of a generations-old family home, and the rooms, some of which are huge, are comfortable and elegant, if not overly sumptuous. It also helps that the inn is located on a hill overlooking the Suwannee, with a wooden stairway leading down to its banks.

White Springs is not known for its nightlife, so you're looking at a quiet night highlighted by a walk among the inn's gardens or in town. Following breakfast in the morning, get back on US 41 and continue east for 22 miles before turning right at CR 240. In another 10 miles, turn left at Southwest Ichetucknee Avenue and drive 5 miles to Elim Church Road (CR 238). Turn left here and look for the north entrance of **Ichetucknee Springs State Park.** Now, before you get to the park, you'll see a string of roadside vendors selling tubes: stop and rent some. Ichetucknee is a beautiful place, a large park with a crystal blue spring-fed swimming pool, picnic areas, beautiful trees, and other fine qualities that hordes of visitors ignore as they rush to get their tubes in the water.

This is Florida's premier tubing destination for good reason. From the northern entrance, you can gently float down the river, a meandering trip that can take anywhere from 45 minutes to three hours, depending on where and when you want to stop. (Don't worry: A tram will take you back to the parking lot.) In summer, this is a wildly popular activity that fills up fast (there is a daily limit on the number of tubes allowed), so make sure you get here early. The pool, with a rocky ledge circling halfway around it, is also a popular place to swim.

From Ichetucknee, head back to CR 238, which will lead you to FL 47, and in just over 2 miles, to US 27/FL 20. Follow US 27 for about 10 miles before reaching **High Springs,** a small town just northwest of Gainesville. You'll stay on US 27, which becomes First Avenue, until you'll get to **The Grady House,** your bed & breakfast for the night. Steeped in history (the home started out as a boardinghouse for railroad supervisors in the early 1900s), The Grady House is an elegant place, with rooms decorated according to their own color theme. Unlike many B&Bs, three of the four rooms here are two-room affairs with adjoining parlors, giving you ample space to spread out. The downstairs has a lovely dining area, a cozy den where you can relax with a book by the fire, and a well-tended garden.

While High Springs enjoyed early prosperity thanks to the railroad, its current claim to fame is spelled out in the town's name: the blue water springs that lie in and around the town. Dasani bottles its water here; the area is known as one of the top cave-diving destinations in the world; and you've already sampled some of its bounty at Ichetucknee. But before you head to your next spring break, you'll want to have lunch.

Besides a few antiques shops, there's not much to downtown High Springs. But most people will agree that the place to go for lunch is **Floyd's Diner.** To get here, head back along US 27 for a few blocks until you get to Ninth Street. Turn right and drive just over a half mile to Northwest Santa Fe Boulevard (US 441). Turn right and look for the restaurant. Floyd's combines quintessential diner food (starring a wide range and variety of burgers) in a quintessential diner setting. Even the jukebox is free.

After Floyd's, check out another spring or two. To get to the first, turn right on Santa Fe Boulevard, heading south for a half mile. Then turn right at CR 236/FL 45/US 41 and drive just under a mile before turning onto CR 340 (also Northwest 182nd Avenue). Drive about 6 miles before turning onto 60th Avenue, which will lead you to Ginnie Springs Road and **Ginnie Springs.** Perhaps my favorite among all the springs in this area, Ginnie is a tubing-rafting-canoeing-snorkeling-swimming-diving destination, spread out over five springs and 2.5 miles of riverfront. Among these activities, the snorkeling and diving is truly exceptional, thanks to its "Devil's Eye" and "Devil's Ear" cave system. Snorkelers and divers are treated to a turquoise-colored yawning chasm that even the casual wader will want to check out.

Ginnie Springs

You could easily spend the day here, but if you're one of those adventurers who likes to check out as much as you can in one area, you might want to hit nearby **Blue Springs** on your way back to High Springs. (You can also get an early start tomorrow and come here before heading south.) From Ginnie Springs, get back on CR 340 and begin retracing your steps to town. In 2 miles, turn left on Northeast 80th Avenue, which curves in about a half mile and turns into Northeast 60th Street, which takes you to the spring.

Blue Springs offers many of the same basic activities as Ginnie Springs and includes a nature trail and boardwalk. The big difference between the two experiences is the diving platform over the crystal blue depths of the main spring's boil. You'll likely find a bunch of kids leaping and somersaulting into the deep blue natural pool when you get here—and if you don't, you should be the one doing it.

After all that activity, you'll probably want to return to The Grady House and freshen up before a solid dinner. Fortunately, there's a place nearby in Alachua that will serve just fine. From the B&B, stay on US 27, heading southeast toward Gainesville. In just under 7 miles, turn right at

Northwest 141st Street/South Main Street. You'll see **Ristorante Deneno** on your right. The menu here is classic Italian in a contemporary setting. As one of a handful of local fine-dining establishments, Deneno's does quite well for itself thanks to solid cuisine (featuring excellent stone-fired pizzas, hearty pasta dishes, and reliable standbys for *secondi*) and live piano music. After dinner, retire to the den or your bedroom at The Grady House.

The spring portion of the tour is not quite over, but your next day will take you away from the water and into a world of museums, gardens, and butterflies.

Enjoy a gourmet breakfast at The Grady House the next morning, and then continue southeast on US 27/FL 20, which later becomes US 441, toward **Gainesville.** Try to time this trip so that this is a Saturday, and take a slight detour about 5 miles into your journey. From US 441, turn left at Northwest 173rd Street (CR 235A). Travel 3 miles until you see the sign for **Mill Creek Farm** on your right. Turn right and follow the driveway to a unique, heartwarming place.

Mill Creek is a retirement home for horses. A labor of love created in 1984 by Mary and Peter Gregory, this is a quiet place where more than one

Butterflies stop for a snack at the Butterfly Rainforest

hundred old, abused, and otherwise unwanted horses come to rest. They are never put to work or ridden, and instead are free to roam and graze on the land or accept your generous admission price of two carrots. Even if you stop by just to have a blind horse nibble out of your hand, it's worth going out of your way to visit Mill Creek.

From here, return to US 441 and continue southeast. In roughly 13 miles you'll turn right at Southwest 34th Street and drive just under 6 miles to reach the University of Florida Cultural Plaza. For a school known nationwide for its football program, UF has also developed into a thriving center for art and culture, and today you'll visit two of its most distinguished landmarks. The first, located in the plaza, is the **Samuel P. Harn Museum of Art,** at the corner of Southwest 34th and Hull Streets. The largest university art museum in the Southeast, the Harn is a spacious, airy gallery focusing on West African, Mesoamerican, Chinese, Indian, and contemporary art.

Next to the museum is the **Florida Museum of Natural History,** a historical, anthropological, and natural treasure. From mastodon bones to a re-created limestone cave to the breathtaking **Butterfly Rainforest,** where hundreds of living butterflies flutter around you, the museum is the kind of place that can captivate you for an entire day. The Butterfly Rainforest is the star of the show, and you can even watch scientists through a glass window as they research and monitor the birth of butterflies in their labs.

After the cultural plaza, head to downtown Gainesville and lunch. Retrace your way along Southwest 34th Street for about a mile, and then turn right at FL 26. In less than 2 miles, turn right at Southwest First Street followed by a quick left at Southwest First Avenue to arrive at the **Paramount Grill.** A cozy bistro that's modern in both decor and cuisine, the Paramount has fantastic, crisp salads and succulent sandwiches for lunch, and a varied, interesting menu for dinner, should you want to visit again.

From here, you're 15 minutes away from the serene, inspiring **Kanapaha Botanical Gardens,** one of Gainesville's best attractions. Continue along Southwest First Avenue, heading east, and make your first left on Main Street (FL 329). Make another quick left to get back on University Avenue (FL 24/FL 26), and in about a mile turn left onto US 441 (Dr. Martin Luther King Jr. Highway). In just over a half mile, bear right onto Southwest Archer Road and drive roughly 4.5 miles to Southwest 58th Street. Turn right here, and in a half mile you'll reach Kanapaha.

Spread out over 62 acres, the park boasts a few special exhibits among its 14 collections. Popular attractions include the giant Victorian water lilies (the largest in the world, visible only from June to October), a must-see sight; the largest public bamboo garden in Florida; and the largest herb garden in the Southeast. There is also a pretty, well-stocked gift shop, and the garden's director, Don Goodman, is a gentleman, a scholar, and an author.

After Kanapaha, you'll follow Archer Road back to US 441 and continue south toward **Micanopy.** This section of 441, from Gainesville to Micanopy, is known as **The Old Florida Heritage Highway,** and along it are natural and cultural treasures. Today, you'll probably only have time to visit one of these: **Paynes Prairie,** Florida's first state preserve. Located 10 miles south of Gainesville on US 441 (turn right on Savannah Boulevard

Kanapha Botanical Gardens

Micanopy's Antiques Shops

Micanopy has become synonymous with antiques shopping in Florida. All but two of the stores along Cholokka Boulevard in the town's historic business district are devoted to antiques. Here are some of the best:

Dakota Mercantile. Featured in *Gracious Living* and *Home & Garden*, the store has a bit of everything, including beautiful home furnishings and bed linens, a line of bath products, handcrafted jewelry, and garden accents.

Delectable Collectables. Housed in the former Strawberry Bank Building (you can still see the marble wainscoting), this store is known for its Flow Blue pottery, Victorian jewelry, and especially for its astounding collection of more than 1,400 cameos.

The Garage. Originally a . . . well, a garage . . . this building has quite the Hollywood resume, with three films under its belt. Today, in-house vendors sell a variety of antiques and collectibles here.

The Shop. Located in the old drugstore, this is one of the more well-turned-out shops in Micanopy, composed of decorated rooms featuring antiques and contemporary furnishings, artifacts, and art.

to get to the park entrance), this 21,000-acre savanna is a piece of natural preservation where nature photographers have come for years to capture alligators, bison, wild horses, and, in winter, more than 270 species of birds (bald eagles are a common sight). See what you can spot from the park's 50-foot observation tower, or hike along one of its eight trails.

If you're tired at this point, you're in luck, because you're about five minutes away from one of Florida's most elegant bed & breakfast inns. You'll be on US 441 less than 2 miles before veering right onto Cholokka Boulevard, which takes you into the heart of quaint Micanopy and **The Herlong Mansion.** The building is an amalgamation of architectural styles that follows the history of its owners; originally built by the Simontons, one of the first families of Micanopy, the building expanded and grew, adding four Corinthian columns, redbrick construction, and a separate carriage house. Today, the six bedrooms, three suites, and three cottages that make up the Herlong give guests a variety of options to suit their tastes. The Victorian decor, meticulous details in each room, and the lovely porch facing the gardens and main street help make this an oasis of Southern hospitality.

The tiny town of Micanopy has a frozen-in-time charm. Its tree-lined main street is filled with antiques shops—Micanopy's primary claim to fame these days, along with being the location for the movie *Doc Hollywood*—and historic buildings. There is little to do here except absorb the quaint beauty of the town and browse its shops, but that's what people love about Micanopy. After settling in at The Herlong, take a walk down Cholokka Boulevard and soak in the atmosphere. There aren't many dining options, but if you don't mind jumping back in your car, you can return to US 441, turn right, and in about 3 miles find yourself at **Blue Highway.** Neapolitan, brick-oven-baked pizzas are the specialty here, and they're crispy, thin-crusted, and delicious.

After breakfast the next morning, hit the shops and enjoy a morning of antiquing, which can all be found on Cholokka Boulevard. Also here is

Old Church in Micanopy

the **Micanopy Historical Society Museum,** housed in the J. E. Thrasher warehouse and general store, once the only place in town where you could buy ice. A modest record of the town's past, the museum includes a talking map, books by botanist William Bartram, Timucuan and Seminole exhibits, and an impressive collection of photographs, maps, and artifacts.

Don't miss a visit to the **Mosswood Country Store,** a general store that specializes in the Old South. You can buy anything from Southern-style dresses and overalls to butter churners, jars of jelly, and oven-fired loaves of bread here, and every Sunday from October to May there's a farmer's market behind the store.

When you're ready for lunch, leave Micanopy by Northeast Second Avenue/Northeast Hunter Avenue, off Cholokka Boulevard, and drive roughly 6 miles (the road becomes CR 346) until the road ends at CR 325. You're now in Cross Creek, the home of renowned author Marjorie Kinnan Rawlings. Turn right on CR 325 and travel less than 4 miles to reach the **Yearling Restaurant,** a landmark named after Rawlings's Pulitzer–winning novel and a place that has been on the list of top 25 eateries in Florida for almost a decade. Enjoy a Cracker-style lunch (which ranges from stuffed flounder to cooter and alligator) amid authentic Old Florida surroundings, and then continue east on CR 325 for a half mile to get to **Marjorie Kinnan Rawlings Historic State Park.**

Even if you aren't familiar with the author's works, a visit to this park is interesting because it gives you a glimpse of life in northcentral Florida at a time when neighbors were few and luxuries even fewer, but nature and inspiration were abundant. Rawlings moved to Cross Creek with her husband in 1928 and continued to live alone in the place she loved after her divorce in 1933. Take the self-guided tour and feel free to talk to the docents in period dress who can be found at Rawlings's home.

Your adventures through northcentral Florida are over, but your journey will make one last stop just south of the region, in **Ocala:** This is Florida's horse country. Continue heading south on CR 325 for 4 miles, until you reach US 301. Turn right here and travel 19 miles to East Silver Springs Boulevard/FL 40 East. Turn right and drive through the center of downtown Ocala, passing the town square and the main shopping district. At Southeast Third Avenue/Watula Street (less than a half mile away) turn right, and in 2 blocks make a left onto East Fort King Street. Drive less than a half mile to reach your final bed & breakfast, which is one of my favorites: the **Seven Sisters Inn.** You might just make it in time for afternoon tea.

Comprising two grand Victorian-era homes, the inn is one of those places that make savvy B&B enthusiasts smile when they see it. It's got all the right elements: a variety of rooms sumptuously decorated, some following an international theme (like the Egypt, India, and China rooms) and others according to the tastes of the original sisters and prior owners. The inn has deservedly won numerous statewide and national awards, but it has also garnered a national reputation for its permanent residents: its ghosts. Said to be one of the most haunted inns in Florida, the inn's staff will happily share their ghost stories with you. When I stayed there, I was told to keep an eye out for orbs, but fortunately I was in the building with the "nice" ghosts. Seriously, it's a lot of fun staying here: Breakfasts are terrific, and there are a slew of packages and events, from ghost tours to murder-mystery dinners to wedding/romance specials. Call ahead to see what's cooking when you'll be there.

Spend the rest of the afternoon and evening strolling or driving around quaint downtown Ocala and checking out the shops (many specialize in antiques, which you may have had enough of by now). For dinner, you'll be treated to one of the best meals on this trip at **Felix's,** a fine-dining restaurant where Marge and Loring Felix have tailored the menu and the experience to their customers. Set in a beautiful pink and teal home on East Silver Springs Boulevard, the restaurant offers an eclectic, sophisticated menu that spans the globe, along with an extensive wine list. Quite wisely, they offer a menu of "petite" portion entrées, allowing you to enjoy a light meal, share a few dishes (no sharing charges apply), or add on an appetizer or salad that you would normally skip. Not to worry, though: the full-portion entrées, labeled "comfort food with attitude," are always available to those with a hearty appetite (and all the petites can be upgraded). Felix's is a short walk away from the Seven Sisters Inn.

On your last day, you can choose from a return to freshwater springs or a day with the horses to end your trip. For the latter, call **Ocala Carriage & Tours** to arrange a horse-drawn carriage ride through country roads past horse farms, or visit **Young's Paso Fino Ranch,** where you can learn how to ride a Paso Fino horse (a breed known for its elegant gait and for offering the smoothest ride in the world). Ocala Carriage & Tours will pick you up in downtown Ocala. To get to the ranch, head back on US 441 and travel north for 5 miles before turning left at FL 326. Travel about 6.5 miles to reach your destination.

Young's Paso Fino Ranch

To continue enjoying Florida's springs, head east on Silver Springs Boulevard/US 40. In about 2.5 miles, you'll come to **The Appleton Museum of Art.** This has nothing to do with springs, but it's a pleasant detour for its eclectic, global collection. About 3 miles from the museum on US 40 is **Silver Springs,** an original Old Florida attraction. The only thing you can't do at this park is swim in its waters, but you can do the next best thing: take a tour in one of their famous glass-bottom boats and see fish darting through the bubbling spring waters of the Silver River, the largest artesian water formation in the world.

The park has a lot to offer for families with small children. This was the site of six original Tarzan movies, along with *The Yearling* in 1946 and *The Creature from the Black Lagoon* in 1954. Native and exotic animals can be found in the park, along with a very cute petting zoo. There are also two additional cruises: the Fort King River Cruise takes you past exhibits where characters in period dress bring to life a Seminole village, military stockade, and archaeological dig, and the Lost River Cruise focuses on the local wildlife and natural environment. The Wilderness Trail is a narrated Jeep tour through a jungle and several animal exhibits. And finally, there are daily concerts here, with well-known stars often on the schedule.

Eat lunch at the park, and then continue east along US 40 into the Ocala National Forest. Twenty-two miles east of Silver Springs, you'll come to **Juniper Springs.** Juniper has nothing on some of the other springs you've visited, but it's a decent-sized natural pool, and the scenic mill and walking trails behind the round basin of the spring make it a worthy stop. Couples may want to skip the park altogether and arrive at Juniper Springs in the morning to take the 7-mile canoe trip down Juniper Creek. (*Note:* This trip is not for beginners.)

Freshwater springs; horses, both retired and in their prime; romantic bed & breakfasts; and the history, art, and culture of Old Florida: You've seen and done it all in the Deep North.

Contacts:

American Canoes Adventures, Inc., 10610 Bridge Street, White Springs 32096. Call 386-397-1309 or 1-800-624-8081. Open daily 10–5 in winter, 9–6 in summer. Web site: www.aca1.com/#WS2.

The Appleton Museum of Art, 4333 East Silver Springs Boulevard, Ocala 34470. Call 352-291-4455. Open Tues. through Sat. 10–5, Sun. noon–5. Closed Thanksgiving, Christmas, and New Year's Day. Web site: www.appletonmuseum.org.

Big Bend Ghost Trackers. Call 850-562-2516. Web site: www.bigbend ghosttrackers.homestead.com.

Blue Highway, 204 Northeast US 441, Micanopy 32667. Call 352-466-0062. Open Tues. through Sat. 11:30–9, Sun. noon–8.

Blue Springs, 7450 Northeast 60th Street, High Springs 32643. Call 386-454-1369. Open March through October, daily 9–7; 9–5:30 in winter. Closed from the week before Christmas to the week after New Year's. Web site: www.bluespringspark.com.

Dakota Mercantile, 114 Cholokka Boulevard, Micanopy 32667. Call 352-466-3006. Open Wed. through Mon. 11–5.

Delectable Collectables, 112 Main Street, Micanopy 32667. Call 352-466-3327. Open daily 10–5.

Felix's, 917 East Silver Springs Boulevard, Ocala 34470. Call 352-629-0339. Open Tues. through Fri. 11–2:30 and 4:30–10, Sat. for dinner 4:30–10. Web site: www.felixsocala.com.

Florida Museum of Natural History, Southwest 34th Street and Hull Road, Gainesville 32611. Call 352-846-2000. Open Mon. through Sat. 10–5, Sun. 1–5 (closed Thanksgiving and Christmas). Web site: www.flmnh.ufl.edu.

Floyd's Diner, 615 Northwest Santa Fe Boulevard, High Springs 32643. Call 386-454-5775. Open Mon. through Thurs. 11–9, Fri. 11–10, Sat. 10:30–10, Sun. 10:30–9. Web site: www.floydsdiner.com.

The Garage, 212 Northeast Cholokka Boulevard, Micanopy 32667. Call 352-466-0614. Open daily 11–5.

Ginnie Springs, 7300 Northeast Ginnie Springs Road, High Springs 32643. Call 386-454-7188. Open Mon. through Thurs. 8–7, Fri. and Sat. 8–10, Sun. 8–8 in the summer; Mon. through Thurs. 8–6, Fri. and Sat. 8–9, Sun. 8–7 in the winter. Web site: www.ginniespringsoutdoors.com.

The Grady House, 420 Northwest First Avenue, High Springs 32655. Call 386-454-2206. Web site: www.gradyhouse.com.

The Herlong Mansion, 402 Northeast Cholokka Boulevard, Micanopy 32667. Call 352-466-3322 or 1-800-437-5664. Web site: www.herlong .com.

Ichetucknee Springs State Park, 12087 Southwest US 27, Fort White 32038. Call 386-497-4690. Open daily 8–sundown. Web site: www.florida stateparks.org.

John Denham House, 555 West Palmer Mill Road, Monticello 32344. Call 850-997-4568 or 850-933-8104. Web site: www.johndenham house.com.

Juniper Springs, 26701 East US 40, Silver Springs 34488. Call 352-625-3147. Open daily 8–8.

Kanapaha Botanical Gardens, 4700 Southwest 58th Drive, Gainesville 32608. Call 352-372-4981. Open Mon. through Wed. and Fri. 9–5, Sat. and Sun. 9–dusk (closed Thurs.). Web site: www.kanapaha.org.

Madison Antiques Market and Interiors, 197 Southwest Range Street, Madison 32340. Call 850-973-9000. Open Tues. through Sat. 10–6, Sun. noon–4.

Marjorie Kinnan Rawlings Historic State Park, 18700 South CR 325, Hawthorne 32640. Call 352-466-3672. Open daily 9–5 (closed August and September). Web site: www.floridastateparks.org.

Micanopy Historical Society Museum, Cholokka Boulevard and Early Street, Micanopy 32667. Call 352-466-3200. Open daily 1–4. Web site: www.afn.org/~micanopy.

Mill Creek Farm, P.O. Box 2100, Alachua 32616. Call 386-462-1001. Open Sat. 11–3. Web site: www.millcreekfarm.org.

Mosswood Country Store, 703 Cholokka Boulevard, Micanopy 32667. Call 352-466-5002. Open Tues. through Fri. 10–6, Sat. and Sun. 9–6, farmer's market Sun. 1–5.

Ocala Carriage & Tours, downtown Ocala. Call 352-867-8717 or 1-877-966-2252. Web site: www.ocalacarriage.com.

Paramount Grill, 12 Southwest First Avenue, Gainesville 32611. Call 352-378-3398. Open Mon. through Thurs. 11–2 and 5–9:30, Fri. 11–2 and 5–10:30, Sat. 5–10:30, Sun. 10–3 and 5–9:30. Web site: www .paramountgrill.com.

Paynes Prairie, 100 Savannah Boulevard, Micanopy 32667. Call 352-466-3397. Open daily 8–sundown. Web site: www.floridastateparks.org.

Ristorante Deneno, 14960 Main Street, Alachua 32615. Call 386-418-1066. Open for dinner Tues. through Sat. 5–11. Web site: www .deneno.com.

Samuel P. Harn Museum of Art, Southwest 34th Street and Hull Road, Gainesville 32611. Call 352-392-9826. Open Tues. through Fri. 11–5, Sat. 10–5, Sun. 1–5 (closed state holidays). Web site: www.harn.ufl.edu.

Seven Sisters Inn, 820 East Fort King Street, Ocala 34471. Call 352-867-1170 or 1-800-250-3496. Web site: www.sevensistersinn.com.

The Shop, 210 Cholokka Boulevard, Micanopy 32667. Call 352-466-4031. Open Mon. through Sat. 11–5. Web site: www.welcometo micanopy.com.

Silver Springs, 5656 East Silver Springs Boulevard, Silver Springs 34488. Call 352-236-2121. Open daily 10–5, extended hours during holidays. Web site: www.silversprings.com.

Sophia Jane Adams House, 16513 River Street, White Springs 32096. Call 386-397-1915 or 1-866-397-1915.

Stephen Foster Folk Culture Center State Park, Post Office Drawer G, White Springs 32096. Call 386-397-2733. Open daily 9–5. Web site: www.floridastateparks.org.

Suwannee River Diner, 16538 Spring Street, White Springs 32096. Call 386-397-1181. Open Sun. through Wed. 5 AM–3 PM, Thurs. through Sat. 5 AM–9 PM. Web site: www.suwanneeriverdiner.com.

Yearling Restaurant, 14531 East CR 325, Cross Creek 32640. Call 352-466-3999. Open Thurs. and Fri. 5–10 PM, Sat. noon–10, Sun. noon–8:30. Web site: www.yearlingrestaurant.com.

Young's Paso Fino Ranch, Inc., 8075 Northwest FL 326, Ocala 34482. Call 352-867-5305. Web site: www.youngspasofino.com.

CHAPTER

11

Hidden Miami

Far from the Tanning Crowd

Overview: Ah, Miami: where the skirts run short and the nights run long. Beautiful Miami, known for its Cuban charm, sexy people, sizzling parties, and general atmosphere of tropical indulgence. Tourists who visit Florida's most electric city tend to come for the South Beach experience: Ocean Drive, Lincoln Road, art deco boutique hotels, and the famed nightlife. But there is a whole city beyond this tiny pocket of hedonism that the average tourist never sees. Even in the heart of South Beach, there are hidden surprises.

I've structured this chapter a little differently because I figured that asking even the most ardent backroader to spend three or four days traveling around Miami while avoiding its hot spots is a little unrealistic. The glitzy hotels, ultrahip lounges and bars, and celebrity-stocked restaurants are all here for a reason: They're pretty darn good. As such, I've organized three day or overnight trips (along with hotel recommendations) to help you explore what the rest of the city has to offer. When you're in town, take a break from the beach, rent a car, and follow the itinerary, or itineraries, that suit your fancy.

Total length of trip: All three trips in this chapter have a starting point of Miami Beach.

Trip 1: The Grove and the Gables. Just under 35 miles in two days.
Trip 2: The Historic Redland Tropical Trail. Roughly 86 miles in one day.
Trip 3: In and around Miami Beach. About 75 miles over two days.

Getting there:

Trip 1: The Grove and the Gables

From Miami Beach, take the MacArthur Causeway (US 41 West) over the water and take exit 2 to get onto Northeast 13th Street. Make a left on Biscayne Boulevard (US 1). Continue to follow US 1 South as it turns into Brickell Avenue, and in a little over 3 miles make a slight left onto South Miami Avenue. In just under a half mile you'll come to the **Vizcaya Museum & Gardens.** Continue along South Miami Avenue, which turns into South Bayshore. In 2.5 miles, the road loops right at MacFarlane Road. Take your first left onto Main Highway and look for signs for **The Barnacle.** After, follow Main Highway to its end (less than a mile) and turn left at Southwest 37th Avenue/Douglas Road. In less than a half mile, make a slight right onto Ingraham Highway and travel under a mile before turning left at Southwest 42nd Avenue/Le Jeune Road, which leads to a roundabout. Take the second exit onto Old Cutler Road and travel roughly 2.5 miles to **The Fairchild Tropical Botanic Garden.**

Follow Old Cutler Road for another mile, and then turn right on Southwest 57th Avenue. Follow this road for less than 6 miles before turning right onto Sevilla Avenue. In under a half mile, turn right at Anastasia Avenue and travel about a half mile to reach **The Biltmore Hotel.** From the hotel, take De Soto Boulevard and travel just over a half mile (at the roundabout, take the third exit to stay on De Soto) to Andalusia Avenue. Turn right and travel just over a half mile to **La Cofradia.**

On your next morning, follow De Soto Boulevard for roughly a half mile to get to the **Venetian Pool.** Then continue on De Soto to the next intersection, which is Valencia Avenue. Turn left here and drive just under a mile to return to Southwest 57th Avenue. Follow this road back toward the Fairchild. In about 5.5 miles, continue straight (heading south) on Old Cutler Road for roughly 4.5 miles before turning left on Coral Reef Drive/Southwest 152nd Street/FL 992. Continue to follow Old Cutler Road for roughly 4.5 miles before turning left on Coral Reef Drive/Southwest

152nd Street/FL 992. In a few blocks, turn right onto Southwest 72nd Avenue and follow the road about a mile to **The Deering Estate at Cutler.** Retrace your steps along Old Cutler Road and, just past the Fairchild, stop at **Redfish Grill.**

Trip 2: The Historic Redland Tropical Trail

From Miami Beach, take the MacArthur Causeway (US 41 West) over the water and take exit 2 to get onto Northeast 13th Street. In less than a half mile, turn right onto Northeast Second Avenue, and after a block make a left onto Northeast 14th Street. Travel 1 mile and turn left at Northwest Seventh Avenue/US 441. In just over a half mile, cross the river and turn left onto South River Drive. Follow the road for a half mile to reach the **Miami River Inn.** From here, continue south on South River Drive/ Southwest Fourth Avenue for a half mile before merging onto I-95 South. In about 1.5 miles, this will merge with US 1/South Dixie Highway. Stay on this road for just over 17 miles before turning right onto Southwest 216th Street/Hamlin Mill Drive. Travel roughly 3 miles to get to the **Monkey Jungle.**

After the Monkey Jungle, retrace your steps along Southwest 216th Street for 2.5 miles, and then turn right at Southwest 124th Avenue. In less than a half mile, turn left at Miami Avenue and travel a few blocks to **Historic Cauley Square.** From here, turn right onto South Dixie Highway/ US 1 and drive just over 2 miles before turning right onto Southwest 248th Street/Coconut Palm Drive. Travel roughly 5 miles to reach the **Fruit & Spice Park.** After, turn left onto Southwest 187th Avenue and head south for 1 mile before turning right at Southwest 264th Street/Bauer Drive. Travel 3 miles and make a left onto Southwest 217th Avenue. Follow this road for 2.5 miles to reach **Schnebly Redland's Winery.** Continue south on Southwest 317th Avenue for just over 2.5 miles and turn left onto Southwest 344th Street/Palm Drive. Travel 2.5 miles to get to the **Robert Is Here Fruit Stand.** Stay on Southwest 344th Street/West Palm Drive for just over 1.5 miles to rejoin South Dixie Highway. Turn left here and head north for roughly 4 miles. Make a sharp left at Southwest 288th Street/ Biscayne Drive and an immediate right onto Old Dixie Highway/West Dixie Highway to reach **Coral Castle,** the last stop on the Redland Tropical Trail.

Trip 3: In and around Miami Beach

From Miami Beach, take the MacArthur Causeway (US 41 West) over the water. Take exit 2 to get onto Northeast 13th Street, and turn left at Biscayne Boulevard/US 1 South. Follow US 1, past American Airlines Arena, for roughly 3 miles and turn left onto the Rickenbacker Causeway (there's a $1 toll) to get to Key Biscayne. Follow this road, which becomes Crandon Boulevard, for close to 8 miles to get to the **Marjory Stoneman Douglas Biscayne Nature Center.** Then return north along Crandon Boulevard and the Rickenbacker Causeway, and take the ramp to Brickell Avenue/US 1 North. Follow the signs to get on Biscayne Boulevard/US 1 North, and travel roughly 5 miles before turning left onto Northeast 36th Street. After a block, turn right at Northeast Second Avenue and travel a few blocks to Northeast 40th Street. Turn left to get to **Michael's Genuine Food & Drink** in the **Miami Design District.**

From here, return to Northeast Second Avenue and turn right. In a few blocks, make a left onto Northeast 36th Street and follow it to the ramp onto I-195 East. Travel about 2.5 miles over the Julia Tuttle Causeway and take exit 5 to merge onto Alton Road. If you're staying at **The Sanctuary,** drive about a mile to 17th Street, turn left, and follow the road for roughly a half mile to St. James Avenue. Turn left and drive a few blocks to the hotel. If you're staying at **Hotel Nash,** stay on Alton Road for about 2.5 miles, and then turn left at 11th Street. Travel just over a half mile to Collins Avenue. Turn left and look for your hotel on the left. To check out **Tobacco Road,** follow the earlier directions and take the MacArthur Causeway to exit 2 and Biscayne Boulevard/US 1 South. Follow US 1 for about a half mile and turn right at Southeast Seventh Street/Claude Pepper Way. Cross the train tracks and turn right at South Miami Avenue to reach the bar.

On your second day, follow 17th Street (if you're staying at the Nash, head north on Collins Avenue to reach 17th Street) for less than a half mile to Convention Center Drive. Turn right, and just past the convention center you'll reach the **Miami Beach Botanical Gardens** and **Holocaust Memorial.** Continue on Convention Center Boulevard and take your next right at Dade Boulevard/Abe Resnick Boulevard. Follow this road for less than a half mile and make a slight right onto Pine Tree Drive. Travel 1 mile and turn right at West 41st Street/Arthur Godfrey Road. Cross the water and turn left onto Indian Creek Drive, which turns into Collins Avenue. In about 8 miles, take the ramp on the left onto Northeast 163rd Street/

FL 826 West/Sunny Isles Boulevard. Stay on this road for about 2.5 miles, and turn right onto West Dixie Highway. In 2 blocks you'll come to the **Ancient Spanish Monastery.** Then return to 163rd Street/FL 826 East and turn left. Make your first left onto Biscayne Boulevard/US 1 North and travel about a half mile to get to **C. Madeleine's.**

After, return to Collins Avenue/FL A1A. Turn right and drive just under 3 miles to 96th Street/Kane Concourse/FL 992. Travel less than a half mile to reach **Caffe Da Vinci.** Return along 96th Street to reach the **Bal Harbour Shops.** From here, you can walk down Harding Avenue to **The Food Gang.**

Highlights:

Trip 1: The Grove and the Gables

Call this the big-budget adventure. Coconut Grove and Coral Gables are among Miami's most long-standing elite neighborhoods, and you'll be visiting some of their most exclusive addresses. (The Grove is actually South Florida's oldest community.) While they don't have (and don't want) the sexiness of South Beach, these areas house Miami's old money (and the Gables, at least, tends to poke a little fun at its glitzy neighbors). They're also home to some of the city's best cultural monuments, lush green tree-lined roads, and posh shopping and dining districts.

Your first stop on this trip is, appropriately, one of Miami's most lavish residences: The **Vizcaya Museum & Gardens** is an exercise in classic European architecture, grandeur, and opulence. The estate overlooks Biscayne Bay and serves as both a private-party and function space for Miami's A-listers as well as a public museum. Don't miss the lovely gardens and statuary, with its beautiful views of the water and the city. Interestingly, the man who built this place, industrialist James Deering, had a half-brother whose tastes were markedly different; you'll be visiting his home on your second day.

From Vizcaya, you'll drive along a scenic road (water on one side, beautiful homes on the other) straight to the heart of Coconut Grove. Once you get to Main Highway, look for a place to park. This is one of the main shopping districts in the Grove. The outdoor **CocoWalk** and **Shoppes at Mayfair in the Grove,** along with the boutiques along tree-lined streets off Grand Avenue, can keep you entertained for a good hour or two. While you're here, don't miss a quick stop at **The Barnacle Historic State Park,** a small but treasured and well-preserved relic of a bygone era. Built in 1891 by Commodore Munroe—a man of many talents but chiefly a yacht builder—this home was once one of the only man-made structures in the area and hidden deep within the Miami Hammock (the ancient remnants of this forest make up the grounds around the home today). The home is decorated with family heirlooms and period furniture. One of the most interesting aspects of its construction was the addition of a second floor in 1908: To achieve this, Munroe had the first floor lifted entirely off the ground and built a new first floor underneath it.

Enjoy the laid-back atmosphere of the Grove and check out **Ginger Grove** at the artistic Mayfair Hotel & Spa for lunch. An Asian-themed restaurant, beautifully decorated with bamboo accents, Buddha statues, crescent-shaped dining booths, and cushioned private rooms, Ginger Grove has a fantastic Express Lunch Menu in the summer, which is a bargain for a place of this caliber.

From here, you'll be going straight down Main Highway, with a right turn at Southwest 37th Avenue to get onto Ingraham Highway. At the roundabout, take the second exit onto Old Cutler Road and follow it to reach **The Fairchild Tropical Botanic Garden.** One of the world's botanical treasures, the Fairchild is more than just a park. Spread out over an incredible 83 acres, it's home to an awesome variety of native and exotic flora, including an unmatched collection of rare tropical plants. It's also a world-renowned center for plant conservation. A stroll through this meticulously preserved Eden is an idyllic way to spend an afternoon, and anyone with even a hint of a green thumb will want to relish the experience. Also, check the Fairchild's calendar for special events. There are always exhibits and fairs going on.

From the Fairchild, head to your hotel. Nothing exemplifies the grandeur of Old Miami better than **The Biltmore,** a short drive away from the Fairchild. Take Old Cutler Road for about a mile until you come to Southwest 57th Avenue. Turn right here and travel about 5.5 miles to Sevilla Avenue. Turn right, followed shortly by a slight right onto Anastasia Avenue, and you'll see the graceful facade of the hotel. The Biltmore is part Gatsby, part country club, and part exclusive retreat. Every aspect of the hotel, from the golf course to the pool to the rooms, is sophisticated, refined, and classy. It's one of Miami's elite addresses for tourists, and if you feel like splurging, this is a good place to do it.

Relax at the hotel for an hour or two, and then head out for dinner. From the hotel, De Soto Boulevard will take you to Andalusia Avenue. Turn right here, and in less than a mile you'll reach the corner of Andalusia and Ponce de León Boulevard, and **La Cofradia.** A newcomer to the Miami fine-dining scene, La Cofradia may not stay tucked away for long. A departure from the traditional Latin cuisine found in the city, this restaurant blends Peruvian, Mediterranean, and Asian flavors. Lima-born chef Jean Paul puts his home-grown signature on his dishes, such as duck magret in a Peruvian *sauco* sauce (a kind of blackberry) and sautéed shrimp with Pisco (a Peruvian brandy), along with classic Peruvian ceviches and *tiraditos*. The decor is minimalist and modern, highlighted by a very chic ceiling mural.

On your next morning, have breakfast at the hotel, and if you're a golfer, try out the Biltmore's course before you depart. Then take De Soto Boulevard again, and just beyond the roundabout, you'll come to Coral Gables' **Venetian Pool.** This natural pool, fed by underground artesian wells, can either be a lovely natural oasis or a kid-friendly aquatic jungle, depending on when you go. Formed out of a limestone quarry, the huge, amorphous pool is deep in places, shallow in others, with caves, waterfalls, trees, and man-made enhancements; all in all, it's quite an unexpected find.

Spend a good hour or two here, and then continue on De Soto to your next intersection, which is Valencia Avenue. Turn left and drive just under a mile to return to Southwest 57th Avenue. Follow this road back toward the Fairchild. In about 5.5 miles, continue straight (heading south) on Old Cutler Road for roughly 3.5 miles, until you get to Southwest 152nd Street. Turn left here, and then make a right on Southwest 72nd Avenue to get to **The Deering Estate at Cutler.** Home of Charles Deering, the aforementioned half-brother of Vizcaya's James Deering, this property is comparatively modest in taste, but it is still a fine example of Florida history. It's also an environmental preserve as well as a working artists' colony.

The estate is made up of several buildings: The Stone House follows the Mediterranean style and decor favored by its founder (the ballroom, with its patterned marble floor and wrought-iron gates, is fabulous), and the adjacent Richmond Cottage was the first hotel between Coconut Grove and Key West. The lands around the estate extend to the water and include a tropical hardwood hammock and an ancient Tequesta Indian burial mound. As unique as this place is, it's amazing that the Deering Estate only opened its doors to the public recently; for decades, the home lay idle and

Venetian Pool

unused. With its artists' village and several tours (nature, bike, canoe, pontoon boat, and historic), this is easily a place that can fill your day.

After the Deering Estate, return to Miami Beach along the Old Cutler Road and Ingraham Highway. Just after you pass the Fairchild garden, you'll see signs pointing you toward Matheson Hammock Park and **Redfish Grill.** Turn right into the hammock and follow the road to get to this hidden-away gem of a restaurant that prefers to remain out of the limelight. The Redfish Grill doesn't advertise and doesn't pick up too much publicity, yet it is a top-class restaurant. The fish and seafood dishes are superb, the service is excellent, and, if you can, try to get a table outdoors, where the yellow lights wrapped around palm trees provide a soft, romantic glow, making for a perfect final destination on your journey to the Grove and the Gables.

Trip 2: The Historic Redland Tropical Trail

Until I started exploring the city of Homestead, located between Miami and the keys, I had no idea the Redland Tropical Trail existed. Essentially a conglomeration of local attractions and businesses, the trail runs along a section of South Dixie Highway/US 1 and includes 10 "stops," some directly on the way and others a bit off the not-so-beaten path. There is nowhere near enough time to visit all of these places in one day, so I've narrowed it down to my favorites. If you're determined to conquer the trail in its entirety, two days should be enough.

Since you'll be out all day, begin by checking in to your hotel. Both because of its more homey ambience (appropriate for this chapter) and for its location away from Miami Beach, head to the **Miami River Inn.** A bit removed from Miami's swanky boutique hotels, the inn skips panache altogether and settles on quaint, historic, and comfortable. The city's only bed & breakfast (a surprise, considering the proliferation of B&Bs in Florida), the inn was built in the early 1900s and still retains some of the city's forgotten history. The 40 rooms, spread across four cottages, are a combination of old and new: hardwood floors, wood and wicker furniture, along with central air and heat, cable TV, and private baths. Between the buildings is a large pool and a dining area for breakfast.

Check in and head out, for you have plenty to see. Your first stop is the longest drive of the day, some 45 minutes away from the inn and a world away from South Beach. For the most part, you'll stay on US 1, heading past Coconut Grove and Coral Gables, until you get to Southwest 216th Street/Hamlin Mill Drive. From here, it's roughly 3 miles to the **Monkey Jungle.** The slogan at this Old Florida attraction is "where the humans are caged and monkeys run wild," an intriguing and appropriate premise. Since its inception in 1935, this park, which has remained a family business, has been all about the conservation, study, and joy of monkeys. Starting out with six macaques, the park is now home to more than 400 primates from 30 species.

The most rambunctious of the lot are the 80-plus java monkeys, who jump, run, hang, and skitter all around you as you walk under a covered wire mesh framework. And yes, the javas, along with the majority of the primates here, roam free outside your "caged" walkway. Dishes hang from the covered ceiling, where you can place food and watch the clever javas pull it up to eat what you've offered. Several shows throughout the day educate you on the behavior of the jungle's residents. Whoever you are, it's hard not to have fun at this unique preserve.

Feeding eager monkeys can build up an appetite; when you're through with the Monkey Jungle, retrace your steps until you get to Southwest 124th Avenue. Turn right and follow the road, which will take you to Miami Avenue and **Cauley Square Historic Village.** Hidden among lush vegetation, this is a quaint village where boutiques, arts and crafts shops, and antiques shops cluster together, a reminder of the way things used to be. The largest structure here is a two-story, stucco-walled flatiron building, and the adjacent houses were hand built by early settlers. Before you hit the shops, stop at the **Tea Room,** Cauley Square's venerable lunchtime restaurant. Inside, the lace-frilled tables and curtains, ceramic teapots, and old-fashioned bric-a-brac adorning the walls will take you back to your grandparents' time. The food lives up to the old-fashioned ambience, with finger sandwiches, spiced tea, ambrosia, and other lunchtime delicacies.

From the Tea Room, wander among garden paths to the small shops in the village before getting back on the road. If you leave here before 2 PM, you'll have time for an extra stop along the Redland Trail. Head back onto South Dixie Highway/US 1 and drive just over 2 miles before turning right onto Southwest 248th Street/Coconut Palm Drive. In 5 miles, stop and smell the mangos (all 125 varieties of them) at the **Fruit & Spice Park.** This colorful botanical garden grows more than five hundred varieties of fruits, nuts, and plants, and there is a guided tour at 1:30 and 3 daily.

After the fruit park, you'll visit a fruit winery. Just a few miles away on Southwest 217th Avenue is **Schnebly Redland's Winery,** an exceptional anomaly among vineyards. The southernmost winery in the country, Schnebly's eschews grapes and makes wines out of a host of other fruits, including guava, lychee (an award winner), and passion fruit (I love their motto: "save the grapes!"). Peter Schnebly and his family, who were in the produce business before a chance experiment got them into wine, use the latest winemaking technology (such as aging the wine in stainless-steel rather than oak barrels—a practice even purist French vineyards have adopted) and have enhanced their winery to include a tiki pavilion, waterfalls, and a five-acre organic farm where the kids can pick fresh fruit. Enjoy the tour, taste the wines, and pick up a bottle or two that your friends have probably never heard of.

From fruit park to fruit wine to fruit stand: so goes the trail. Five miles from Schnebly's, on 344th Street/Palm Drive, is perhaps the most famous fruit stand in the world: the **Robert Is Here Fruit Stand.** The story of the man behind the stand is one that belongs in the annals of "the American Dream" tales. One fine day in 1959, six-year-old Robert stood on this corner and attempted to sell cucumbers from his father's crop. On his first day, he sold zero. On his second day, he employed some strategic marketing and advertising, adding a sign that read ROBERT IS HERE. It was an instant success. From these humble beginnings, Robert's fruit stand has grown exponentially and now offers a range of fresh, homegrown produce unmatched in the best grocery store. The most popular items here are the mangos, but you can buy anything from apples and oranges to durian, star fruit, mamey, and other exotic fruits you may have not tried. (What's not in season is imported.) Robert's is also the place to try arguably the best milk shakes on the planet (strawberry is the crowd favorite). Robert is still here, and his four children help him run his fruit stand; say hello, and ask him to carve out a sample of fruit for you.

As the afternoon winds down, you'll begin the journey home and return to South Dixie Highway. Before you leave this region, however, you

Robert Is Here Fruit Stand

have one last stop, and it might be the most bizarre of all (stranger than free-ranging monkeys, guava wines, and an über-successful fruit stand combined). From the road, you'll see signs for it on the parallel-running Old Dixie Highway/West Dixie Highway. Pull over and walk through the gates of **Coral Castle,** a place that no one has been able to fully explain. While theories abound about how this structure came to be, the prevailing wisdom is that the "castle" was carved and shaped out of coral by a single man. Edward Leedskalnin was not a large man by any accounts, so how he could have created this monumental masterpiece, using homemade tools and not a forklift or crane in sight? That's the big mystery. There are elements of the castle (most notably the 9-ton gate that Leedskalnin made with such precision that it can only be duplicated today by laser-controlled drills) that absolutely defy the belief that one man alone was responsible for its construction, and yet, here it stands, a fitting finale on your journey.

You've seen most of what the Historic Redland Tropical Trail has to offer, but you also missed a few stops: alligators and orchids, bonsai trees, and Italian cuisine are what another day along the path will yield. It might be enough to warrant another day of exploring this little-known stretch of South Florida, just a few miles from Miami Beach.

Trip 3: In and around Miami

You don't have to travel far from Ocean Drive to see a whole new side of Miami. Quirky museums, an ancient monastery, ecotourism, and the city's design district are all a short drive away. To enjoy this other Miami, we have to take some liberties: The city's most well-known attractions, like the Miami Seaquarium and the Lincoln Road promenade, have been skipped in favor of less-prominent destinations. And the first of these is so little known that all the South Florida residents I spoke with had never heard of it.

Its location, however, is quite famous. Key Biscayne is a resort destination known around the globe. However, its **Marjory Stoneman Douglas Biscayne Nature Center,** located on Crandon Boulevard (take the north entrance just across from the golf course), is not. But this is a terrific place to spend the morning, for many reasons. For one, the focus here is as much on environmental education as it is on tourism. As such, there are always special programs and events on the schedule, from fossil reef exploration to beachcombing to hammock hikes to (in season) turtle-awareness programs. And that's in addition to the regular activities that you can enjoy with **Miami-Dade Parks Eco-Adventure Tours,** which offers bike tours of the park and beach, canoe trips, and kayak and snorkeling tours. While you're here, don't forget to check out what I call mini Jurassic Park: In the fields around what used to be the zoo, you'll see hordes of iguanas perk their heads up from the tall grass, looking like nothing so much as tiny dinosaurs.

After an active morning, you'll be ready to eat, but here comes the hardest part of this journey, because I'm making you wait about 40 minutes before you have lunch. That's how long it should take to reach the **Miami Design District** and its gastronomic star, **Michael's Genuine Food & Drink.** Fortunately, Michael's is more than worth the wait. The restaurant, a bright and airy place, could easily belong in New York's Meatpacking District; it has that combination of laid-back yet sophisticated air and outstanding, inventive cuisine. From never-before-done pizza combinations (an example: slow-roasted Berkshire pork with mission figs, grilled onions, Fontina cheese, and arugula) to gourmet salads, sandwiches, and entrées (the steamed mussels on a bed of sticky black rice makes a perfect light meal), you can't go wrong here. It would be wrong of me not to add that at Michael's I had what may be the best dessert I've eaten in Florida: Chef Michael Schwartz's Chocolate Cremoso (think of it as a deconstructed chocolate pretzel) is out of this world.

After Michael's, take some time to explore the Design District, which has had an up-and-down history but seems to be thriving these days, thanks to an influx of hip new restaurants and a revitalized arts scene. Its annual event, Design Miami (www.designmiami.com), brings together a world-class gathering of designers, collectors, curators, and critics. Browse among the diverse, high-end furniture stores and visit art galleries like the **Miami Art Group Gallery, LLC** and **The Moore Space,** an art gallery on the second floor of the Moore Building (check out the fascinating interior design in the lobby and the ultracool modern rain forest garden lounge next to the building).

Since this trip has you shuttling around Miami Beach, it makes sense that your hotel should be there. Again, in keeping with the theme of this book, I've bypassed listing the ultrafamous Delano and Loews Hotels, as well as anything on Ocean Drive. Instead, here are two boutique hotels in the heart of South Beach that you may not have heard of, but they exemplify the Miami ambience. **Hotel Nash,** located in a beautiful white building on Collins Avenue, is a hip and modern place. Every guest room is unique, but all share the same design theme: light wood furniture and soft off-white, sea green, and blue hues. One of the masterstrokes of the hotel is the trio of outdoor saltwater, mineral water, and freshwater pools. The hotel's restaurant, Mark's, is something of a Miami staple.

Your other option is a hotel that doesn't advertise a whole lot, whose occupancy is based mainly on word of mouth, and yet stays busy (and hot) enough to warrant the attention of tourists, celebrities, and critics alike. **The Sanctuary** on James Avenue has only 28 suites surrounding a bamboo courtyard. Each suite is furnished in typical Miami style, with soaring frosted-glass headboards behind the beds and stylish but functional furnishings. Not to be aquatically outdone, its rooftop pool and lounge are very inviting, with views of some of the city's most iconic buildings. The Sanctuary also has a fantastic restaurant in **Ola.**

Relax at your hotel for an hour or two and recharge for the long Miami night. When you're ready for dinner, I'd recommend Ola for some of the best nouveau-Latino cuisine you'll find. The restaurant is the latest addition to celebrity chef Doug Rodriguez's resume (of Patria fame in New York, among other culinary hits), and the food continues his personal brand of pan-Latin cuisine infused with creative twists from around the world. Start your night with a Rodriguez Mojito and move on to appetizers like Mystery Meatballs (the mystery is that they're made with Kobe beef) and mahimahi mini tacos. The main courses are huge, so a few tapas followed by a shared main course (the churrasco steak is to die for) is a good way to go.

A less expensive and more casual option is **Tapas y Tintos** on Española Way, just off Washington Avenue (you can walk here from the Nash). Serving an extensive menu of authentic Spanish tapas accompanied by excellent wines and sangria, this is a loud and fun place in one of Miami Beach's most colorful alleys. There's something going on every night, with tango, salsa, and flamenco lessons throughout the week, and the bar stays open late into the night.

After dinner, check out the exotic, intriguing, and outlandish **World Erotic Art Museum.** A four-thousand-piece collection amassed by Naomi Wilzig (Miss Naomi to her friends), this is quite an experience, but the aim of this museum is not to shock, but rather to educate and appreciate erotic art. Sure, it's cheeky (anyone who has seen the replica of Catherine the Great's vividly carved love-chair would agree), but it's also quite interesting. One of the coolest themes here is art from around the world with hidden erotic imagery, from naughty nuns to finely carved Japanese porcelain figures with a revealing underside. It's not for the kids, but it's a fun place that stays open late.

For a (complete) break from the South Beach scene, hop in your car and head back across the Rickenbacker Causeway to downtown Miami. Just minutes after you take the exit onto Biscayne Boulevard, you'll find yourself at **Tobacco Road,** a local legend. Miami's oldest bar, Tobacco Road has a special reputation, charm, and history. It stayed open through Prohibition (ask to see the secret passage behind the bar); it's been a gay bar, a strip club, and now a home of good music; and its old-fashioned upstairs lounge (love the tables with posters of jazz greats) has seen the likes of John Lee Hooker, Albert Collins, and Buddy Guy, to name a few. It continues to remain open until 5 AM, so if you get hungry late at night, try one of their excellent burgers (the kitchen closes at 4 on weekends).

On your second morning, head to Convention Center Drive, where you'll find the small but picturesque **Miami Beach Botanical Garden** and, next door, the dramatic **Holocaust Memorial.** Then travel on along leafy Pine Tree Drive and Collins Avenue into North Miami. At 163rd Street, turn left and travel to West Dixie Highway to reach what is, amazingly, the oldest building in the Western Hemisphere: **The Ancient Spanish Monastery.**

Originally built in Segovia, Spain, from 1133 to 1144, the monastery, along with its neighboring buildings, was bought by William Randolph Hearst in 1925 and shipped to the United States. The shipment languished in a storehouse for more than two decades before it was purchased in 1952 and relocated to Miami. St. Bernard's Church (as it is known today) includes a chapel (an active church) and chapter house. As you stroll through the serene cloisters, look out for the marble reliefs and statues along the walls. The telescopic stained-glass windows above the altar in the chapel are two of the only three such windows known to exist today.

Just minutes from the monastery on Biscayne Boulevard, you'll change scenery from old cloisters to old clothing. **C. Madeleine's** is very well known to its rather impressive client list. Celebrities and some heavy-hitting fashion designers have shopped at this vintage-clothing boutique, which *Forbes Traveler* named one of the world's top 10 hot spots for vintage clothing. At "the world's largest designer showroom," you'll find a huge variety from different countries, fads, and eras dating back to the

The Ancient Spanish Monastery

1920s. You can hunt for one-of-a-kind pieces by Gucci, Chanel, Louis Vuitton, and their peers; pick up those platform shoes you always wanted; or perhaps purchase a 1950s ball gown for your next party. The options are almost endless, and consignment never looked so good.

From here, stop for lunch at the unpretentious and welcoming **Caffe Da Vinci,** where you can dine on authentic Italian cooking in a romantic setting. Owner Alex Portela is a charming and affable host, and the restaurant serves nothing but homemade pasta (along with flavorful salads and entrées). After lunch, you'll go from the best of the old clothing to the best of the new at the **Bal Harbour Shops.** Miami's most exclusive shopping mall, Bal Harbour ·is home to Dior, Dolce, and Giorgio. For those with lighter wallets, it's also home to Banana Republic and Gap. Because I've seen what Bal Harbour does to people, I've devoted several hours to it; all the way up to dinner, as a matter of fact.

When the shopping bug has finally abandoned you, you can walk down Harding Avenue for what I feel is one of Miami's most exciting restaurants. Fans of Bravo TV's *Top Chef* may remember Chef Howard from season three. He was the chef at **The Food Gang.** Howie moved on from the restaurant after the show's end, but you're moving in, at least for dinner. The decor is a funky orange color but is otherwise minimalist: The focus is all on the plate, where the varied menu explores French, Mediterranean, Continental, and Latin flavors. What makes the food so good here is how well the dishes are balanced; the day boat scallops, for example, are perfectly paired with gnocchi, wilted spinach, and a champagne beurre blanc. For the dry aged rib eye, the chef sticks to the basics, serving it up with fries and letting the quality of the meat do the talking.

The Food Gang ends your final journey in and around Miami on a triumphant note; South Beach wouldn't have it any other way.

Contacts:

Trip 1: The Grove and the Gables

The Barnacle Historic State Park, 3485 Main Highway, Coconut Grove 3133. Call 305-442-6866. Open Fri. through Mon. 9–4; house tours at 10, 11:30, 1, and 2:30. Web site: www.floridastateparks.org.

The Biltmore Hotel, 1200 Anastasia Avenue, Coral Gables 33134. Call 305-445-8066 or 1-800-915-1926. Web site: www.biltmorehotel.com.

The Deering Estate at Cutler, 16701 Southwest 72nd Avenue, Miami 33157. Call 305-235-1668. Open daily 10–5 (closed Thanksgiving and Christmas); house tours at 10:30 and 2. Web site: www.deeringestate.org.

The Fairchild Tropical Botanic Garden, 10901 Old Cutler Road, Coral Gables 33156. Call 305-667-1651. Open daily 9:30–5 (closed Christmas). Web site: www.fairchildgarden.org.

Ginger Grove, 3000 Florida Avenue, Coconut Grove 33133. Call 305-779-4580. Open daily 7–11 AM and noon–3; for dinner Sun. through Wed. 6–10, Thurs. through Sat. 6–11. Web site: www.mayfairhotel andspa.com/dining.

La Cofradia, 2525 Ponce de León Boulevard, Coral Gables 33134.
Call 305-914-1300. Open for lunch Mon. through Fri. noon–2:30;
for dinner Mon. through Thurs. 6–10, Fri. and Sat. 6–11. Web site:
www.lacofradia.com.

Redfish Grill, 9610 Old Cutler Road, Coral Gables 33156. Call 305-668-
8788. Open for dinner Tues. through Thurs. 6–10, Fri. and Sat. 5–10.
Web site: www.redfishgrill.net.

Venetian Pool, 2701 De Soto Boulevard, Coral Gables 33134. Call 305-
460-5306. Hours vary depending on the season. Web site: www.coral
gables.com.

Vizcaya Museum & Gardens, 3251 South Miami Avenue, Miami
33129. Call 305-250-9133. Open daily 9:30–4:30 (closed Christmas).
Web site: www.vizcayamuseum.org.

Trip 2: The Historic Redland Tropical Trail

Cauley Square Historic Village, 22400 Old Dixie Highway, Miami
33170. Call 305-258-3543. Open Tues. through Sat. 10–5, Sun. noon–5.
Web site: www.cauleysquare.com.

Coral Castle, 28655 South Dixie Highway, Homestead 33033. Call 305-
248-6345. Open Sun. through Thurs. 8 AM–6 PM, Fri. and Sat. 8 AM–
9 PM. Web site: www.coralcastle.com.

Fruit & Spice Park, 24801 Southwest 187th Avenue, Miami 33031. Call
305-247-5727. Open daily 10–5. Web site: www.fruitandspicepark.com.

Miami River Inn, 118 Southwest South River Drive, Miami 33130. Call
305-325-0045 or 1-800-HOTEL89. Web site: www.miamiriverinn.com.

Monkey Jungle, 14805 Southwest 216th Street, Miami 33170. Call 305-
235-1611. Open daily 9:30–5. Web site: www.monkeyjungle.com.

Robert Is Here Fruit Stand, 19200 Southwest 344th Street, Homestead
33034. Call 305-246-1592. Open daily 8–7; closed September and
October. Web site: www.robertishere.com.

Schnebly Redland's Winery, 30205 Southwest 217th Avenue,
Homestead 33030. Call 305-242-1224. Open Mon. through Fri. 10–5,
Sat. 10–6, Sun. noon–5. Web site: www.schneblywinery.com.

The Tea Room Restaurant, 12310 Southwest 224th Street, Miami 33170. Call 305-258-0044. Open Sun. through Wed. 11–6, Thurs. through Sat. 11–7.

Trip 3: In and around Miami

The Ancient Spanish Monastery, 16711 West Dixie Highway, Miami Beach 33160. Call 305-945-1461. Open Mon. through Sat. 9–5, Sun. 2–5.

Bal Harbour Shops, 9700 Collins Avenue, Miami Beach 33154. Call 305-866-0311. Open Mon. through Sat. 10–9, Sun. noon–6. Web site: www.balharbourshops.com.

C. Madeleine's, 13702 Biscayne Boulevard, North Miami Beach 33181. Call 305-945-7770. Open Mon. through Sat. 11–6, Sun. noon–5. Web site: www.cmadeleines.com.

Caffe Da Vinci, 1009 Kane Concourse, Bay Harbor Islands 33154. Call 305-861-8166. Open for lunch Mon. through Fri. 11:30–2:30; for dinner Sun. through Thurs. 5:30–10:30, Fri. and Sat. 5:30–11:30. Web site: www.caffedavinci.com.

The Food Gang, 9472 Harding Avenue, Surfside 33154. Call 786-228-9292. Open Tues. through Sun. 11–midnight. Web site: www.thefood gangcompany.com.

Holocaust Memorial, 1933–1945 Meridian Avenue, Miami Beach 33139. Call 305-538-1663. Open daily 9–9. Web site: www.holocaust mmb.org.

Hotel Nash, 1120 Collins Avenue, Miami Beach 33139. Call 305-674-7800. Web site: www.hotelnash.com.

Marjory Stoneman Douglas Biscayne Nature Center, 6767 Crandon Boulevard, Key Biscayne 33149. Call 305-361-6767. Open daily 10–4. Web site: www.biscaynenaturecenter.org. Call 305-365-3018 for **Miami-Dade Eco-Adventure Tours** or visit www.miamidade.gov/parks/eco adventures.htm.

Miami Art Group Gallery, LLC, 126 Northeast 40th Street, Miami 33137. Call 305-576-2633. Open Mon. through Sat. noon–7. Web site: www.miamiartgroup.com.

Miami Beach Botanical Garden, 2000 Convention Center Drive, Miami Beach 33139. Call 305-673-7256. Web site: www.miamibeach botanicalgarden.org.

Michael's Genuine Food & Drink, 130 Northeast 40th Street at Atlas Plaza, Miami 33137. Call 305-573-5550. Open for lunch Mon. through Fri. 11:30–3; for dinner Mon. through Thurs. 5:30–11, Fri. and Sat. 5:30–midnight, Sun. 5:30–10. Web site: www.michaelsgenuine.com.

The Moore Space, 4040 Northeast Second Avenue at the Moore Building, Second Floor, Miami 33137. Call 305-438-1163. Open Wed. through Sat. 10–5 and by appointment. Web site: www.moorespace.org.

Ola Restaurant, 1745 James Avenue at The Sanctuary, Miami Beach 33139. Call 305-695-9125. Open for dinner weekdays 6:30–11 PM, weekends 6:30 PM–1 AM. Web site: www.olamiami.com.

The Sanctuary, 1745 James Avenue, Miami Beach 33139. Call 305-673-5455. Web site: www.sanctuarysobe.com.

Tapas y Tintos, 448 Española Way, Miami Beach 33139. Call 305-538-8272. Open Mon. and Tues. 4 PM–1 AM; Wed. noon–1 AM; Thurs., Fri., and Sat. noon–2 AM; Sun. noon–1 AM. The bar stays open until 5 AM. Web site: www.tapasytintos.com.

Tobacco Road, 626 South Miami Avenue, Miami 33130. Call 305-374-1198. Open daily until 5 AM. Web site: www.tobacco-road.com.

World Erotic Art Museum, 1205 Washington Avenue, Miami Beach 33139. Call 305-532-9336 or 1-866-969-WEAM. Open daily 11 AM–midnight. Web site: www.weam.com.

Miami Beach Botanical Gardens

Ocean Drive

Opulence along the Coast

Overview: Save this one for a special moment with your special someone: an anniversary, proposal, or one incredible Valentine's Day weekend. This is the only chapter in this book that centers on a hotel, but **The Breakers** is worth it. For an unmatched setting, outstanding service, top-class dining, and sheer pamperability, you just can't beat this place. Very few hotels can live up to this standard, and fortunately this one is a mere hour away from Fort Lauderdale. And, when you feel like leaving the hotel, the many benefits and attractions of Palm Beach and West Palm Beach await you. When you're ready to forgo budget, forget expenses, and simply have an unforgettable weekend, read on.

Total length of trip: About 50 miles, spread over a weekend (most of the driving is there and back).

Getting there: From I-95 in Fort Lauderdale, take exit 31A for Oakland Park Boulevard East. Merge onto the road and travel about 3.5 miles to reach Ocean Boulevard/FL A1A. Turn left and travel 36 miles to Palm Beach. At this point you'll reach a roundabout. Take the first exit to stay on A1A/South Ocean Boulevard. In just over 2 miles, turn left on Royal Palm Way, and make the next right onto South County Road. Travel a half mile to the entrance of **The Breakers.**

From here, return to Royal Palm Way, turn right, and travel a half mile. Turn right at Four Arts Plaza to reach **The Society of the Four Arts.** Continue north on Four Arts Plaza and make the next right at Seaview Avenue. At the next intersection, turn left onto Cocoanut Row and travel a half mile to get to the **Henry Morrison Flagler Museum.** From here, make your way back along Cocoanut Row for about a half mile to Royal Palm Way. Turn left and make your first right onto Hibiscus Avenue. Travel a few blocks to reach the shops along Worth Avenue.

On your second day, take County Road to Royal Palm Way and turn right. Travel just over a mile, crossing Lake Worth and continuing along FL 704, before turning right at Rosemary Avenue to reach **CityPlace.** Head north on Rosemary Avenue for about a half mile before turning right at Clematis Street. Travel to the water's edge to reach **E. R. Bradley's.**

Highlights: Once you hit A1A and drive out of the main residential area of Fort Lauderdale, you'll feel like you're in one of those early race-car games. The winding road takes you along the ocean and past some flamboyant mansions fronting the ocean on one side and the Intracoastal on the other. You'll hit stretches of condos along the way, but much of this drive is through multimillionaire territory, as the homes and yachts anchored on your left will attest to. This would be a good time to roll down the windows or the roof of your convertible, if you have one, and enjoy the drive.

Your destination lies in the very ritzy address of Palm Beach, but along the way you'll cross some pretty exclusive neighborhoods. Just after Deerfield Beach is Boca Raton, where some of South Florida's established gentry resides. Continue north, past Red Reef Park and Spanish River Park. After Boca comes Deerfield Beach, followed by Boynton Beach. Keep driving, and soon you'll be on a narrow strip of land, the ocean stretching away on your right and more grand mansions on your left. You'll travel past Lake Worth and the Palm Beach Par-3 Golf Course, until you come at last to West Palm Beach.

A quick left at Royal Palm Way, followed by a right at South County Road, and you'll arrive at the stately gates that front the estate grounds and the path that leads, rather majestically, toward **The Breakers.** The Rolls Royce of Florida hotels since the 1890s, this Italian Renaissance–style building stands at the edge of the ocean, with a generous private beach lapping against its foundations. The Breakers itself is actually much larger than the

The Breakers

main hotel, occupying 140 acres of prime real estate. But the principal building provides the most breathtaking initial welcome. The lobby is a gorgeous, chandelier-laden affair with vaulted ceilings and columns resembling a cathedral, rich carpets, plush furnishings, and some lovely artwork. Check in and take your special someone to your room, which is a blend of personal comfort, warmth, and extravagance. If you can, try to get a room with an oceanfront view so you can hear the surf break on the rocks and remember where the name of the hotel came from.

After settling in, explore The Breakers, which can by itself take up the weekend. Eleven exclusive shops, eight restaurants (some off-property), two championship golf courses, state-of-the-art gym and spa, and a marvelous area for children are among the amenities here. But perhaps the greatest perk is what lies at the water's edge. In addition to a large private beach dotted with colorful umbrellas, The Breakers offers not one but five separate, heated, oceanfront pools, including one specifically for relaxation, one for kids, and one for more active guests. In addition, a new feature of the hotel is the addition of beach bungalows, which are available for daily rental and allow people spending the day on the water to cool off, take a shower under the open sky, check e-mail, watch TV, and essentially get all the comforts of home without the bedroom.

Tour the property and relax until dinner, and then take your pick of the award-winning restaurants in the main building. Your top choice is **L'Escalier,** The Breakers' signature restaurant, AAA Five Diamond winner, and recipient of *Wine Spectator*'s highest honor, the Grand Award. You have a choice at L'Escalier of selecting a dining experience of a more casual Parisian bistro (with classic bistro fare like duck à l'orange and bouillabaisse) or elevating the meal to the artistry of the main restaurant. Accompany your meal with a wine from one of the nation's most impressive cellars, which features close to 28,000 bottles ranging in price from a decent $35 to you-better-be-proposing. After dinner, retire to the adjacent and opulent **Tapestry Bar,** where 15th-century tapestries hang from the walls of a living room setting suited for a royal family.

On your next day, you might want to indulge in the hotel's amenities in the morning (check out the scuba and snorkel services) or play a round of golf before hitting the town for some sight-seeing and shopping. Before you go, grab lunch at **The Seafood Bar,** a casual restaurant offering wonderful views of the ocean and specializing in seafood. (Crabcake lovers will want to know the coveted, one-hundred-year-old recipe served here.) The decor centers on the one-of-a-kind bar, which is actually one long wraparound aquarium.

Now you're ready to hit the town. Just a few minutes from the hotel are two of Palm Beach's best cultural highlights. On Royal Palm Way are the lovely, diverse gardens of **The Society of the Four Arts.** This quiet sanctuary includes a botanical garden and the **Philip Hulitar Sculpture Garden.** From here, you're a stone's throw from the **Henry Morrison Flagler Museum,** named after the man who built the railroads in Florida, brought the first rail car to Miami and facilitated its settlement, spurred the growth of St. Augustine into a bustling tourist capital, and developed Palm Beach (including the hotel that would come to be known as The Breakers).

The museum is located at **Whitehall,** the Flaglers' one-time winter retreat. (When your winter retreat has 55 rooms, there's a good chance you'll be in a guidebook one day.) The grand building, designed in the beaux-arts style so in vogue among the elite of the era, is a luxurious place, and the tour takes you through its main rooms, including the renaissance-style Grand Hall, sumptuously red-hued library, an amazing music room (also an impressive art gallery), and the aptly named Grand Ballroom. Outside the house you'll find Flagler's private railcar, a comfortable way to travel even by today's updated standards.

After Whitehall, drive south to Worth Avenue, the Rodeo Drive of West Palm Beach. Gucci, Tiffany, Bulgari, Chanel, and other high-end boutiques line the road, and if you're out to spoil your loved one, this is the place to do it. From Worth Avenue, stroll among the shops, beautiful tropical architecture, and gardens and plazas that make up this ritzy neighborhood. My favorite hidden enclave here is **Pan's Garden,** just off Worth on Hibiscus Avenue. A small oasis defined by the beautiful statue of Pan playing his reed flute above an entrance pool, the garden showcases native flora, including gumbo limbo trees, saw palmettos, and bald cypress trees.

Stick around until dinner and head to **Ta-boó,** on Worth. A Palm Beach legend, this funky restaurant has a jungle feel, especially in the tropical, leafy decor. The menu has a little bit of everything, but its true fame stems from its popularity as a place to see and be seen. Celebrities—among them John F. Kennedy and Frank Sinatra in its heyday—have dined here.

Return to the hotel and enjoy a moonlit walk along the beach for a romantic conclusion to your night. On Sunday, make sure you've reserved brunch at the architecturally breathtaking **The Circle.** Sunday brunch is a tradition here, and the hotel does it in grand style, with literally hundreds of breakfast and lunch specialties on offer. Then check out from The Breakers and spend the day in West Palm Beach. Take Royal Palm Avenue across Lake Worth and follow the road to get to Rosemary Avenue, which is the entrance to **CityPlace,** a pleasant outdoor shopping complex (with much more modestly priced retailers than the ones on Worth Avenue). This is also home to an outdoor concert pavilion and the beautiful **Harriet Himmel Theater,** a performing arts center and the architectural crown jewel of the complex.

Spend the day here and follow Rosemary Avenue to Clematis Street, a more bohemian section of town where many of West Palm Beach's clubs and music venues are located. At the top of the street, near Centennial Square (where during summer days you'll see kids skipping through a water fountain), is the **Cuillo Centre for the Arts,** a modern but intimate theater that has staged some well-known musicals and plays. Check out what's playing when you're in town. If you're sticking around for a show, then walk toward the water and, at the edge of the street, you'll find **E. R.**

CityPlace

Bradley's, a casual local institution known for its amiable vibe, hearty food, and fantastic setting on the water.

This weekend is not designed with the budget traveler in mind, but it does include some of the best cultural, dining, and lodging options available at one of the nation's most exclusive addresses. If you want to be spoiled, or if you want to spoil someone, let Palm Beach and The Breakers take care of it.

Contacts:

The Breakers, 1 South County Road, Palm Beach 33480. Call 561-655-6611 or 1-888-BREAKERS. Web site: www.thebreakers.com.

The Circle, 1 South County Road at The Breakers, Palm Beach 33480. Call 561-655-6611 or 1-888-BREAKERS. Open for breakfast Mon. through Sat. 7–11 AM, Sun. 7–10 AM; Sun. brunch 11 AM–2:30 PM. Web site: www.thebreakers.com.

CityPlace, 700 South Rosemary Avenue, West Palm Beach 33401. Call 561-366-1000. Open Mon. through Thurs. 10–9, Fri. and Sat. 10–10, Sun. noon–6.

Cuillo Centre for the Arts, 201 Clematis Street, West Palm Beach 33401. Call 561-835-9226. Web site: www.cuillocentre.com.

E. R. Bradley's, 104 Clematis Street, West Palm Beach 33401. Call 561-833-3520. Open daily 8 AM–4 AM. Web site: www.erbradleys.com.

L'Escalier, 1 South County Road at The Breakers, Palm Beach 33480. Call 561-659-8480. Open for dinner Tues. through Sat. 6–10. Web site: www.thebreakers.com.

Henry Morrison Flagler Museum, 1 Whitehall Way, Palm Beach 33480. Call 561-655-2833. Open Tues. through Sat. 10–5, Sun. noon–5 (closed Thanksgiving, Christmas, and New Year's Day). Web site: www.flaglermuseum.us.

Pan's Garden, 386 Hibiscus Avenue, Palm Beach 33480. Call 561-832-0731. Open daily 9–5.

The Seafood Bar, 1 South County Road at The Breakers, Palm Beach 33480. Call 561-655-6611 or 1-888-BREAKERS. Open daily 11–1 AM. Web site: www.thebreakers.com.

The Society of the Four Arts, Four Arts Plaza, Palm Beach 33480. Call 561-655-2766. Open Mon. through Fri. 10–5, Wed. until 6, and from November through May on Sat. 10–3. Web site: www.fourarts.org.

Ta-boó Restaurant, 221 Worth Avenue, Palm Beach 33480. Call 561-835-3500. Open weekdays 11:30–10, Fri. and Sat. 5–11, Sun. for brunch until 3. Web site: www.taboorestaurant.com.

Index

Orlando Science Center, 153, 158
Orman House Museum, 101, 119
Osceola County Historical Society and Pioneer Museum, 142–43, 158

P

Palace Saloon, 19, 20, 37
Palacio, 106, 119
Palm Beach, 244
Palmdale, 162–63
Palmira Golf Club, 69, 72
Panama City, 102
Panhandle, 97–119
Pan's Garden, 247, 249
Paradise Coast, 57, 69
Paramount Grill, 209, 218
Park Plaza Gardens, 148, 158
Park Plaza Hotel, 147–48, 158
Pat Croce's Pirate Soul Museum, 50–51, 55
Paynes Prairie, 210–11, 218
Pensacola, 105–12
Pensacola Cultural Center and Pensacola Little Theater, 106, 119
Pensacola Lighthouse, 109
Pensacola Museum of Art, 106, 119
Pensacola Victorian Bed & Breakfast, 106, 119
Pepsi 400, 125
Perdido Key, 106
Petrello's at the Olde Boarding House, 189, 199
Philip Hulitar Sculpture Garden, 246
Pho Cali, 87, 93
Pigeon Key, 46
Pines and Palms Resort, 44, 55
Pinewood Estate, 181
Pioneer Settlement, 128, 137
Piper, Joan, 130, 136
PLaE (Peolple Laughing and Eating), 21, 37
Planter's Exchange, 115, 119
Pleasure Island, 154
Polk County, 175–85
Polk Museum of Art, 178, 184
Polk Outpost 27, 176, 184
Polly the Trolley, 17, 37
Ponce de León Hotel. *See* Flagler College

Ponce de Leon Inlet Lighthouse & Museum, 123, 137
Ponce Inlet, 122, 123–24
Port St. Joe, 102

Q

Quilt Shop of DeLand, 128, 137
Quincy, 113–14

R

Radisson Resort Orlando-Celebration, 140, 158
The Rain Barrel Sculpture Gallery, 43, 55
Ramrod Key, 48, 53
Raptor Bay Golf Club, 69, 72
Rawlings, Marjorie Kinnan, 213
Red Barn Bar-B-Q, 112, 119
Redfish Grill, 228, 238
Renninger's Antique Center, 151, 158
Restaurants: Alachua, 208; Alys Beach, 103; Amelia Island, 15, 19–20, 21; Apalachicola, 101–2; Arcadia, 168; Big Pine Key, 48; Captiva, 82–83; Carabelle, 101; Cassadaga, 131; Cedar Key, 194, 195–96; Celebration, 142, 146; Coconut Grove, 226; Copeland, 78; Coral Gable, 227; Crawfordville, 100; Cross Creek, 213; Daytona Beach, 122–23, 126; De Leon Springs, 127–28; DeLand, 128; Everglades, 63, 74; Gainesville, 209; Gibsonton, 90; Grayton Beach, 104; Havana, 115; High Springs, 206; Islamorada, 44, 45; Key Largo, 41–42; Key West, 50, 52; Kissimmee, 146; LaBelle, 168; Lake Helen, 129; Lake Placid, 165; Lake Wales, 180–81, 183; Lakeland, 178, 179; Miami, 229, 230, 233, 235, 237; Miami Beach, 228, 234; Micanopy, 212; Milton, 112; Mount Dora, 151, 152; Naples, 66–67, 68, 70; Ocala, 214; Ochopee, 74–75; Orlando, 153–54; Palm Beach, 246, 247; Pensacola, 105, 107–8, 111–12; Polk City, 177; Ponce Inlet, 123–24; Ramrod Key, 48; Sanibel Island, 81; Santa Rosa Beach, 102–3; Sarasota, 86–87, 88–89, 90; Seaside, 104; Sebring, 165; St. Augustine, 24, 27, 30, 31; Steinhatchee,

Steinhatchee River, 190, 192
Stephen Foster Folk Culture Center State
    Park, 204–5, 219
The Sugar Festival, 171
Sugarland Tours, 171, 173
Summer Beach Resort, 16, 37
Suwannee River, 201, 204–5
Suwannee River Diner, 204, 219
Suwannee Valley Quilt Shoppe, 189, 199
Swamp buggy rides, 61–62, 63–64, 144
The Swamp Cabbage Festival, 171
Swamp Water Café, 63

T

T. T. Wentworth, Jr. Florida State
    Museum, 106, 119
Ta-boó, 247, 249
Tabu, 154, 159
Tamiami Trail (US 41), 57, 73–90
Tapas y Tintos, 234, 240
Tapestry Bar, 246
Tarpon Bay Explorers, 82, 95
Tarpon Bay Road Beach, 81
Tarpon Springs, 197
Tavernier, 42
The Tea Room Restaurant, 230, 239
10,000 Islands region, 76, 77, 78
The Terrace Hotel and The Terrace Grill,
    177, 179, 184
The Theater of the Sea, 44, 55
Thursby House, 132
Tiburón Golf Club, 69, 72
Tigertail Beach, 78
Tin City, 68, 72
Tobacco Road, 235, 240
Toby's Clown School, 165
Tony's Seafood Restaurant, 195–96, 199
Towles Court Arts District, 86, 95
Treasure Village, 43
Trendy With a Twist, 67, 72
Trenton, 188, 189
Très Jolie, 183, 185
Trolley and train tours: Amelia Island, 17;
    Key West, 50; Mount Dora, 152;
    Naples, 68; St. Augustine, 24, 26
Truluck's, 66, 72
Turtle Beach, 89
'Tween Waters Inn, 82–83, 95

U

Universal's CityWalk, 154
University of Florida, 201, 209

V

Valencia Golf & Country Club, 69, 72
Venetian Pool, 227, 238
Versailles Restaurant, 74, 95
The Village of South Walton Beach, 102
Vizcaya Museum & Gardens, 225, 238

W

Wakulla Springs State Park, 99, 119
Wallaby Ranch, 140, 147, 159
Wanderings, 114, 119
Warbird Adventures, 143–44, 159
Watercolor, 102
The Watering Hole, 165, 173
Waterside Shops, 70, 72
Weeki Wachee Springs Park, 188, 199
Wekiwa Springs State Park, 151, 159
West Palm Beach, 243, 247
Westgate River Ranch, 181–83, 185
Wheeler's Café, 168
White Springs, 204–5
Whitehall, 246–47
Wicked Davey's Fancy Saloon, 20, 37
The Windsor Rose Old English Tea
    Room, 152, 159
The Wine Room, 150, 159
Winter Haven, 179–80
Winter Park, 147–51
World Erotic Art Museum, 234–35, 240
World's Smallest Police Station, 101
Worldwide Sportsman, 44, 55
Worth Avenue, 244, 247
Wright, Capt. Charles, 77
Wright, Frank Lloyd, 178–79

Y

Yearling Restaurant, 213, 219
Young's Paso Fino Ranch, Inc, 214, 219